MOORCROFT
A New Dawn

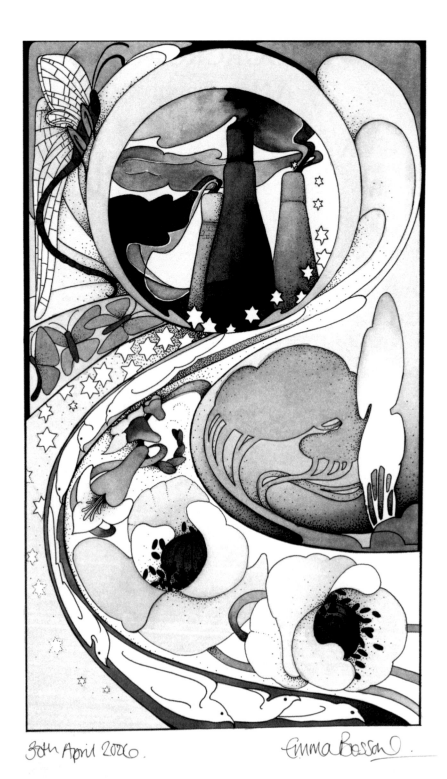

30th April 2006.   Emma Bossons.

For a moment the old collector allowed his imagination to drift back in time. From the gaping
mouths of the bottle ovens, dark grey, almost black sulphurous smoke laced with sparks billowed
high into the night sky in huge clouds rolling and heaving on their journey towards a sea of stars
spread out across the heavens. For people who are able to dream, those same stars would sink
slowly back to earth in a sparkling spiral of light, mutating as if by magic into images of dragon-
flies, birds, flowers, trees, and butterflies. Hugh Edwards. Moorcroft Newsletter: May 2006.

Fraser Street

MOORCROFT

A New Dawn

With best wishes

Hugh Edwards.

22. 10. 2006

WM PUBLICATIONS

First published in 2006 by W M Publications Ltd
5 Town Street, Thaxted, Essex CM6 2LD
Distributed by W M Publications Limited
Phoenix Works, Nile Street, Burslem, Stoke-on-Trent ST6 2BH

Printed in Great Britain by Butler and Tanner, Frome and London

Editor: Ann Geneva
Design: Peter Campbell
Photographic Records and Captions: Elise Adams
Photography: Gary Leggett Studios; Andrew Eeley at The Image Factory,
Barrington Kaufmann-Wright Bsc; Richard Blower; Burghley House.
Index: Margaret Crowther

Moorcroft Pottery can be found
on Sandbach Road, Burslem, Stoke-on-Trent ST6 2DQ
Telephone: + 44 (0) 1782 214 323 Facsimile: + 44 (0) 1782 283 455
Moorcroft Collectors' Club Telephone: + 44 (0) 1782 820 510

Contents

This book would not have been possible
without the help and encouragement of many people.
I must thank, in particular, Rachel Bishop and the Moorcroft Design Studio,
Lynn Cooper, Peter Donovan, Maureen Edwards, Elisabeth Haldane,
David Holland, David Johnson, John Moorcroft and the late Walter Moorcroft
OBE, Sian Parry, Ruth Ratcliffe, Kim Thompson, Mr and Mrs Tilstone, Robert
Townsend, Gloria Withington and, most specially the physician who recently
saved my life, Professor Stephen O'Rahilly, and without whom this book
would never have been completed.

H.R.E.

TO MY WIFE, MAUREEN

YOU ARE WITH ME IN MY WORK AND IN MY DREAMS

ONE

New Millennium, New World

The sky was grey, tinged with ominous streaks of red, but with sufficient patches of pale blue to add a note of cheer to the dawn of a new millennium. For many in England the celebrations had been a disappointment, an expensive anticlimax. A millennium dome destined to cease trading for its original purpose on commercial and economic grounds after just one unhappy year; a millennium bridge that wobbled and had to close for safety reasons; not to mention the London Eye, that enormous wheel which was simply unable to turn. The detritus of alcohol-driven festivities in London included thirty-two thousand empty champagne bottles scattered over pavements. Lying in gutters smelling of stale beer were more empty lager cans than could be accurately counted. Fireworks on the Thames were to have become a river of fire, but some failed to ignite. They had been spectacular, but not as spectacular as the fireworks that lit up the Eiffel Tower for more than five glorious minutes, or those seen exploding into a myriad of coloured stars of fire in Beijing or fired from Sydney harbour bridge in Australia. So much money seemed to have been spent on so little worth remembering, or which simply failed to function.

In modest contrast, the artists, tube-liners, designers and all the skilled men and women who worked at Moorcroft had every reason to be pleased with the small art pottery's own special contribution to the millennium festivities. With her 2000 year plate, designer Nicola Slaney had accurately picked up the opening millennium theme with her prophetic image of a Kiribati islander blowing a shell horn to greet that great dawn. Within twenty-four momentous hours the same image had been televised from Kiribati itself to every corner of the globe. Nicky's work had been completed a year earlier following her visit to the South Pacific islands in search of inspiration in the company of fellow Moorcroft designer, the young Emma Bossons. Ultimately the Moorcroft millennium plate became a joint effort, with design lines coming from Nicky herself, but not the colour. That came from the legendary Wendy Mason, a Moorcroft painter acknowledged by her colleagues at the Works to be the art pottery's greatest colourist of all time.

The new year also brought a wave of good press for Moorcroft. A millennium masterpiece from Nicola Slaney featured in a number of national newspapers with

FACING: *Birth of Light (1999-2000). Diameter 20cm (8")*

its theme of reconciliation for the most troubled city on earth. Jerusalem, which took the designer more than six months to draw and colour, featured three panels showing the Wailing Wall, the Dome of the Rock and the Church of the Holy Sepulchre, each separated by three panels of elegant white flowers. Moorcroft had tried to be different, and in its own peculiar way it had succeeded.

Perhaps not surprisingly, letters arrived on the chairman's desk in considerable quantity praising the Moorcroft vision for the millennium. Hugh Edwards was pleased, not only with the compliments showered on Moorcroft's young Design Studio, but also because he knew that friendly press backed by spontaneous letters of praise from Moorcroft collectors gave a good indication that the art pottery was still moving in the right direction. For all those who wrote or took the trouble to telephone, the answer was the same. We keep innovating: our eyes are fixed on the future; we leave the past to those who cherish it. Our purpose is to succeed by driving our art forward in the pursuit of excellence. The message was clear. For a Design Studio with an average age at the millennium of under thirty and a workforce with an average age of less than twenty-seven, the Moorcroft chairman could look with justifiable pride at a group of young people who had created probably the best and most successful art pottery in the world.

Never be ashamed to see how things were done in the old days, Hugh had told his designers more than once. Never follow others, nor become a slave to transient fashion; be true to yourselves and your own art; map your own way and ignore those who try and pull you back. Designers must show they can do even more than their predecessors. Design never stands still, he would tell them. On the day that it does, for whatever reason, Moorcroft will stand still as well. Hugh tried to avoid making speeches at Design Studio meetings, and whenever he over-stepped the mark he always found himself on the receiving end of a glare from the senior designer, Rachel Bishop. Her devout belief was that Moorcroft should never follow popular trends, that the purpose of design was to create pots that were timeless. It is a philosophy central to Hugh's own dream for the future, one of the reasons he had given up four-fifths of his income as a commercial lawyer in the City of London to work full-time for the art pottery in Stoke-on-Trent. He believed in the ability, vision and inspiration of the Moorcroft designers with a passion, supporting them at every stage, and protecting them from those who might attempt to denigrate their work. Hugh had no time for those who suffered from what he called 'the English disease' – people who can only deride success, and whose only reaction to those who succeed is to attack. Every month he received letters of criticism, dislike and even hate from people in the ceramic industry, antique dealers, failed artists and failed designers. If arrows of hate or envy were fired at himself he took no notice. If they were fired at any one of his beloved designers or any member of the Moorcroft workforce, all hell would let loose, and Hugh never let go until an apology had been received. He had been born with an unforgiving nature. Similarly, his colleagues were very protective of him. Those who worked at Moorcroft had freedom. Freedom to design, freedom to work and achieve their best, and freedom to take full credit for their work. The old days when a skilled workforce was not given full credit for its contribution to a business had long since come to an end.

Not everything, even in the recent past, had been entirely happy or successful. Back in the late summer of 1999, Peter Hughes, then sales director at Moorcroft and managing director at Okra Glass Studios, a Moorcroft subsidiary, had advised the Moorcroft board about a potential export market for its pottery in North America. His overall scheme was interesting, but it generated a certain amount of unease in Hugh's mind. Okra Glass, although producing superb art glass, was not doing well financially. Moorcroft decided that Peter should concentrate on Okra's problems and not on a new North American market. That would be for others to explore. Peter was told to carry out his managing director's responsibilities and improve Okra's performance. As the summer moved on and lurched into an uncertain autumn, more problems surfaced. Almost inevitably, at the end of the year, Peter Hughes left the troubled glass company by mutual consent. The following August, Moorcroft sold Okra Glass Studios back to its founder, Richard Golding.

Soon after Peter's departure Moorcroft made two important decisions, both of which were to influence the company's corporate strategy but not its art. In January 2000, veteran sales agent Alan Wright, together with the company's sales representative in Scotland Donald Reid, attended the Atlanta International Gift Fair in the United States to make their own assessment of export potential in North America. It would not be easy, Peter had said. Sacrifices would have to be made. For Alan and Donald the Moorcroft exhibition stand in Atlanta was little more than a few tables covered with plastic sheets. It had been an eleventh hour decision, but the shortcomings of the stand did not deter American retailers. When the two returned, their colleagues back home learned that enthusiasm for Moorcroft on the other side of the Atlantic was not just warm but positively boiling. That was welcome news, but it triggered another potential problem. The Moorcroft workforce was already producing pottery to full capacity. It would be necessary to recruit and train additional staff to satisfy North American demand. Training was an expensive burden for a small company, but expansion into North America would not only provide new jobs in Stoke-on-Trent, said to be the second poorest city in the United Kingdom, but would also increase Moorcroft's security. As a result, those at home in Stoke-on-Trent set about recruiting new painters and tube-liners, while Alan Wright and Donald Reid made plans for a summer sales trip to the United States and Canada in July 2000. This time Alan had requested an all-singing, all-dancing exhibition stand at the summer trade show in Atlanta, on which to display the designs which had made their proud debut in the Moorcroft millennium catalogue. Trestle tables and plastic covers may have served well at the beginning of the year, but they were scarcely in keeping with the Moorcroft image. Sal Bakhsh, a young trade stand designer of outstanding ability, had set the Birmingham National Exhibition Centre alight with well-earned praise for his work on the new millennium exhibition stand. What Alan asked for and received was a smaller replica of the Birmingham stand with Sal himself personally on hand throughout the Summer Fair in Atlanta to look after it. Much to everyone's pride and delight, Moorcroft carried away from Atlanta the 'Stand of Show' award. Decades earlier the company would have received a gold medal. In July 2000, the Stand of Show award came in the form of a simple blue rosette!

When Hugh told them about the North American initiative, the designers were curious. Should they design with American and Canadian collectors in mind? Would there be Collectors' Days in North America with a special Collectors' Day vase just as there was in the United Kingdom? Would they be asked to tour North America? The answer in every case, Hugh told them, was 'yes.' Always to the point, Rachel Bishop asked when the new venture was due to start. Hugh's reply came as something of a surprise. Alan and Donald were already in the United States taking orders for Moorcroft. Plans were already afoot to display Moorcroft at trade shows in Atlanta and New York twice a year, and later in San Francisco. A trade show presence in Canada was also necessary, but the location had yet to be identified. It was only a matter of time, Hugh surmised, before North American design themes entered into the Moorcroft collection, but that would be largely a matter for the designers.

What Hugh did not tell the Design Studio was that he was about to serve notice of termination of the distributor's agreement in New Zealand, just as he had done a year earlier for distribution in the United States. The way had to be cleared to enable the Moorcroft sales team to sell directly to overseas markets. After New Zealand, others would be looked at. Moorcroft would have to enter a new era of direct selling, but he kept that thought to himself. For the moment it was enough to acknowledge that selling overseas through a distributor had become an anachronism. Hugh was a collector, and he saw no reason why overseas collectors should pay a much higher price for a piece of Moorcroft than their counterparts in the United Kingdom. More importantly, overseas collectors had the right to expect design themes emanating from their own native countries as well as the United Kingdom. New Zealand was a case in point.

Until they ceased acting as Moorcroft's distributors, Manufacturers' Agencies had served the art pottery well. Leading retailers in New Zealand were encouraged to assume responsibility for special limited editions; flexible stock arrangements facilitated promotion of their own special events, and the ethos of collecting was preserved throughout the country in the nicest possible way. The only problem was that New Zealand collectors were among those who had to pay a significantly higher price for a piece of Moorcroft. A distributor had to take a profit. After that, retailers would add their own profit margin. It was a system of two-tiered cost that had to stop. Global market opportunities which followed the arrival of the Internet had already enabled New Zealand collectors to buy their Moorcroft anywhere in the world. Admittedly they did so without the opportunity of appraising a piece before purchase, but the price paid was often lower. In a competitive market, that fact on its own weighed heavily against New Zealand retailers, who had to face the real possibility that the Internet would cause their collector base to melt away. As a good manufacturer, Moorcroft had to help them.

Fantail (2004)
Diameter 20cm (8")

It took time to organise a visit to New Zealand retailers after Manufacturers' Agencies had been moved out of the distributor frame, and it was not until May 2002 that the energetic Donald Reid and Kim Thompson, a Moorcroft director, visited twenty-six potential New Zealand retailers over a period of almost three weeks. New Zealand collectors themselves had supplied the names of potential retail customers, and amazingly the two Moorcroft travellers opened accounts with all twenty-six retailers introduced to them. Moorcroft Collectors' Club Secretary, Elise Adams, was over the moon. It was time, she said to Hugh, for Moorcroft to welcome the return of New Zealand collectors with something special. In practical terms, that 'something' had to be ready to introduce in New Zealand by June 2003. Hugh approached

The New Zealand Collection (2006)
From left to right: Kotare Ltd.Edn.100
Kotare plaque Ltd.Edn.150 and
Ribbonwood. Tallest vase 18cm (7")

Philip Gibson, a senior Moorcroft designer and one who to this day still talks of the privilege of working with the late Susie Cooper at William Adams, a Wedgwood company. Phil was experienced in his design work and thorough in his research. What emerged over the months that followed was an inspired collection of designs based on New Zealand themes. As a starting point, Phil decided that New Zealand was synonymous with spectacular scenery, magnificent trees, shrubs and flowers, and with wildlife unlike anything else in the world. Even for those who live far away from the Land of the Long White Cloud, there is a deep feeling of mystery and romance for a country whose southern shores reach out toward the icy waters of the Antarctic. In simple terms, New Zealand is admired for its unique evolution, its beauty and its heritage, as much by strangers as by those who are privileged to live within its coastlines. With this firmly in mind, the Moorcroft designer set to work to create a collection which reflected the colour and imagery of New Zealand. The result was The New Zealand Collection, initially a set of five pieces.

Kowhai, the national flower of New Zealand, was the first design theme Phil created. On an elegant and popular strap-handled jug, the soft green, semi-stylised leaves gave the flower an almost fern-like appearance. The lemon coloured kowhai flowers shade almost into gold, making it one of the best-known and most popular flowering trees in New Zealand. The result was a powerful piece of ceramic art, as was Poor Knights Island, Phil's second design, which cleverly combined two native New Zealand flowers. The first was the southern rata, which when seen flowering en masse in the forests of the South Island can provide one of New Zealand's most spectacular experiences. The second was the poor knights lily, a flower found mainly along the rugged coastline of some of the more isolated northern islands. Untouched by the passing of time, Poor Knights Island is one of only two islands on which this rare flower can be found. Rarity on its own was enough to provide Phil with his inspiration and his superb design with its name.

The New Zealand Collection would have been incomplete without the country's famous tree fern, a native plant better known for its status as the national emblem.

Using soft, subtle colours, Phil successfully captured the various stages of a tree fern unfurling in the sun. This added a touch of artistic magic to the smallest piece in the collection. In the wild, the warm, red and gold shoots mutate into lush green tree fern fronds as they mature. The kaka beak flower is a popular garden plant in New Zealand, seldom found growing in the wild. Lake Waikaremoana is said to be virtually the last place that the kaka beak was ever seen in its natural habitat. After a successful conservation program, the kaka beak has now re-established itself in the wild. This red and white flower derives its name from petals that are beak-like in shape, which Phil twisted around the slim vase he had chosen to great effect.

It was at this point that the designer turned his attention to New Zealand collectors. In the past, small but very successful limited editions had been launched into the New Zealand market. To make his collection especially attractive to local collectors, Phil created an eight-inch plate featuring the tui bird and koru flower. The koru is never easy to find. Usually hidden away in secluded places on the banks of streams or shallow woodland gullies, the plant is attractive to the nectar-loving tui. With the overhanging flowers of the koru acting as a floral umbrella, the nectar literally drips directly into the tui's eager beak. The plate turned out to be pure Moorcroft magic. It was the only piece in the New Zealand collection to arrive as a limited edition, and one which New Zealand retailers could have sold twice over. Following heavy orders for urgent dispatch, those incredible far away New Zealand collectors who had done so much to keep the Moorcroft name alive were rewarded for their patience. Apart from the Tui plate, all pieces in the inaugural New Zealand collection were open editions, and from the date of its release in June until the end of the year, the collection remained exclusive to New Zealand.

Because the Tui plates had all sold out within a few weeks of their launch, a replacement became an urgent necessity. The result was Fantail inspired by another exotic native bird often found among tree fern fronds where it usually makes its nest. The bird's name is derived from a set of beautiful tail feathers which spread out into a shape reminiscent of an aristocratic Victorian lady's fan. The Fantail plate was both exciting and colourful and was approved as an open edition.

As planned, The New Zealand Collection was

The New Zealand Collection (2005) Clockwise from top: Puriri Tree, Poroporo and Violet. Lidded jar 13cm (5")

launched to the world in the 2004 catalogue with the Fantail plate substituted for the Tui plate. Sales were strong, so much so that Phil was persuaded to design the Puriri Tree, Violet and Poroporo for the following year. When 2006 arrived, the designer added his celebrated Ribbonwood and Kotare vases and a Kotare plaque. Kotare is the Maori name for the New Zealand kingfisher, a bird which they regard as sacred. For some inexplicable reason it was the Kotare images which convinced everyone that the world had changed. There were kingfishers flying in New Zealand, two islands on the other side of the world, just as there were kingfishers in the United Kingdom. Art had to encompass all kingfishers wherever they appeared in the world. In an age of global trade, overseas distributorships had outlived their purpose. In their place, the era of direct selling to even the remotest corners of the earth had begun. For designers, the culture, images and art of distant countries had to be taken into account. To ignore the outside world was no longer an option.

The New Zealand Collection (2003). Clockwise from top: Kowhai Flower, Tui Ltd.Edn.150, Tree Fern, Kaka Beak and Poor Knights Island. Jug 24cm (9.5")

TWO

Shock Waves

Towards the end of April in the millennium year, a potential Moorcroft drama moved suddenly and unexpectedly centre stage. Always alert, Kim Thompson was among the first to comment that for some mysterious reason incoming orders were falling slightly below forecast. Millennium indigestion everyone said jokingly, but Kim saw amber lights flashing. It was already increasingly difficult to match incoming orders to production capacity, and from time to time a significant shortage of work among the painters in the decorating shop had occurred. To correct the decline in orders, veteran sales supremo Alan Wright was put in charge of trade sales at Moorcroft as a director. He remained upbeat. Alan's advice was that retailers no longer saw it necessary to lodge one huge order for Moorcroft at the beginning of each year, in the hope that at least some of it would have arrived by early autumn in time for Christmas trade. Fresh orders for the autumn and winter seasons would once again become the norm. Everyone had to be patient and wait for them to arrive. It would all come right in September during the Autumn Fair at the National Exhibition Centre. Alan's thoughts were measured, logical and based on a lifetime's experience in sales. There was a great deal of wisdom in what he said, and even Hugh had to admit there was little else to go on. Everyone agreed that collectors' credit cards were probably suffering fatigue as a result of the millennium celebrations. Nobody dared say too loudly that there was a shortage of cash in the retail system, a shortage aggravated by a glut of millennium stock from other manufacturers which had failed to sell. Most of it was of poor quality, and much of it made in China or around the Pacific Rim.

A few months later, in the early autumn of 2000, disaster struck the quiet, colourful world of the Potteries, a shock that caused even Moorcroft to shudder. Major players in the British ceramic industry went into sudden and steep decline, some of them lurching from crisis to crisis one after another. Other manufacturers described sales as 'hitting a wall, particularly in North America'. The news turned Hugh's stomach upside-down. This time it seemed there might be no escape for Moorcroft. Not since he first joined the company as a shareholder in 1986 had the outlook seemed so bleak. Orders for the pre-Christmas trade failed to materialise as Alan Wright had forecast, and many which did were cancelled well before Christmas arrived. By the end of October there were even insufficient orders on the Moorcroft books to keep everyone busy, the opposite of recent trends. Each day it became more and more difficult to match orders against pots. Nobody had ever been laid off or put on short time at Moorcroft since the mid-1980s, but there was now a serious risk that everything was about to change. James Macintyre & Co, the Leeds retailer owned and run by the Edwards' youngest daughter Debbie, weighed in with its full quota of autumn orders. Macintyres are the only independent retailer in the world who sell nothing but Moorcroft, but even their business had slowed down. Hugh had to act quickly. B & W Thornton in Stratford-upon-Avon were sharply down on their autumn order as were Talents of Windsor, another major Moorcroft customer. Ominous signs were everywhere. Only Collectables in Newcastle added their name to that of James Macintyre, ordering in significant quantity. Hugh's idea was to head off the crisis by design. It was time to call in the designers.

At the crisis Design Studio meeting the old lawyer gave little away. Even so, a questioning look in Emma Bossons' eye made it clear she understood Moorcroft had a real problem. Many of her friends in the decorating shop had commented on the growing quantities of unallocated stock hanging about the Works, which production director Keith Dawson had continued to make without orders. A few of the staff had seen it all before in the mid-1980s when the cash ran out leaving a huge mountain of unwanted stock in its wake. This recollection troubled them deeply. Hugh knew that history was not about to repeat itself. In common with others it had a problem, but Moorcroft was strong enough to cope. In theory, Hugh told the Moorcroft designers, any company in the ceramic industry could design itself out of trouble. How local companies hated his theories! 'Arrogant' was the word they often used. Now his design theory would be put to the test.

Within a week, senior designer Rachel Bishop came forward with a stylised design inspired by the star of Bethlehem, one of the most beautiful of all small flowers. Her selected colours came in shades of red, orange and green with faint hint of yellow. Generally, Rachel told Hugh, star of Bethlehem was a white flower with dark green, linear, strap-shaped leaves, which she had twisted to highlight the delicate flowers. The senior designer paused, largely to make sure that the Moorcroft chairman was still listening. Without waiting to be asked why white flowers had been coloured orange, Rachel volunteered the answer herself. What colour would the flowers be with glowing, yellowish orange beams of evening sunlight shining on

FACING: *Favrile (2001). Tallest vase 20cm (8")*

*Star of Bethlehem (2000) Ltd. Edn.250
Height 15cm (6")*

them? For good measure, she seized the opportunity to remind the Moorcroft chairman that the art pottery had never really been in the business of reality design. Nevertheless, Hugh had a different kind of reality to worry about. It remained for him to ask James Macintyre & Co to take on Rachel's Star of Bethlehem ginger jar as a limited edition and the very real financial risks that went with it. It was a big favour to ask of James Macintyre & Co in the circumstances, but Debbie answered for her company by giving her father a big hug. Things were moving, but not enough to steer Moorcroft to safety. Hugh had another favour to ask of his daughter.

Nicola Slaney's new Favrile range drew inspiration from Clara Driscoll's famous dragonfly design for the American art glassmaker Tiffany, and Favrile needed a home. Nicky had designed it as a range of thirteen pieces, and never before in its history had Moorcroft asked a single retailer to take on board and market a whole range. Seeing a look of real fear in his daughter's eyes, Hugh changed tack. James Macintyre & Co in Leeds could become lead retailer for Favrile, not sole retailer. There was a possibility that Geoff Taylor (China) in Reigate, Surrey and Lewis Goldinger's Stockwell China Bazaar in Glasgow would join forces with Macintyres. To Hugh's unmitigated relief, both Geoff Taylor and Lewis Goldinger of Stockwell China Bazaar agreed and Favrile was launched to an enthusiastic public early in 2001 from all three shops simultaneously.

Hugh had thought long and hard about a suitable name for Nicky's design. In 1902, Louis Comfort Tiffany had become vice president and art director at Tiffany Studios in the United States. While the labelling of the Tiffany Dragonfly design as 'Favrile' is a well-documented historical fact, it is less well-known that four years earlier Tiffany had started a small decorative enamel workshop and art pottery which he called Favrile. The pottery featured moulded plant forms with both plain and textured surfaces, many of which Tiffany designed himself. Tiffany pottery under the Favrile label was first introduced to potential buyers at the same 1904 Louisiana Purchase Exposition in St Louis at which a young William Moorcroft won his first

FACING: *(top left) Cleopatra (2001). Tallest vase 23cm (9") (top right) Cleopatra (2001). Tallest vase 28cm (11")
(bottom left) Pheasants Eye (2001). Jug 24cm (9.5) (bottom right) Pheasants Eye (2001). Tallest vase 30cm (12)*

Pheasants Eye (2002)
Ginger jar 15cm (6")

gold medal. Take the Favrile name from the Tiffany Dragonfly lamp labels, take the word 'Favrile' used for Tiffany pottery and the name Favrile for Nicky's innovative dragonfly range became inevitable.

There were important lessons learned from Favrile. While a retailer might baulk at assuming the financial burden of either a special limited edition or range, there was nothing to prevent that burden being spread among a number of retailers as far apart as possible geographically for the convenience of collectors. Debbie's decision both to take Star of Bethlehem and share Favrile had been a courageous one. Hugh was delighted when he later learned that her shop, James Macintyre & Co, had toppled Liberty of London as leading retailer in the world of Moorcroft. At a more personal level, Hugh was proud of his daughter for the support she had given.

By November, even an outsider visiting Moorcroft could scarcely fail to notice the telltale signs about the Works that the art pottery had a fight on its hands. Stock was accumulating everywhere, stock which lacked orders from retail customers. If sales to retailers were falling away, sitting still and hoping things would improve was not an option. The art pottery had to be proactive. If retailers were not buying, the shortfall could be made up by selling special designs direct to Collectors' Club members. Thus the idea of a Collectors' Christmas Weekend was conceived; but to become reality much more had to be done. Unfortunately Moorcroft had very little time. The Design Stu-

Kingfisher (2001)
Length 40cm (16")

FACING: *(top left) Kingfisher (2001) Ltd.Edn.350. Height 20cm (8") (top right) Odyssey (2001) Ltd.Edn.500. Height 18cm (7") (bottom left) Tamarin (2001) Ltd.Edn.300. Height 25cm (10") (bottom right) Cetona (2001) Ltd.200. Height 25cm (10")*

dio started to work immediately on seasonal designs for an inaugural Christmas Weekend. It was a tall order, but potentially the only way to avoid a crisis.

Quite separately, and with attention still focused on a handful of courageous retailers, Sian Leeper designed Cleome. It was an unassuming vase with red flowers set against a backcloth of rolling green hills. Connaught House took up the challenge to sell it. Hugh was grateful, and told proprietor Peter Allsopp so. The placing of Star of Bethlehem with James Macintyre & Co and Cleome with Connaught House would be a great help, but even with the addition of Favrile, it was still not enough. To keep people working productively, a number of pieces already designed for the new catalogue were put into production. Among them were Tamarin, a classic Sian Leeper jungle scene, and a Kingfisher jug and plaque from Philip Gibson. It was significant that the moment the new year arrived, Kingfisher jugs and plaques raced off shop shelves on delivery. Cetona and Odyssey, both by Beverley Wilkes, were two designs which caught Hugh's eye. There was a touch of William de Morgan about Odyssey with its Islamic colour palette. As with Phil's Kingfisher pieces, a totally new field of design had started to open up. Both colour and subject matter were undergoing a process of change. In keeping with the new mood, Beverley's Cetona captured the rural spirit of Umbria in Italy to perfection. For Moorcroft, townscape had been added to traditional landscape.

At the Works everyone was in agreement about Wolfsbane, an Anji Davenport limited edition. It

Juneberry (2002). Vase 15cm (6″)

was old-style Moorcroft, and for Moorcroft traditionalists an absolute classic in linework, colour and shape. Whatever a collector's preference, Hugh was confident that all limited editions of the quality of Wolfsbane should be moved out of Moorcroft's storage pens as soon as the new year arrived. Time was of the essence.

After Wolfsbane, Anji started work on a new design different in structure from anything she had ever attempted. Juneberry featured pure ivory bands, outside which the designer had drawn deep purple berries, striking white flowers and greenish brown leaves. The base colour was a faded dark blue. Indeed, Juneberry was so

FACING: *(above) Juneberry (2001). Tallest vase 23cm (9″) (below) Juneberry (2001). Candlestick 20cm (8″)*

Wolfsbane (2001) Ltd.Edn.350. Height 30cm (12")

different from anything Moorcroft had ever produced that Hugh decided to take a sample to a leading tableware manufacturer for their opinion. 'Still Moorcroft', was the immediate response, 'and before you ask we are not yet ready to manufacture Moorcroft designs!' What else should the Moorcroft chairman have expected? At least he knew that Juneberry was not a tableware design. More importantly, collectors liked its novel style and pressed retailers to take it into stock.

Sian Leeper's Cleopatra Blues arrived at the same time as Juneberry. Like Odyssey, it also had a faint Islamic aura about it, but Hugh was relaxed. During his career as a commercial lawyer, colour combinations derived from Middle Eastern mosaic themes in shades of jade green, aquamarine, purple, mauve, oatmeal and blue had been a familiar sight on his travels throughout his working life. He knew that the Moorcroft designers were not copying William de Morgan. Just as de Morgan himself had done, the Design Studio had started to absorb the distinctive colour and style of the Middle East as a source of inspiration. Ultimately it would be Shirley Hayes' magnificent Saadian design which would inextricably link Moorcroft to the Islamic colour palette, but in the post-millennium year Saadian was not even a twinkle in Shirley's eye. That year her Pheasants Eye design scooped up retailer praise by the bucketful, especially when it appeared as lamps. In the world of Moorcroft lamps tend to be regarded as furniture, with a completely different market place from the pots. The John Lewis Partnership took Pheasants Eye as a lead design in table lamps, and as a result sales were strong. It was a design which fascinated collectors of pottery and excited customers who wanted fine lamps to complement their homes.

Largely because week after week seventy-year-old Alan Wright and the ever-optimistic Donald Reid were giving their all in the United States and Canada, Moorcroft's infant export business across the Atlantic was holding up well despite the transatlantic recession. New orders from new accounts arrived as welcome substitutes for those which had failed to materialise in the home market. Although his colleagues were not to know it at the time, Alan Wright's heart was in a serious condition, so serious that in April 2001 he almost died after a triple heart by-pass operation. Back in the late '80s and early '90s, in a virtuoso sales performance without parallel in the art pottery's long and colourful history, Alan had helped put the Moorcroft name back on its pedestal with a reputation for quality work and design excellence. At an age when most people

Cleome (2000) Ltd.Edn.250
Height 20cm (8")

would have retired, he was still travelling all over the United States, giving his all to open up a new and potentially huge market.

From the Atlanta and New York trade shows, plus subsequent follow-up calls on potential customers, a new millennium in-flow of orders from North America arrived by the bucketful. As a result, a potential crisis at Moorcroft disappeared. If there had existed a brick wall in America against which other manufacturers had crashed, Alan Wright and Donald Reid had played a significant part in knocking it down for Moorcroft all on their own. It was a sales performance of which the trumpeters at Jericho would have been proud.

Year Plate (2001) Ltd.Edn.750
Diameter 20cm (8")

THREE

Christmas Cheer

For as long as Hugh could remember, open weekends at Moorcroft had always provided a happy hunting ground for special editions and rare, one-off designs. Few doubted that the inaugural Christmas Weekend scheduled to take place at the end of the millennium year would be any different. By the end of October, it was looming large on the horizon. The Moorcroft Design Studio had already achieved a great deal, but the designers were tired and there were limits on how far Hugh could push them. Design is not something that you can turn on like a tap and expect to see linework and colour come gushing out. It can sometimes take months for a good idea to mature. As a job, design never operated on conventional nine-to-five principles, and if pushed too far there was a risk that one or more designer would slide into a black spell devoid of inspiration and colour. Hugh need not have worried. The Design Studio responded as it had always done and delivered in a way that made the inaugural Christmas Weekend an occasion to remember.

In contrast to the rain, wind and dank gloom of a typical late November day, the glitter and glow of new pots, Christmas trees and colourful decorations in the Moorcroft factory shop seemed all the more welcoming. Journalist Ann Geneva commented that not only was there a physical glimmer about the place, but this time round there seemed to be an inner gleam as well. On entering the shop, a collector was heard to comment that it was 'like dying and coming into paradise'. The journalist elaborated on her theme. 'Speaking of paradise, Oh the pots! Oh the temptations! So proficient has the Design Studio become in creating new beauties that the impression is of tube-lined clay pigeons flying past almost faster than they can be taken in!' The mood throughout the weekend was one of real excitement, spurred on by an enlightened preview of new Moorcroft scheduled to appear in the new year. It was a real tonic. The special pieces designed for Christmas Weekend showed just how much support the designers had given Moorcroft, and that support was converting into unbridled enthusiasm among collectors before Hugh's very eyes.

As a small Christmas keepsake, leading tube-liner Marie Penkethman designed a Moorcroft mug decorated with stylised snowflakes, a mug somewhat unimagi-

Caper (2000) Ltd.Edn.100
Width 20cm (8")

natively called Snowflake. It had become a tradition that Marie would design mugs for the May Open Weekend, and nobody saw any good reason why the inaugural Christmas Weekend should be different. Interestingly, it was that simple Snowflake mug which sowed the seeds of another new idea. Pots with Christmas themes should become a recurring feature of the Moorcroft calendar, but the dying days of a millennium year was not the moment to bring forward such thoughts. There was no time.

Writing about the Christmas Weekend in the Collectors' Club newsletter, Ann Geneva continued to enthuse. 'At the risk of using yet another superlative, the atmosphere could only be described as one of pure happiness.' Ann made the remark after spending time with collectors admiring Sian Leeper's two Passion for Red pieces. With a degree in design, Sian had arrived at Moorcroft as an experienced tube-liner and painter after a varied career which took her from Somerset to Stoke-on-Trent and from Stoke-on-Trent back to Somerset, before leaving to spend a considerable time successfully designing and making pots in the United States. Passion for Red attracted collectors. Sian's arrival had been noticed.

Two mysteries surround that inaugural 2000 Christmas Weekend. The first centres on a Nicola Slaney design aptly named Shooting Star. What is quite clear is that only 55 pieces were made: Shooting Star was literally a weekend wonder. For a long time Hugh convinced himself, wrongly as it turned out, that Shooting Star was something Nicky had designed to become the 2001 year plate. It was a muddle. As a result, Shooting Star as a vase made its Christmas debut with a lively name attached, whereas the hapless year plate with a delicious design based on American cranberries appeared in the 2001 catalogue without any name at all! It was the only time a piece of Moorcroft was ever launched without being christened, and to this day nobody is quite sure why. The other mystery centred around Anji Davenport's Caper vase. The approved trial had remained in Hugh's room at the Works for well over a year. There was no particular reason why Caper should have emerged at Christmas. If anyone should have known it would have been Hugh, but he still persists in maintaining a discreet silence. 'It's a barometer matter,' is all he will say.

Another of Anji's Christmas designs that year was Begonia. As a piece of

Moorcroft it was well thought through in both style and colour, and its arrival caused scarcely a ripple. Anji had carefully bent small, orange flowerbuds over delicate variegated leaves to make a simple but very attractive design. Begonia was very much a favourite of Kim Thompson, who spoke strongly in its favour at the time it came up for design approval. 'Without a shadow of a doubt', she announced to a startled meeting, 'Begonia is a classic!'

A third contribution for the occasion from the industrious Anji was novel. Woodside Farm as a range had sold well and retailers continued to chirp happily that it was 'right for us'. Deep down, Hugh had serious doubts as to whether Wood-

Christmas Collection (2001). Clockwise from top: Love's Lace Ltd.Edn.30, Cymbidium blue and green Ltd.Edn.30, Wood Blewit Ltd.Edn.50, Michaelmas ivory and green Ltd.Edn.100, Scarlet Star Ltd.Edn.30, Southern Magnolia, Chinese Lantern Ltd.Edn.50, Honesty Ltd.Edn.50, Tiger Butter Orchid Ltd.Edn.50. Tallest vase 25cm (10")

Christmas Collection (2000)
Clockwise from top: Begonia, Passion
for Red vase and coaster and Shooting
Star. Tallest vase 20cm (8″)

side Farm was a design at all. There was a strong argument that it was more akin to a picture image in the Moorcroft style than a design. Those lingering doubts turned into a certainty when Anji introduced her six Woodside Farm eggcups, all of which were to remain available for collectors to order until January 2001. Kim was ecstatic. Rachel may well have wondered what William Moorcroft would have thought. Elise mourned what appeared to be the passing of an era in Moorcroft design, while Hugh, in a gesture which some felt to be hypocritical, purchased a complete set for his home. 'Eggcups are for eggs', he was happy to tell the world, 'and eggs are laid in farmyards. What on earth was wrong with Woodside Farm eggcups?' Happily, Moorcroft collectors agreed.

The following year, Collectors' Christmas Weekend came and went so fast that those involved had to really concentrate to convince themselves it had taken place at all. North America had saved the day and sales were strong worldwide. Moorcroft was enjoying itself once more. To mark the occasion, Emma Bossons' Honesty, Southern Magnolia and Wood Blewit all made an appearance. All three designs had been considered for release at least once, and each time they had been passed over for reasons which had nothing whatever to do with their quality. When the time came, Honesty and Wood Blewit almost flew out of the factory shop. Collectors loved them with the same passion they showed for Emma's Southern Magnolia coasters. Moorcroft coasters had always been strong collectors' items. With a virtually unlimited capacity to carry every kind of design theme, and blessed with a shape and size that made them popular additions to sideboards, shelves and favoured mantelpieces in collectors' homes, coasters had almost become the ultimate Moorcroft collectable.

It would be a mistake to assume that whenever designers have no new work on show, something is wrong. Design availability is an erratic process. It can depend on rejections by the design approval committee, on-going work which has to be completed, or even a designer's 'black spell', that recurring nightmare where

design inspiration withers and dies. With a good supply of approved work already available, it was relatively easy for Emma to add Michaelmas to her three other pieces earmarked for a Christmas debut. Curiously, Michaelmas arrived with two alternative colourways, green and pink, while the seemingly tireless Anji offered Mistletoe on a small ginger jar with an unashamed and familiar seasonal image. Although lacking an overt Christmas theme, Scarlet Star pleased Elise with its climbing clematis. A greater cause for anxiety arose because Scarlet Star arrived as a tiny limited edition of thirty pieces, as did Anji's more sophisticated Cymbidium with line-work paying homage to orchids, one in a shade of lime green and the other in soft pink. A limited edition of thirty pieces is always good news for collectors lucky enough to find one, but less welcome to the Moorcroft tube-liners and painters who had to familiarise themselves with new patterns more frequently than was sometimes reasonable. Sian Leeper's Love's Lace was a design which used that flower as its main theme, making its appearance limited to thirty pieces. With Moorcroft looking only fractionally less timid, Debbie Hancock's Chinese Lantern and Shirley Hayes' Tiger Butter Orchid were both approved as limited editions of fifty. Chinese Lantern carried bold orange flowers, while Tiger Butter Orchid showed a flower with rich scarlet petals and a cream-coloured centre cleverly set against a woodsmoke ground colour. Interestingly, those same colours were to reappear on Shirley's vibrant Fleur Rouge, a significant vase in the 2004 Innovation by Design collection.

In total, no fewer than ten new designs (plus a mug) had been offered to add quality and colour to what was already a sparkling occasion, but for

(Top) Woodside Farm (2000). Height 5cm (2")
(Middle) Woodside Farm (2002). Height 15cm (6")
(Bottom) Snowflake (2000). Height 9cm (3.5")

Mistletoe (2001). Height 10cm (4")

Hugh it provoked the start of an underlying and prolonged anxiety. Some of those ten new designs had been sold with tiny edition numbers attached. If this turned out to be the thin end of the wedge, retailers would legitimately increase their own demands for something special and exclusive. Worse still, they might be tempted to ignore the risk involved. Until that risk materialised, retailers would enjoy the fruits of success and ask for more. If a failure to sell ever entered into the equation, some retailers would stamp their feet and ask Moorcroft to take unsold pieces back because the design was 'not right for us'. Another less obvious possibility was that the potentially voracious appetite of the Collectors' Club for new work might increase still further. Theoretically, trade sales and sales in-house offered a system of commercial checks and balances. If one fell down, the other could be allowed to rise. Hugh began to realise that it was not as simple as that. Moorcroft was now involved in a risky game.

Those leaving the Sandbach Road factory at the close of the 2001 Christmas Weekend were happy collectors who had all enjoyed a second Moorcroft Christmas experience together. That same happiness reverberated throughout each year that followed. The formula on each occasion was friendly and familiar: mince pies and mulled wine; special designs created for the occasion; and for Moorcroft, a means of securing new work at a time when retailers were busy with their Christmas trade. Apart from 2004, it was all good-humoured seasonal fun. That was the year when Moorcroft learned the hard way that it served no useful purpose to give away a free piece of pottery to Collectors attending a Christmas Weekend. The seasonal gesture was abused. Dealers attending sold their Christmas gifts on the Internet a day or so after the event closed. It was a sad experience for all concerned, and inevitable changes were made the following year. Even so, Collectors' Christmas Weekends at Moorcroft had come to stay.

One Christmas Weekend turned out to be especially memorable. The 2003 event was brought forward a week to give collectors the opportunity to enjoy the BBC's Children in Need auction in Stoke-on-Trent on Friday 21st November. Moorcroft had teamed up with the BBC to raise money for this most worthwhile charity, and its commitment was to make sixty-six unique pots for Antiques Roadshow celebrity Eric Knowles to auction. It is not generally known that Eric is also a professional auctioneer and a very fine one at that. To aid the cause, the BBC persuaded Stoke-on-Trent City Council to host the auction free of charge in Stoke's massive Kings Hall. For the Moorcroft production team, the occasion had all the qualities of a potential nightmare.

The BBC raked in potential designs by the sackful, these would-be Moorcroft designers paying five pounds a head to Children in Need for the privilege. Literally thousands of designs had come in from all over the country, and it fell to the Moorcroft Design Studio to appraise each one. The sixty-six best entries were selected for production. As a final auction lot, Elise added an eight-inch Owl and Pussycat ginger jar for good measure, and in just eighteen days those incredible tube-liners and painters at Moorcroft were coaxed and cajoled into making all sixty-six winning entries plus the ginger jar in time for the auction. Then, with Eric Knowles at his best, and with Hugh, Elise and Works Manager Gloria Withington all dressed up as porters for the occasion, the auction started. By the time it finished two hours later, the BBC's Children in Need Charity was almost £40,000 better off. As a special treat for Elise, the unique Owl and the Pussycat ginger jar sold for a healthy £3200! The excitement at Moorcroft touched everyone as it swept through the Works and into the factory shop. It also swept Hugh, Elise and the Design Studio into the new year with a firm belief that Moorcroft had a vibrant and happy future to look forward to.

A small part of that future identified itself as a result of the auction. A series of nursery rhyme ginger jars, starting with The Owl and the Pussycat by Nicky Slaney, was launched that same November and sold out in less than a month. Introduced as a replacement for the earlier crèche pieces, nursery rhyme ginger jars proved to be just as popular. In June 2005, Hickory Dickory Dock achieved an identical reception. Little Miss Muffet has yet to appear, but for a designer more on maternity leave than not in the recent past, Nicky surpassed herself.

Nursery Rhyme Collection. From left to right:
Hickory Dickory Dock (2005) Ltd.Edn.250 and
The Owl and the Pussycat (2004) Ltd.Edn.250
Height 15cm (6")

FOUR

Prestigious Rewards

The provision of subsidised crèche facilities at Moorcroft had acquired a grudging notoriety in the Potteries, but they were not an example other pottery manufacturers chose to follow. Among those planning to use the Moorcroft facility after completion of her maternity leave was designer Nicola Slaney. While Nicky would never claim to be the instigator of the idea, second time round she was certainly the one on whose shoulders the burden of designing a millennium crèche piece had fallen. What arrived on a small version of the popular Moorcroft ginger jar was Nicky's aptly-named Wish Upon a Star. Within a matter of weeks, trialing had been completed and production underway. As soon as the launch of the little ginger jar was announced, orders arrived from collectors in their hundreds. Wish Upon a Star provided a morale boost for Hugh and the innovative ideas on which he had relied all his life began to take shape in his mind once more.

Wish Upon a Star (2000) Ltd. Edn. 400 Height 10cm (4")

Elise Adams was also an innovative thinker, and it was she who suggested that Moorcroft collectors deserved recognition for their loyalty. Elise knew that collectors were the lifeblood of the art pottery. At a meeting Hugh, Elise and Kim Thompson agreed there should be some form of tangible reward for long service to the Collectors' Club, with each third year of membership triggering the right to buy a special design. In practice this meant that after three years' continuous membership the right to buy the first vase would arise; after six years the second vase, and so on up to fifteen years. The words 'Star Award' would be used, and as the Collectors' Club had been in existence since 1987, only the first four categories of member required Star Award designs. For One Star members Rachel was the first

FACING: *First Collection of Star Awards (2001). Clockwise from top: Kaffir Lily (2 Star), Soldiers Grass (2001-2003), Honeysuckle (4 Star), Lizard Orchid (3 Star) and Sweet Thief (1 Star). Tallest vase 20cm (8")*

to come forward with a relatively small, but totally effective design featuring hearts-ease, a wild flower dubbed by William Shakespeare as Sweet Thief, and from which the senior designer had taken her design inspiration as well as a potential name. Shirley Hayes offered Kaffir Lily which was allocated to Two Star members, while Philip Gibson's Lizard Orchid was earmarked for Three Star members. That left only Four Star members, and for them an altogether different treat was in store.

As custodian of design at Moorcroft, Hugh often received frequent career details from designers wishing to secure a place in the Moorcroft Design Studio. Occasionally watercolours would be included, but these were rare. Each application was taken seriously. Sometimes Hugh would consult Rachel, although perhaps not as often as he should have done. Occasionally there would be an interview, but mostly a kind but firm rejection. One such application arrived from a designer named Sarah Brummell-Bailey, and it stood out from all the others in two significant ways. First, there was no request to become a member of the Moorcroft Design Studio. Second, the nine watercolours submitted showed a very distinct and very personal design style. Echoes of Florianware, Hugh remarked to Rachel, calling to mind early design work of the founding father of Moorcroft, William Moorcroft. It was also significant that Sarah lived in Norfolk and showed not the slightest inclination to leave East Anglia.

To mention a more delicate point, Sarah was somewhat older than all other Design Studio members. Even the eldest, Philip Gibson, had to defer to the years of Sarah Brummell-Bailey. After discussions and trials, and yet more discussions and trials, Sarah's Remember vase passed through an enthusiastic design approval meeting. All five hundred pieces in the edition were destined to sell out before 2001 was more that a few weeks old. At the same meeting, a six-inch ginger jar covered with Honeysuckle in Sarah's inimitable style was also approved. Hugh's wife Maureen suggested that Honeysuckle should be used as the piece available to Four Star members. Everyone agreed, and on New Year's Day all four Star Award designs were launched to a delighted Collectors' Club. A year later, the four original Star pieces were joined by Emma Bossons' Soldiers Grass, designed for those who had been club members for more than fifteen years. Lucky are those who purchased Soldiers Grass as the Five Star member's piece. Only twenty nine were ever made!

Soon after the millennium introduction of Anna Lily as a range, Hugh received a letter of complaint from a collector. The thrust of the complaint was that as the design had first appeared on the 1999 year plate, it was wrong to bring the same design forward a year later as a range. By so doing Moorcroft had denied the collec-

FACING: *Remember* (2001) Ltd.Edn.500. Height 35cm (14″)

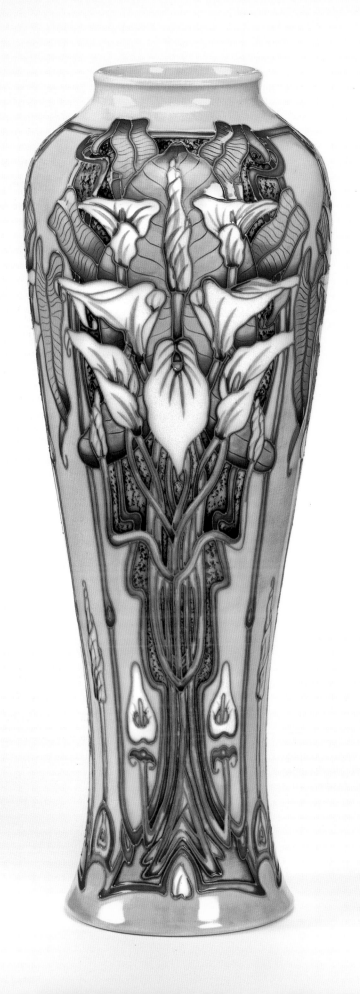

tor the potential fruit of his investment in the year plate. Hugh answered by saying that if the same argument had been applied to Lamia several years earlier, the world would have been deprived of one of the most successful Moorcroft designs of all time. Rachel Bishop's Lamia range was to enthral everyone for a decade, yet it had been preceded by a prestigious limited edition. Rather as Lamia had done, Anna Lily displayed all the hallmarks of a design with a long future ahead, and like everyone else in the Design Studio, Nicky Slaney would regularly refresh her work by removing less popular shapes in a particular range and introducing new ones to take their place. Because of the complaint, Hugh always felt a perverse twinge of satisfaction every time Nicky designed new pieces to enhance the appeal of Anna Lily. In 2001 eight new shapes, a handsome lamp and a mug were all approved. At the same time the problematic 8/6 vase disappeared. Still in the mood to refresh existing work, Nicky turned her attention to Fruit Garden, a millennium range featuring strawberries and strawberry blossom as its design theme. As a result, 2001 witnessed the arrival of three new Fruit Garden vases and a lamp. It was enough to ensure survival of Fruit Garden for another year.

Nicky was not alone in her labours. Shirley Hayes increased the appeal of Palmata with an attractive clock and three new vases, and the following year an additional vase and jug were added to the range. All in all, 2001 turned out to be a productive year for a group of designers in the mood to refresh

FACING: (top left): Fruit Garden (2001). Tallest vase 15 cm (6")
(bottom left) Woodside Farm (2001). Diameter of plate 25 cm (10")
(right) Montana Cornflower blue (2001) Height 40 cm (16")
Montana Cornflower pink (2001). Height 40 cm (16")
Woodside Farm (2000). Height 20 cm (8")

(Above) Anna Lily (2001). Tallest vase 25 cm (10")
(Below) Anna Lily (2001). Tallest vase 15 cm (6")

their existing catalogue designs. Anji Davenport introduced four new pieces into her Woodside Farm collection, a range further enhanced in 2002 by the addition of a new six-inch vase. Rachel was not far behind. She and Hugh both believed with a passion that Gypsy was a great Moorcroft design, but whatever their personal opinions, it was one which retailers assiduously ignored. If retailers decided not to take Gypsy into stock, collectors would be denied the opportunity of buying it. The thought almost made Hugh weep. One day Gypsy would be seen for what it was – one of the great Moorcroft designs of all time. In a gesture of defiance, Rachel put Gypsy onto a new lamp. To do so, she used a shape much loved by collectors; but the senior designer was fighting a losing battle. The following year, Gypsy disappeared.

It was, Rachel reminded Hugh late one evening, a fact of life that some collectors were running out of display space in their homes. Lilliputian Moorcroft enamels had gone some way to redress the balance, but there was no reason why Moorcroft should not become more imaginative and concentrate on decorative tiles. Tiles, or 'plaques' as Elise primly tells everyone to call them, had been around for a year or two, but attempts to make them successful had come to nothing. As if to emphasise her point, the senior designer produced drawings of two double tile panels illustrating her Montana Cornflower, one pink and one blue. Tiles made a slow start, but the solution arrived on its own the following year. Emma Bossons introduced a Calla Lily tile which revolutionised attitudes to decorative tile work. Rachel had been right. There was a place for decorative tiles at Moorcroft.

An incorrigible collector himself, Hugh had al-

Palmata (2001). Tallest vase 23cm (9")
Palmata (2002). Jug 24cm (9.5")

Simeon (2001). Diameter 43cm (17")

ways approached his work at Moorcroft from the perspective of a collector. In 1986, when he acquired his first shares in the company, he was a collector. By 1993, when he and Maureen acquired a controlling interest in Moorcroft together, he was still a collector. Collectors were his kind of people and Moorcroft Collectors' Club members were his friends – each and every one of them. Hugh knew that collectors loved a challenge. There is no equivalent thrill to finding a unique piece of Moorcroft. In the past, the sale of trials had given collectors the opportunity of finding potential 'one-off' pieces, but trials tended to be erratic and of variable quality. If a designer or painter struggled with a design in the early, formative stages of their work, trials were plentiful but weak. Conversely, if a designer was quick to bring a new piece to production, trials were inevitably rare but of high quality. Hugh's final millennium idea was to harness the collector's genuine drive to find examples of Moorcroft that were outside the catalogue. To a certain extent the special pieces created by Design Studio members both for open weekends and for selected retailers satisfied that passion, as indeed did quality trials; but even at open weekends the pure elation at finding an 'off-catalogue' piece was rare. The characteristic of the special pots Hugh had in mind, which would distinguish them from all others, was that they should be large. Prestige pieces, he called them.

Early thinking at Moorcroft was muddled with very little distinction drawn be-

tween prestige versions of catalogue designs and new prestige pieces derived from fresh design inspiration. Large moulds had to be made quickly, something much easier to say than do. Master mould-maker Trevor Critchlow will always say that he is one of the busiest people at the Works, and for Trevor to find extra time for new work had always been an uphill struggle, but on this occasion, as with others, he succeeded. By the time the 2001 International Spring Fair opened at the National Exhibition Centre in Birmingham, five prestige pieces were ready to meet their public. Two of the designs had never appeared in a Moorcroft catalogue. Both were larger versions of the original 576/9 Meknes 'Day' and 'Night' vases designed by Beverley Wilkes. Another two were substantial Queens Choice vases designed by Emma Bossons, while a particularly large and elegant Simeon bowl from Philip Gibson completed the first Moorcroft prestige collection.

It was at this moment that the art pottery realised it had a problem. Nobody had thought about exhibiting prestige work at the N.E.C. As a result there was no room on the stand to display the new collection. Out of necessity, each new prestige piece was placed on high shelves in the 'office', a small box room which doubled as a kitchenette hidden behind the far wing of the new and futuristic Moorcroft millennium exhibition stand. The sight of the pride and joy of all Moorcroft prestige art standing on shelves among packets of orange juice, potato crisps and biscuits was faintly amusing to those who regard trade shows as the high altar of sales activity. Moorcroft had always been different, even in failure. There they all were, the best that the art pottery could design and make, sitting among the tea mugs, sugar, milk and tea bags, illuminated

(Above) Meknes Night (2001). Height 38cm (15")
(below) Meknes Day (2001). Height 38cm (15")

by nothing more than a small, flickering strip light. Retailers loved the new prestige pieces; they made notes, took photographs and talked happily about customers who would die to lay their hands on such magnificent works of art. To buy prestige pieces was a significant financial commitment for a retailer to assume, but they did. By the time the show closed, Moorcroft had more ex-catalogue prestige orders on its books than anyone could have imagined.

Among all the excitement it was easy to overlook the fact that Montagnac, Emma Bossons' lead piece in that year's catalogue had virtually sold out before the Spring Fair closed. Admittedly a significant number had been put on one side at Donald Reid's request to satisfy the North American market, now opening up on a number of fronts. Hugh loved Montagnac. As a thirteen-year-old, he had stayed at a farm in the Dordogne for several long, rather lonely months. The farm had been called Montagnac, and its name had been annexed to Emma's design of vineyards, juicy purple grapes and a chateau at the foot of distant hills under an azure sky. Later that same year Emma travelled to France

Queens Choice (2001). Height 40cm (16″)

where she saw for herself the Montagnac farmhouse in which Hugh had stayed all those decades before, and much to his surprise she called him on her mobile phone to tell him where she was. Later that same summer Hugh celebrated his sixtieth birthday. Unknown to him, Emma had designed a one-off Montagnac vase based on the old Dordogne farmhouse. The vase was presented to Hugh with best birthday wishes from everyone at the Works, together with Emma's original watercolour.

For a few months after the Spring Fair closed, a small amount of retailer confusion wafted around the prestige pieces. Moorcroft was forced to admit this confusion was certainly not the retailers' fault. From the outset the art pottery had made a fumbling attempt to distinguish between large pieces based on catalogue designs and those which were not. In reality there should have been no distinction. The thinking was that a piece was prestigious if it was large, and large meant fifteen inches (38 centimetres) or more in height. A good example surfaced nine months

Queens Choice (2001). Height 38cm (15")

FACING: *Montagnac (2001) Ltd.Edn.100. Height 60cm (24")*

later in Rachel Bishop's Bullerswood carpet vase, an adaptation of a design on a William Morris carpet discovered in the Australian outback early in 2001. The shape selected by the senior designer was not a prestige piece by any definition operating at the time. As if to highlight the point, Rachel modified the Bullerswood design and transferred it to a much larger version of the same shape. This time Bullerswood fell unambiguously into the prestige category.

Rather like the Collectors' Club Star Award pieces, the Moorcroft prestige collection developed a life of its own. Both were destined to become permanent features of Moorcroft life. More significantly, Hugh had been forced to recognise that however much he might wish otherwise, he could never again rely solely on retailers in the United Kingdom to sustain his much-loved art pottery, particularly those retailers who stacked their shelves with jokey pots and plaques, cold-cast resin models of animals and birds, not to mention rubber dinosaurs, teddy bears, dollies and other miscellaneous giftware imported from China and the Pacific Rim. There was nothing wrong with any of these products, but if a specific collectables market collapsed for whatever reason and retailers ran short of cash as a result, Moorcroft would suffer even if its own art pottery was selling as strongly as ever. The living proof of that argument is to be found in Leeds' Victoria Quarter where James Macintyre & Co. entered the year 2001 stronger than they had ever been, devoutly thankful that only work from Moorcroft stood proud on their shelves.

(Above) Detail of the William Morris 'Bullerswood' carpet
FACING: Bullerswood (2001). From left to right: Ltd.Edn.100 and Ltd.Edn.10.
Tallest vase 50cm (20")

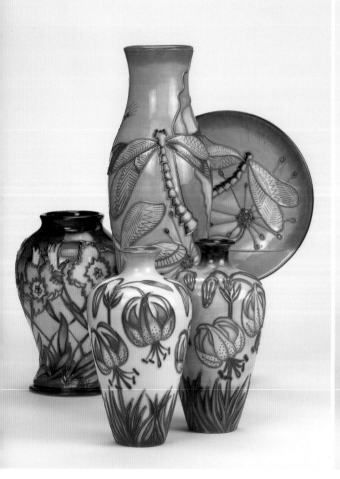

FIVE

Out in the Works

Hugh had never pushed the Design Studio so hard for a May Open Weekend as he did in the millennium year. Most designers responded by bringing forward a fresh crop of designs for that all-important event. The quality had to be high, he told them. That much was clear. Collectors had become increasingly discerning in defining design in terms of quality. To make his point, Hugh spent a great deal of time discussing design ideas on a one-to-one basis. Because of ongoing work for the following year, Hugh's demands for the May Open Weekend might have been seen as an artistic intrusion into an already busy schedule. When Open Weekend finally arrived, Moorcroft literally rolled out the red carpet for a record one thousand collectors. Elise and Kim hired a huge marquee for the occasion, which they decorated with an impressive forest of blue and gold balloons, as well as floral displays that would have done credit to the Chelsea Flower Show. The mood was festive. Even the Moorcroft museum adjacent to the factory shop had a special sparkle all its own. Museum advisor Kathy Niblett confessed she and Barbara Mountford had cleaned the entire exhibition area 'from top to toe'. By consolidating shelves and cabinets, Kathy made it possible for a significantly larger open display. Although the exhibition was restricted to examples of discontinued work, she somehow contrived to show a complete set of Collectors' Club pieces dating back to 1987. In this way Club members were able to see museum examples of their own pots at a glance.

African Savannah from Anji showed a fabulous weaverbird building a rock-the-cradle hanging nest. Her second contribution, Myth, also found itself the centre of attention with its alternative brown and blue versions. During the course of the weekend all available pieces disappeared at a speed that caused finance director Ted Turner to blink with disbelief. Debbie Hancock's Pastimes with its conkers and mushrooms proved to be an instant hit, as did both versions of Rachel's Martagon lilies, their blooms nodding gently on their perches. Philip Gibson's Maiden Pink showed just how popular the only male in the Moorcroft Design Studio had become with Club members, while Nicky's Heralds of Spring featured winter iris and a mass

FACING: (top left) Angels Trumpets pink (2000). Height 18cm (7") (top right) Open Weekend Collection (2000) Clockwise from top: Heralds of Spring, Etoile orange, Etoile gold, Myth blue, Myth brown and Sunray. Tallest vase 15cm (6") (bottom left) Open Weekend Collection (2000). Clockwise from top: Lords and Ladies vase and coaster, Martagon yellow, Martagon orange and Maiden Pink. Tallest vase 23cm (9")
(bottom right) Open Weekend Collection (2000). Clockwise from top: Correa green, Correa turquoise, African Savannah and Correa blue. Tallest vase 13cm (5")

of snowdrops bending their delicate white heads around the base of the vase. In contrast, Emma's new-look Sunray followed the path of her more abstract Indigo design introduced at the beginning of the year. Still in the heavens, two Etoile pieces from Debbie Hancock left the firmament at high speed and started a more earthly journey into collectors' homes. Both had been designed in two different colourways, each as popular as the other. In contrast, a futuristic Lords and Ladies vase and coaster from Jeanne McDougall offered few clues about her impending departure early the following year. One of the surprises of the occasion was tucked away in one of those intriguing corners found only in the Moorcroft factory shop. From its discreet hiding place, Sian Leeper's Correa in no fewer than three colourways attracted sufficient admirers to ensure that all pieces on offer sold out. It was the same with Shirley Hayes' Centary which also arrived in three different colourways. Both designs resulted from one of the more indecisive moments in the life of the design approval committee!

Back in the magnificent marquee, raffles with prizes much coveted by Moorcroft collectors caused great excitement, while a quantity of Anji Davenport's superb Angels' Trumpet vases in a rare rose colourway were presented to overseas collectors

Thaxted (2000) Ltd.Edn.250
Height 20cm (8")

Thaxted charger (2000). Diameter 35cm (14")

Thaxted Collection (2000). Clockwise from top: Phlox, Nouveau Lily, Black-Eyed Susan and Abbey Rose Tallest vase 20cm (8")

who had travelled all the way from their home countries to Sandbach Road. There were more international collectors present than ever before, hailing variously from New Zealand and Australia, the Netherlands, Luxembourg, Canada, Italy and the United States. A much larger number of special presentation vases were required than in 1999, when Debbie Hancock's Woodland Flora was given to a handful of international collectors who had crossed the seas to celebrate the Moorcroft centenary. It was important for everyone at the Works to realise just how much the Collectors' Club had grown in popularity over the intervening period.

Moorcroft had every reason to be pleased at the way the millennium year was developing. A rewarding Easter Weekend at Thaxted had preceded the successful

May Open Weekend. With early morning queues stretching from Thaxted's six-hundred-year-old guildhall right up to its magnificent cathedral-like church, the consensus was that it had been more memorable in both numbers and interest than any previous event held in the ancient town. Limited to sixty visitors at any one time, Thaxted guildhall was continuously full to capacity. Glorious sunny weather and a light, warm breeze blowing from the southwest contributed to an atmosphere full of genuine excitement among the three thousand or so visitors. Even Patrick Haylock at Thaxted Galleries had reason to smile. His delightful antique shop had been commandeered by Kim Thompson and her determined team as a second retail outlet. The shop doorbell rang constantly. Collectors talked happily together while they exercised the privilege of choice between Philip Gibson's Thaxted vase, Shirley Hayes' Phlox pot, an attractive Nouveau Lily from Debbie Hancock and Black-Eyed Susan from Anji Davenport. Interestingly, Phil's Thaxted vase had first appeared in a modified form on a Moorcroft charger made especially for the inhabitants of St Vrain, a small French hamlet twinned with the old Essex town. Moorcroft records show that only one trial of the Thaxted charger was ever made, making it most rare among trials. For collectors, one of the most interesting of all the pieces on offer at Thaxted was Elise Adams' Abbey Rose, the first design ever brought forward by a Moorcroft Collectors' Club Secretary for her own members.

As visitors milled together in the Thaxted sunshine, other plans started forming in Hugh's mind. The Thaxted event had been the first serious occasion on which Moorcroft had gone out to meet its collectors. For administration supremo director Kim Thompson the effort involved had been enormous. But even as collectors were enjoying themselves in seemingly endless circular tours of the windmill, church, guildhall, Patrick Haylock's shop and Michael and Pepe's tearooms, Hugh's mind had already travelled into the future in pursuit of another new idea. A list of famous stately homes had taken shape in his brain, and top of that list was Chatsworth. Nestling in the heart of Derbyshire dales, Chatsworth was steeped in history, full of priceless works of art and with restaurant, café and shop facilities of more than adequate calibre and capacity to cater for visiting hoards of Moorcroft collectors. After the Thaxted experience, Chatsworth at Easter would make a great weekend for collectors, preferably embellished with a quality lecture and perhaps an exhibition. Hugh decided to make an appointment to see the Duke and Duchess of Devonshire with his old friend, television personality Eric Knowles, who knew Their Graces personally.

Hard on the heels of the first idea came another which was more complex and

(Above left) Torridon (2004). Tallest vase 25cm (10")
(Below left) Trout (2001). Diameter 35cm (14")

(Above right) Trout (2001). Tallest vase 20cm (8")
(Below right) Torridon (2004). Diameter 20cm (8")

Hidcote (2004) Ltd.Edn.250
Height 30cm (12")

far reaching. Designers at Moorcroft enjoyed almost total freedom from the endless inane demands imposed on those employed in some other companies by management untrained, unskilled and often devoid of ideas of how to harness the benefit design could deliver to their business. Indeed, one managing director working in the applied arts had once boasted proudly to Hugh that he had never read a book on design in his life! That made Hugh tremble, but designers themselves also have responsibilities, and now and then it is necessary to remind them of this. One of the most important is a need to be aware of the wishes of those who ultimately pay their salaries. In the real world they are called customers. At Moorcroft they are called collectors. What Hugh asked was that each designer should commit a fair share of their time on centre stage meeting their public. Designers were Moorcroft ambassadors, and to be an ambassador was part of the responsibility they had to carry out as designers.

Design on its own was not enough. It was essential that Moorcroft designers travelled out into the world to meet collectors as part of their jobs.

Throughout the Easter event at Thaxted Hugh had been watching visitors buying numerous examples of Phil's Thaxted vase. Unfortunately, no Phil was present to greet them, talk to them or even simply smile and say 'hello'. It was hardly surprising. Neither Hugh nor Elise had thought to ask Phil to come along in the first place. The whole idea of a designer taking centre stage suggested something beyond personal appearances. Struggling a little, Hugh managed to catch hold of the direction his thoughts were taking him. Every so often designers should be asked to create a signature collection on their own. It would be a real challenge for them all. Hugh made up his mind. As always, the first person to consult was senior designer Rachel Bishop. The conversation which took place between them was animated and constructive. Reflections of a Decade, a Rachel Bishop solo collection, became a reality in 2003 as a result. Phil followed suit in 2004 with Philip Gibson Presents, while Emma Bossons was to consolidate her reputation with Hidden Dreams in 2005.

Perhaps the most intriguing of these three collections was the one which came

FACING: *Hidcote (2004) Ltd.Edn.75. Height 45cm (18")*

(Above) Pink Damask (2004)
Diameter 15cm (6")
(Below) Pastimes (2000) Ltd.Edn.250
Height 10cm (4")

from Phil in 2004. During the latter part of 2003, Phil had become anxious that he might be losing his design edge. This was not good news, and a mere trickle of work from Phil was a worrying development. There was nothing for it. Hugh asked Phil to stop all new work and take a break. It was all he could do, and for the custodian of Moorcroft design it seemed precious little. Phil drifted through Christmas and into the New Year almost a shadow of his former self. The design fires seemed to have died, his famous enthusiasm gone. It was a new dilemma, but one which Phil resolved entirely on his own. He recalled a time when he had hit a similarly poor creative period as a freelance designer. A client had suggested that he should flood new design work with colour. Phil did so, and it worked. The time had come to do the same thing again.

The result was Phil's great Hidcote vase which carried an incredible mix of vibrant colour. The designer was back on form. The Hidcote vase turned out to be the catalyst for six out of eight designs in the 'Philip Gibson Presents' collection. The autumnal Dahlia was a firm favourite of the Moorcroft chairman. During a tour of New Zealand in March 2006, Hugh found several Dahlia vases sitting hopefully on retailers' shelves without a single collector in sight. Hugh gave each one he came across a pat just to show that he had noticed them. Another Hidcote theme was picked up on Ivory Bells which used campanula flowers on a set of three small pieces. Pink Damask, a numbered edition, featured day lilies, while an elegant jug which Phil called Wyevale almost came to life with its subtle pink clematis flowers. To round off the Hidcote part of the collection, Phil designed a colourful Hidcote tile plus a ginger jar decorated with bright red peonies. 'We'll call the jar Tree Peony. Why be complicated?' Phil said. As for the Hidcote tile, Elise's persistence changed several hundred years of history in ceramic art. By the year end, all Moorcroft tiles were called 'plaques'.

Moving in a slightly different direction within his collection, Phil used two fish,

FACING: (top left) Dahlia (2004) Ltd.Edn.250. Height 23cm (9") (top right) Tree Peony (2004) Height 15cm (6")
(bottom left) Derwent (2004) Ltd.Edn.200. Height 20cm (8") (bottom right) Wyevale (2004) Numbered.Edn. Height 27cm (11")

Centary in three colourways (2000). Height 20cm (8")

roach and perch, to decorate a sturdy pot with a strong design which he asked to be called Derwent. A year earlier, Hugh would have deemed it impossible to contemplate a solo collection from Phil, but to round it off the designer introduced his Torridon loons, diving birds that inhabit a Torridon loch and there command attention with their amusing rituals and black and white plumage. Two Torridon vases made an appearance accompanied a modest eight-inch plate. The whole collection had Phil's collector fan club in raptures.

The millennium catalogue had been hard to produce, and the number of design discontinuation proposals which surfaced during the year had been more numerous than anyone predicted. A decline in sales to unacceptable levels was generally

Ivory Bells (2004). Tallest vase 15 cm (6")

the yardstick against which discontinuation decisions were made. Armed with only a calculator, designers would reach the same conclusions themselves. Limited editions always had to be replaced. Additionally, less popular shapes within a continuing range were regularly weeded out and replaced with something new. Old favourites which made an exit in this way included the Dateline Series, Jeanne McDougall's Balloons, Flame of the Forest by Philip Gibson and Debbie Hancock's Gustavia Augusta. Even Oberon, a perennial Moorcroft favourite designed by Rachel, was moved out of the catalogue to make way for new arrivals. For good measure, Arizona, California and Florida joined the millennium exit list. So too did every one of Rachel's Islay shapes. Philip Gibson's Trout lamps and two vases were added to the exit list late in the day. To keep his 1999 Trout design alive, Phil decided to bring forward two new vases and a fourteen-inch charger.

A new design that surfaced around that time caught Hugh's eye. It featured some striking blue Himalayan poppies, but that was not the only thing which commanded attention. The unusual structure of the design and the way the stems bent at almost 90° reflected Sarah Brummell-Bailey's earlier work on Remember with its strong Art Nouveau style; but there the similarities ended. Phil's Himalayan poppies were dramatic, where Sarah's lilies were gentle, almost soothing, in comparison. The blue used on the poppies was electric while the leaves shaded from a soft fawn to a muted purple. It was ceramic design at its best, and a fine example of how similar design techniques can produce totally different results. Before his meeting with Phil came to an end, Hugh was smiling. So was Phil. From out of the blue, they joked together, had come a potential Collectors' Club piece for the post-millennium year. It would be a worthy successor to Anji Davenport's Angels Trumpets. For a while Hugh and Phil argued about the name. On this occasion Phil had his say, but Hugh had his way. It would be called Blue Rhapsody.

Woodland Flora (1999). Height 15cm (6")   FACING: *Blue Rhapsody (2001). Height 25cm (10")*

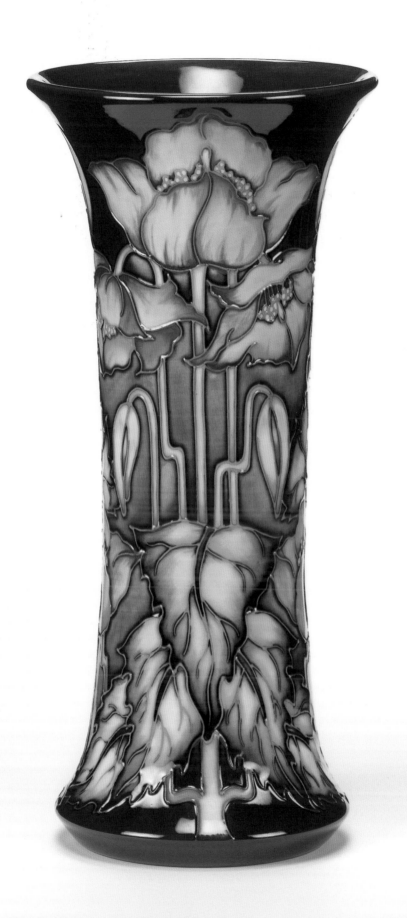

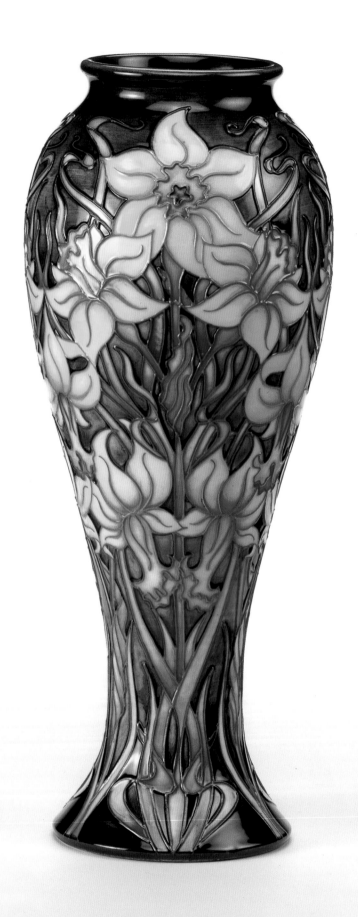

SIX

Innovation by Design

Chatsworth at Easter was not to be. The foot and mouth epidemic in the United Kingdom put an end to Hugh's original idea. In its place the first Moorcroft Spring Festival arrived, but to make the occasion a success Moorcroft needed yet more new designs. It was the only way that the theory of a Spring Festival would translate into a successful reality. For this to happen the Design Studio had to be told of the decision and the implications for their work schedules. Rachel Bishop's famous 1995 Daffodil vase had been one of the most successful limited editions ever to emerge from Moorcroft. Originally priced at £375, by 2001 some collectors were reputed to have paid in excess of £1500 to secure a piece in the secondary market. Rachel was not the slightest bit interested in secondary market values, but she liked the suggestion that she should design a second vase carrying a daffodil image. Before her conversation with Hugh came to an end, the senior designer had already decided to use the shape of a vase first made by William Moorcroft a hundred years earlier. The elegant 75/10 with its classical contours was the perfect vehicle for a successor to Rachel's 1995 Daffodil. When it arrived, she named her new design Jonquilla.

Emma Bossons' Hepatica design had been one of the great successes of the millennium year, with order books showing that more pieces had been sold than any other design. Initially 2001 showed Hepatica heading for a repeat performance, but by February it was Emma's new design Queens Choice which started to take up the running, gently overtaking Hepatica as it did so. Emma was now competing with herself to become the most successful Moorcroft designer two years in succession. Hugh decided that the time had come to test the Design Studio's youngest member a little harder with a task to be completed in a hurry. As a result, Emma was asked to be ready with a spring flower design for the inaugural Spring Festival. It remained to be seen whether she would cope with the challenge as promptly as Rachel had done. Easter Saturday fell on the 14th April that year leaving less than ten weeks to complete design work and trials, as well as manufacture enough pieces for collectors to take home. Kim Thompson had already decided that the Spring Festival would run

FACING: *Jonquilla (2001) Ltd.Edn.200. Height 23cm (10″)*

*Elisha's Tears (2001) Ltd.Edn.20
Height 40cm (16")*

from the 31st March to 28th April, with new items of interest introduced each weekend to make April a month offering something fresh and stimulating every week.

While Kim moved into action to stage a month of surprises, Hugh set about encouraging Moorcroft designers in every way that he could. All of them had to work around the clock on their personal contributions for an event which, with luck, would feature daffodils from Rachel, a familiar spring flower from Emma and a set of six Easter eggcups from Rachel, Emma, Sian Leeper, Philip Gibson, Angela Davenport and Shirley Hayes, each individually decorated with a spring flower.

When it arrived, the first day of the Spring Festival was attended by a crowd of dedicated collectors. A queue had lined up patiently outside the Works since the early hours of the morning. Every one of them wanted to be the first inside. There was plenty for everyone to enjoy, including the first comprehensive exhibition of the 2001 Moorcroft catalogue collection. The walls of the packing warehouse had been temporarily swathed in blue silk by Kim to 'create atmosphere'. In addition to the new collection were some of the first pieces of the art pottery's Prestige Collection. Not surprisingly, this ad hoc exhibition room became affectionately known as 'The Blue Room' at the Works.

Back in December 2000, Nicola Slaney's innovative Waters of Time had captured the imagination of collectors. Housed in the Blue Room were the prestige pieces which followed, including Shirley Hayes' Venice, Philip Gibson's superb Mediterranean Doves, Rachel Bishop's Sun God and Anji Davenport's Elisha's Tears. Elise Adams was not the only person who enthused about Shirley's Venice pieces. The movement of freehand-painted water and the detail of the Venetian buildings and bridges combined to create a piece of ceramic art where every feature worked in perfect harmony. Venice sold out by lunchtime on the first day, leaving Kim Thompson to rue the moment she forecast that five pieces were all that Moorcroft would sell!

FACING: *Mediterranean Doves (2001) Numbered Edn. Height 38cm (15")*

Venice by Day (2001) Ltd.Edn.5
Height 45cm (18″)

Venice by Night (2001) Ltd.Edn.5
Height 45cm (18″)

Two collectors confided in Elise that they had been swept away by Venice, and looked forward to the moment when a piece they had ordered assumed pride of place in their home. To avoid collector disappointment, Shirley Hayes agreed to convert her design into a different colourway, later called Venice by Night. The reworked Venice by Night was also limited to just five pieces and sold out as quickly as its predecessor.

Emma finally decided to introduce a Bluebells vase for the occasion. It was a sheer delight. A designer for whom the arrival of Spring had always been a source of inspiration, the task of creating a special piece had not proved difficult. The design was launched on Saturday 7th April, with many collectors vowing to return to the factory shop before the end of April to make absolutely certain they secured a Bluebells vase. Indeed, so infectious was the overall enthusiasm of collectors that twelve casual visitors who stumbled in on the first day of Spring Festival joined the Collectors' Club there and then. Among both casual visitors and dedicated collectors alike, the Springtime eggcups proved popular. As each eggcup had been designed by a different member of the Design Studio, the sets proved particularly attractive. The lids of the presentation boxes in which they nestled were soon snapped shut and carried to the till.

Perhaps the most unusual, even intriguing item of Moorcroft on display was dark blue, triangular in shape, and emblazoned with the words 'Moorcroft Pottery'. The new Moorcroft name plaque was dressed with the succulent fruit of Queens Choice. Although still at the trial stage, the name plaque was scheduled to appear on the shelves of Moorcroft retailers well before Christmas. It would be good work for the art pottery at the tail end of the year, but it was the instinctively inventive Elise Adams who suggested that the design on the name change every year, making it collectable in its own right. Only a few months after its arrival, a Queens Choice name plaque was sold on the Internet for £182 – an instant premium on the original retail price of £125. Elise had been vindicated.

Although Emma's Queens Choice range had sold consistently well from the date of its introduction, Moorcroft never took into account the possibility that the new triangular name plaques would become seriously collectable, but that is what happened after Elise intervened. Sian Leeper recognised that name plaques had become popular and adapted her Sophie Christina design to replace Emma's inaugural Queens Choice. Watching the moves with some amusement, Emma returned to name plaques in 2003 with her innovative Hartgring design.

Throughout the Spring Festival the Moorcroft factory shop was decorated with bright, colourful daffodils of the horticultural kind. In contrast, daffodils of the ceramic kind from senior designer Rachel Bishop soon disappeared. Jonquilla was cov-

Queens Choice (2001)
Length of name plaque 18cm (7")

Sungod (2001) Ltd.Edn.15
Height 45cm (18")

ered with nodding heads of golden narcissi, and because of the success of her 1995 Daffodil vase, it was almost inevitable that Jonquilla would assume a special place in Moorcroft collectors' affections. Daffodils are said to represent rebirth, a symbol of a new beginning that comes with Spring. The flowers are also said to be a sign of good fortune and hope for the future. Those collectors who walked away with a Jonquilla vase in their bags at the opening of the first Spring Festival would have agreed. Others who found themselves watching the Richard and Judy show, 'This Morning', on their television screens later the following week also saw Rachel's Jonquilla, Emma's Bluebells and the Springtime eggcups. Every piece was described in glowing terms. No better advertisement could have been devised by the most prestigious agency. Pandemonium followed, with phone lines at Moorcroft jammed solidly for three days.

The life of an art pottery is never simple. Kilns collapse or misfire; flu epidemics can run rife throughout the workforce; snow can close the Works overnight. For Moorcroft, the outcome of the Spring Festival became a matter of considerable jubilation. Rachel's Jonquilla vases and Emma's Bluebells vases all sold out long before the festival closed, while orders for the designers' egg cups would take until at least midsummer to fulfil.

With visitors to the inaugural Spring Festival milling all around her, everything that happened in 1999 might well have happened in another age as far as Elise was concerned. In 1999 Nicky and Emma made one of their designer visits to Ashwood Nurseries. It had been a fruitful trip. Both were given access to John Massey's world-famous hellebore house. For Nicky as well as Emma, inspiration from Ashwood Nurseries was like a breath of fresh air. By 2000, Nicky's five original Hellebore pieces had made their debut in the millennium collection, but by 2001 she decided that the time had come to enhance the range with six new ones. As soon as the new pieces made their debut, everyone loved them, and the strength of the 2001 catalogue was considerably enhanced.

On the 18th September 2000, Hugh had been appointed a director of the Ceramic Industry Forum, an entity backed with government cash whose task was to try and halt what the popular press said was a decline in the British ceramic industry. This was a totally different world from the one in which Emma and Nicky lived. Even as Hugh arrived at his first board meeting, talk in the Potteries was of 'lean manufacturing', 'down-sizing', 'machine processing', and 'unfair competition from the Far East'. To Hugh the mood seemed to be one of defeat and excuses. He had no wish to become part of a process of negative thinking and defensive attitudes. Many

Pheasants Eye (2001). Height 50cm (20")   *Palmata (2001). Height 50cm (20")*

Bluebells (2001) Ltd.Edn.250
Height 15cm (6″)

of those present knew people who had presided over the decline. How on earth could the same people ever be expected to reverse it? Largely absent, it seemed to Hugh, were designers, innovators, and entrepreneurs.

The inevitable happened. In front of the great and the good in the ceramic industry, the men and women of power and influence in Stoke-on-Trent, Hugh exploded. He would not become part of an apologia for everything that had gone wrong in the closed world of ceramics, a world that talked of 'traditions' and the 'way things are done in this city'. The ceramic world had to go out and fight its competition head-on, using weapons understood by other industry sectors in Britain better than any in the world. Design, innovation and marketing were the tools of growth and expansion, not lean manufacturing, down-sizing or at worst an expatriation of British ceramic manufacturing capacity to China and the Pacific rim. The Potteries had artistry and ceramic skills ten generations deep. Those skills should be harnessed and used to add value to ceramics made in Britain, not discarded like some item of obsolete machinery. A machine was a machine wherever it was installed. The only difference lay in the level of wages paid to those who worked the machines – perhaps a few dollars a day and a bowl of rice in the Far East; a dignified living wage in the United Kingdom.

Only design, innovation and marketing could turn the tide by adding value to each piece of ceramic produced in the United Kingdom: lean manufacturing, at best, would only postpone the inevitable. There had been occasions in the recent past when it seemed as if management in Stoke-on-Trent were short of new ideas and lacking in direction. It was time to move on. The passionate, sometimes arrogant Hugh Edwards was in full flight, and he was offending people left, right and centre. To succeed, he boomed, managerial culture needed to change. Innovation and design had to shine like twin beacons. Design to sell, manufacture to deliver, the Moorcroft chairman told them. It was Moorcroft's own motto, though none of those present knew it. Instead of taking direct action itself, the Government had given a one-off opportunity to proprietors and management to change the ceramic world in which they worked and lived and donated millions of pounds to prove their point.

As he spoke, Hugh watched the stony faces of the ceramic industry's chairmen, chief executives and finance directors all looking at him without the flicker of an eye-lid. He was ready to stand up and walk, his new directorship of the Ceramic Industry Forum lasting just one day. Nobody would submit to such a lambasting. The moment Hugh stopped the silence was ominous. Then the man from Aynsley spoke. 'I agree', he said. Portmerion, Wedgwood and Bridgewater Pottery followed suit, as did Royal Worcester and Dudsons. Surprised, Hugh remained seated but still watched the door marking the way out of the boardroom. Perhaps he had misjudged them. Doubt set in.

Then a voice said, 'Well, you appear to have made your point, Hugh. What do we do next?' It was David Ritchie, director of the West Midlands Government Office. 'Redraft the funding bid', the Moorcroft chairman suggested, 'and include design, innovation and marketing, whatever the rule book says'. A junior civil servant present protested that to do so was impossible. Those items were outside the remit of the funding model to be used when bidding for Government cash. Hugh was becoming angry again, and his voice started to wobble. 'Nothing in this world is impossible provided you are willing to try. Write everything into the bid whether in the funding model or not'. And they did. Design, innovation and marketing were written into a revised draft of the bid. On that day the ceramic industry in Britain refocused itself fundamentally.

When he came to Stoke-on-Trent to announce the success of the 'lean-manufacturing' part of the bid, Secretary of State for Trade and Industry Stephen Byers invited the second, unofficial part of the bid for design, innovation and marketing to be officially resubmitted. Six weeks later the additional part of the bid was handed in. Design, innovation and marketing featured on every page. Despite a belated rearguard action from the Civil Service, against which Hugh intervened personally with the Secretary of State, more money arrived to back design, innovation and marketing than had been made available for lean manufacturing and machine processing.

Those who knew Hugh well were not surprised. The reasoned arguments of an old commercial lawyer, the sudden, unpredictable bursts of emotion and anger, and above all a deep love for anything of quality made out of clay all played their parts. Design improved quality and added value, and Britain's designers and innovators were among the best in the world. It was something Hugh believed in with a passion, and his beloved workforce at Moorcroft proved it. As further proof, in November 2005

Emma Bossons won the annual Innovation Award in the Potteries for her Hidden Dreams collection. Hugh and Maureen attended the presentation ceremony in the King's Hall, Stoke-on-Trent with Emma and her parents. Warm applause showed how well Emma's work reflected on Moorcroft and the ceramic industry. She was an innovator who knew how to use her art both for Moorcroft and her country.

Painters and tube-liners working for the art pottery were paid the highest wages in the ceramic industry, its workforce was happy and Moorcroft was profitable. It was a company which recruited and used the highly-skilled and artistic labour readily available in Stoke-on-Trent. It was a unique community, and their skills lay many generations deep. Hugh used those skills on his journey to perfection in ceramic art. That was how he led Moorcroft and its design process, and not long after his outburst in the Ceramic Industry Forum there were signs everywhere that other great names in the Potteries had started to do likewise.

When Hugh arrived in Stoke-on-Trent in 1997 to work for Moorcroft full-time, he made a vow not to become engaged in the business of the city other than with Moorcroft. The commitment made to the Ceramic Industry Forum forced him to acknowledge that he had broken his vow, but it was a worthy cause. Indeed, in the long term there would be precious little future for Moorcroft or any other ceramic company if the city lost its skilled workforce, its colour and clay suppliers, kiln builders and repairers, and other key support industries. Moorcroft was plainly unable to provide all these companies with enough work on its own to enable them to survive. In comparison with the big ceramic names in Stoke-on-Trent, Moorcroft was still a very small company. 'A mighty mouse', Elise Adams had once called it. The Collectors' Club Secretary was right. Moorcroft was a little company with a big name, something that forced it to behave like a big company, even if most of the time it felt like a very small art pottery indeed.

For Elise to put together detailed plans for Open Weekend in May, barely a month after the close of the Spring Festival, was a daunting prospect. It was the same for the designers, all of whom had to switch from their early work on the 2002 catalogue to consider their contributions to this important occasion. For many collectors, Open Weekend is seen as the highlight of the year, and a great deal of hard work goes into its preparation. Since 1993, managing the Moorcroft design process had been Hugh's responsibility and pleasure. The art pottery had the benefit of his ideas, managerial skills and commercial expertise, and in return he took personal and very firm control of the design process. At heart Hugh was an incorrigible Moorcroft collector, and only a real Moorcroft collector would understand the happiness derived from the arrival of a good piece of new Moorcroft. Phil Gibson's first official prestige vase, Mediterranean Doves, had sent an unmistakable shiver through Hugh's emotional system as soon as he saw the watercolour, a piece of original artwork he later acquired at a high price from Moorcroft and which now hangs in pride of place above the lounge fireplace in his home in Stoke-on-Trent. Tellingly, the legendary Moorcroft painter Wendy Mason had burst into tears painting the first trial of Mediterranean Doves. The sheer size of the vase, the unusual shades of colour and intricate linework almost defeated an artist whom colleagues deem the greatest Moorcroft painter of all time. Despite the quality of its many prestigious contemporaries and successors, Mediterranean Doves would always remain on a pedestal of its own. For Hugh, it symbolised success and the triumph of magnificent human endeavour in the applied arts. Best of all, it exemplified an inner spirit strong enough to overcome all difficulties. It also demonstrated how frustration and tears can be beaten by sheer skill, artistry and perseverance.

After Mediterranean Doves, a continuous stream of fine prestige pieces began to emerge from the Design Studio. Anji Davenport used exactly the same shape, linework and colour to enlarge her successful Wolfsbane design. It was a simple but successful ploy. Even better was her new Elisha's Tears. Unlike Wolfsbane, Elisha's Tears was not a straightforward adaptation of an existing design, but something totally new, something colourful, elegant and worthy of the genuine praise it received. On a smaller scale, Emma toyed around with her Hepatica design in an attempt to fit the small, delicate flowers onto a twelve-inch vase. It was available only for a very short time, and only a handful were made.

Sungod was a Rachel Bishop prestige classic. She loved it; others were not so sure. Ultimately an example ended up in the lounge of the British Pottery Manufacturers' Federation Club in Stoke-on-Trent, silencing all potential critics at a stroke. Behind the scenes, Shirley Hayes was working hard on two prestige pieces of her own, Palmata and Pheasants Eye. Both pieces proved popular with collectors, and the fact that both were derived from existing catalogue designs appeared to make no difference at all.

Springtime (2001). Height 5cm (2″)

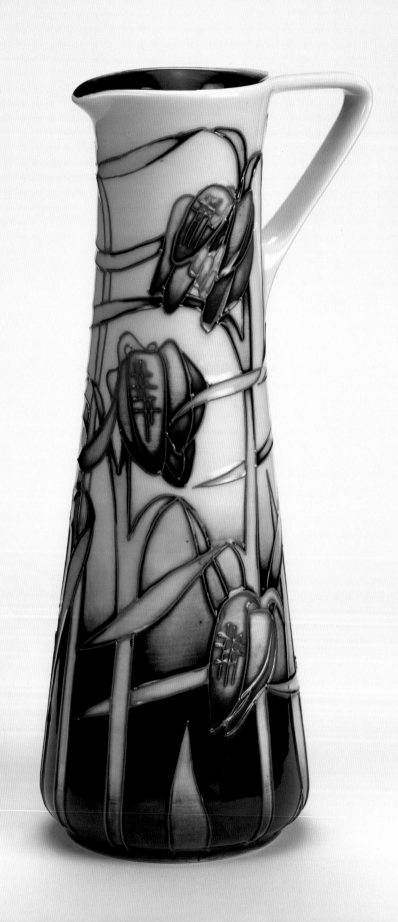

SEVEN

American Tragedy and Triumph

Rachel had watched the design activity around prestige pieces with considerable interest. Eventually she suggested that every range would benefit from the existence of a 'lead' prestige piece to catch people's eye. To prove her point she designed a prestige version of Prairie Summer before turning her attention to a full range. Hugh had a particular affection for Prairie Summer for a rather curious reason. At the time of its arrival the American sales team were positively bursting with enthusiasm about the reception of Moorcroft in the United States and Canada, and had suggested Hugh make a short tour of selected stores to sign his books, Moorcroft, The Phoenix Years and Moorcroft, Winds of Change. In this way he could meet collectors as Fraser Street, and meet American and Canadian retailers as the chairman of Moorcroft, hopefully to the benefit of both. After animated discussion, Hugh agreed that September 2001 would be the ideal month to travel. High summer temperatures would be falling, retailers would be thinking about Thanksgiving and Christmas, while that energetic army of North American collectors would be on the prowl for pots after the close of the summer vacation season.

The landscape that included the small town of Oglethorpe, Georgia, was a land of a thousand salt-water creeks, forests and friendly people. Hot in summer and pleasantly warm in winter, facts which explain the silent mansions scattered among the forests. Even though it was early September they were still mostly empty, waiting patiently for their millionaire migrant owners to return from industrial areas further north. Snowbirds, they were called. Hugh and his travelling companion, Donald Reid, had driven up to Oglethorpe from Jacksonville, Florida for the day. Donald carried his salesman's case of Moorcroft samples; Hugh was laden with Phoenix Years and Winds of Change for a signing at Oglethorpe Antiques.

By lunchtime the ebb and flow of Moorcroft collectors appraising and buying pottery and books had eased off a little, giving Hugh an opportunity to stretch his legs and look hard at the Moorcroft on offer in Oglethorpe Antiques. An hour or so earlier he had noticed a curious vase shaped vaguely like an old fashioned bottle and decorated with no more than a simple greenish-orange lustre glaze. It was time to

FACING: *Cricklade (2001). Height 24cm (9.5")*

take a closer look. Give or take a few months either way, the seven-inch vase would have been made at Moorcroft's Sandbach Road factory in around 1916. For Hugh, the vase had a special significance. In more than thirty years of devoted pot hunting he had never seen that particular shape before. It was the kind of discovery that excited the collector inside him. It was also a shape with considerable potential, and one which had to be secured for the Design Studio's library of shapes. The possibilities provoked by the discovery were significant, but Hugh and Donald were faced with a problem. To buy the vase from Oglethorpe Antiques was essential. Unfortunately the two Moorcroft visitors had both left credit cards and cash behind at their hotel in Jacksonville.

After turning his pockets inside out Hugh found two ten-dollar bills. Donald Reid had a single hundred dollar bill. The supply of available cash was obviously not enough. It was time to take stock of other Moorcroft assets and try to make a deal. A spare Emma Bossons Cricklade jug made exclusively for Moorcroft Collectors' Days that year lay wrapped in the boot of their car. It had not been put out on display because it was unlikely that the inhabitants of Oglethorpe would have even heard of England's snakeshead fritillary, still less of Cricklade meadow where these rare flowers bloom each year in their hundreds of thousands. The first objective was to beat the price down, something difficult to achieve without causing offence as a guest in the owner's store – doubly so when the owners are also Moorcroft retailers. An asking price of six hundred dollars was on the high side for an undecorated vase c1916. This suggested a first pitch at around five hundred and thirty dollars.

Hugh made the move with modest success. It would have been rude to try and beat down Gordon Guess and John Rushs's five hundred and fifty cash counter-offer because Hugh and Donald had only a hundred and twenty dollars between them. Without a commodity called cash, there are things you cannot do. Fortunately Donald had already filled the Moorcroft hire car with gasoline. There was more than enough 'gas' in the tank to see the pair of them back to Jacksonville, and there rejoin both credit cards and money. A hundred and twenty dollar cash contribution saw Gordon and John soften, more out of surprise at the lack of Moorcroft credit cards or money than anything else. Even so, five hundred and fifty dollars had suddenly become four hundred and thirty dollars.

Hugh relaxed, prematurely as it turned out. The Cricklade jug might have been worth US$ 330 to an English collector who knew all about snakeshead fritillaries, but it was worth much less to Gordon and John who had a profit margin to consider. Working on the assumption that they would double their price, Hugh and Donald were still short of their target by US$165 dollars, and both were becoming visibly disappointed. But then inspiration struck! Oglethorpe Antiques would take free of charge the first-ever piece of Moorcroft to carry a design on the shape of the old lustre vase. Oblivious to her potential views on the matter, Hugh added rashly that the first design would be from Rachel Bishop. Gordon, Donald, John and Hugh all shook hands. The deal was done.

With the Oglethorpe vase securely packed in his hand luggage, Hugh watched the remainder of the Moorcroft suitcases disappear on a noisy conveyor belt through hanging strands of heavy-duty rubber. The check-in desk at Jacksonville airport was like any other. The only difference was that it was 9am on 11th September 2001. Hugh and Donald's luggage would not travel far on its journey across the airport before it was on its way back again. The World Trade Centre mass-murder was minutes old, and all civilian aircraft across the United States had been called down from the skies. As details of the

372 shape discovered in 2001 at Oglethorpe Antiques in Georgia

massacre emerged, thousands of shaken Americans and two shaken British travellers could scarcely believe their ears. For Donald and Hugh it was surreal.

Hugh had looked forward to reminding Californians about Moorcroft's long association with the state. It had been a brave decision for a little company like Moorcroft to resume selling its pots in the United States for the first time since the Second World War. Only recently had the art pottery created sufficient additional capacity to make and sell its magic into the North American market. Now a murderous act of terrorism planned and executed by psychopaths had destroyed those dreams. Canada's border with the United States had been immediately closed. The Canadian leg of Hugh's book signing tour became impossible. It could only be a matter of time before the Tamsen Munger Gallery in Fresno, California cancelled their event scheduled for the 13th September. Donald's adrenaline-driven optimism was fast joining Hugh's downright depression, but in all of this both of them were wrong.

Everyone was saying that life had to go on. To do otherwise would hand terrorism victory on a plate. Donald's mobile phone sprang to life. Assurances were

sought by the Tamsen Munger Gallery that if at all possible Donald and Hugh would come to Fresno for the event. Everyone wanted the show to go on. Within an hour the two of them were driving from Jacksonville to Atlanta. Eight hours later they arrived, first tying up the leasing arrangements for the new Moorcroft showroom in the city, before catching the first available internal flight from Atlanta to San Francisco. Several hours in the air were followed by a four-hour drive to Fresno, but in spite of everything the Moorcroft duo arrived with an overnight to spare!

It was one of those rare occasions when Hugh had to pinch himself to be sure that what was happening was real. Books were coming through for signature in a continuous stream, but it was a surge of genuine pleasure which welled up inside him as he watched Moorcroft collectors enjoying themselves in the same warm, sometimes competitive, and always friendly way that their counterparts in the United Kingdom tend to do. The evening before the Fresno event Donald and Hugh noticed that the symbol of a nation's grief had been a silent candle vigil on street corners throughout the city. The very next day, some of those same American people were in the Tamsen Munger Gallery to make sure that the losers were the terrorists and not a small British art pottery swept up in the wake of it all.

It was a matter of particular pleasure for Hugh to watch the way Emma Bossons' designs were received. Fresno welcomed the young designer's work with open arms. Famous for its fruit, particularly its wine grapes, Californians took to Emma's massive Montagnac vase with a passion. Nobody knew that Emma's hugely successful Queens Choice range had only just made the new catalogue. At the final design approval meeting she had produced an eight-inch Queens Choice ginger jar, which stopped all those present dead in their tracks. As a result, the design door was held open for a further two weeks, during which Emma worked night and day drawing Queens Choice, destined to become a best-selling range, onto a further fifteen shapes. The previous year her Hepatica range had been top design, and in 2001 it was deservedly freshened with three modest vases and a small ginger jar. Significantly, a new Hepatica teaset made an appearance – the first teaset design to appear since Oberon and Violet were discontinued at the end of 1999.

Emma and Hugh had spent a pleasant half hour together identifying a suitable name for her new fruit design. As so often happens at Moorcroft, words from Shakespeare's A Midsummer Night's Dream came to their aid. They were words which inspired Emma when she created her original artwork. Every fruit mentioned by Shakespeare features in Emma's Queens Choice design.

FACING: *Queens Choice range (2001) (top left) Ginger jar 20cm (8") (top right) Tallest vase 25cm (10") (bottom left) Charger diameter 35cm (14") (bottom right) Candlestick 20cm (8")*

(Top left) Hepatica (2001). Diameter of plate 15cm (6") (top right) Ginger jar 10cm (4")
(Bottom left) Blakeney Mallow (2002). Tallest vase 25cm (10") (bottom right) Ltd.Edn.150. Height 35cm (14")

Blakeney Mallow (2002). Tallest vase 25cm (10")

Be kind and courteous to this gentlemen;
Hop in his walks and gambol in his eyes;
Feed him with apricots and dewberries
With purple grapes, green figs, and mulberries....

Sitting at his desk in the Tamsen Munger Gallery, these memories all came flooding back. Out of the corner of his eye Hugh noticed the senior partner of a San Francisco law firm and his wife leave as proud owners of a Sarah Brummell-Bailey Remember vase, both clearly delighted at the elegant addition to their collection. A year after her success with Remember, Sarah was to move on and design Blakeney Mallow with a special, co-ordinated limited edition vase included in the range. In a far corner of the store a young couple were examining two superb Queens Choice vases. Hugh

desperately wanted them to buy both pieces. Emma's career was heading for the stars. Yet for all the praise heaped upon her, despite the success she had already earned all over the world with her work, the designer never sought to exercise power or influence. Popular with her colleagues at work, her family and friends, the young designer quietly enjoyed her success and the reputation that came with it. At that moment, almost on cue, the two young Fresno collectors carried the pair of Queens Choice vases to Tamsen Munger's till.

Nicola Slaney was Emma's great friend in the Design Studio. Each has a design style all her own. Emma's work draws strength from organic form and a strong sense of colour. Nicky derives her inspiration from the great wealth of knowledge locked away in a mind that produced eight GCSE passes, including five 'A' grades, four A grades at A level and perhaps not surprisingly a university degree which saw her graduate in design at the top of her year. In contrast, Emma had left school at seventeen, after which she painted for Wedgwood on a work experience scheme. Frustrated with her lack of opportunity, at nineteen the young artist applied to join Moorcroft as a painter. By the age of twenty-

(Above) Serendipity (2001) Ltd.Edn.300. Height 35cm (14")
FACING: (above) Prairie Summer (2002). Tallest vase 30cm (12") (below) Tallest vase 23cm (9")

Prairie Summer (2001). Height 50cm (20″)

four she had become a leading light in the Design Studio, and at twenty-six was elected the youngest Fellow of the Royal Society of Arts, a great honour.

Donald Reid's personal favourite in the 2001 catalogue was Nicky's Serendipity vase. Towards the end of the Fresno event, Donald was seen working long and hard in what turned out to be a futile attempt to persuade a wealthy raisin grower to buy what he knew to be the only example still sitting on a retailer's shelf. To his disappointment he failed, but what the Moorcroft salesman had not noticed was that the young couple who had earlier purchased the Queens Choice vases had overheard his Serendipity eulogy. 'He who hesitates is lost' is an apt phrase in the serious business of collecting pots. No sooner had the raisin grower put the Serendipity vase back on its perch than a large young hand reached out, picked it up and carried another prize away to the till.

'Never put a piece down until you have decided not to buy', Hugh muttered to himself. Many years earlier he had been in the position of the raisin grower. A particularly fine William Moorcroft Wisteria vase c1912 had surfaced in Bermondsey market in southeast London. Hugh had baulked at the fifteen-pound asking price and backed off the dealer's stall in concern. Another collector swooped on the piece and paid the dealer his asking price before walking away with the Wisteria vase wrapped up in old newspaper, nodding at a disappointed and inexperienced Hugh Edwards as he did so. Two things happened a quarter of a century later. Hugh had to pay a thousand pounds for the same vase, and in that same year the Bermondsey Market stallholder was appointed a director of Christies, the famous London auction house.

Flying back to the United Kingdom after the Fresno trip, neither Donald nor Hugh had much to say. Hugh spent an age considering how best to persuade Rachel Bishop to use the Oglethorpe vase for a contemporary design, but he need not have worried. Rachel liked the shape a great deal and successfully persuaded Hugh to commission it in four different sizes. She then proceeded to use two for her Prairie Summer range, and within weeks the first Prairie Summer vase on the new Oglethorpe shape was winging its way to Georgia free of charge. In doing so, the outstanding commitment to Gordon and John of Oglethorpe Antiques was honoured.

By the time Hugh approached her with his Oglethorpe proposition, Rachel had already completed trials for her prestigious Prairie Summer vase. It made its debut with a clutch of other prestige pieces early in 2001 and was firmly held 'off catalogue'. Only after completing her work on the prestige version of the design did the senior designer rework her Prairie Summer images onto a modest range of nine pieces. In this way she achieved all she had set out to do. The prestige version of the Prairie Summer design became the herald of a range.

EIGHT

A Debt and Two Designers

The year 2001 delivered an exceptionally successful May Open Weekend, recalled Collectors' Club Secretary Elise Adams with some pride. It was a weekend of contrasts. At one end of the scale Emma had introduced her May Lily coasters. These were presented as gifts to collectors attending the event. As the May Lily coaster came in four colourways, it was a matter of chance which of them a collector received. Not unnaturally this provoked considerable 'exchange' activity among collectors, but it was seen as good fun. At the other end of the scale came Emma's handsome Himalayan Honeysuckle, a tall slim vase with a black ground. It featured fully open coral and pink honeysuckle flowers growing from the base of the vase and becoming smaller, finer and less open towards the neck and rim. Cleverly shaded red berries hung from trailing honeysuckle stems in delicate clusters. Himalayan

Honeysuckle was a joyous, colourful and vibrant celebration of movement. Both before and after the 2001 May Weekend Elise rued the day the edition had been fixed at a miserable 30 pieces. For Hugh, number twenty-nine has pride of place in his personal collection. To this day he sees it as one of the great vases made by Moorcroft in recent years, one which helped identify Emma as a world-class ceramic designer.

Open Weekend was supported by work from everyone in the Design Studio, including Nicky Slaney who had been away on maternity leave since January. Her pre-confinement legacy had been Paradise Fruit. Although absent in person, the small vase was there to remind everyone of her continued involvement in Moorcroft as a designer of proven ability. Anji Davenport's Dryandra turned up in a

FACING: *Himalayan Honeysuckle (2001) Ltd.Edn.30*
Height 40cm (16")

May Lily (2001) in four colourways
Diameter 20cm (4")

colourway different from that approved as a limited edition to travel with her to Australia later that same year, while Romulea, the May Open Weekend Mug designed by Marie Penkethman, saw collectors queuing patiently to hand in their personalised message to be fired underglaze on the base. If Nicky's absence passed by unnoticed, the name of Sally Guy did not. An attractive set of small, limited edition ginger jars decorated with unusual, wine-coloured pansies designed by Sally, entered into the May collection almost unnoticed at first. Sally, an able freelance designer, had originally offered her design services to come up with ideas for the Queen's Golden Jubilee celebrations. Although of high quality, her initial designs were never followed up, and Emma's Golden Jubilee collection was the only one ultimately accepted. To his great regret, shortly after the 2001 May Open Weekend closed, Hugh lost contact with Sally Guy.

Occasionally it becomes necessary for a designer to take up a special project to celebrate a particular occasion. This happened when Emma was originally asked to come up with a Golden Jubilee design. Behind the scenes Sally Guy was also instructed to come up with possible design themes. If the truth were known, Hugh had probably given her the commission as a sophisticated insurance policy to cover the possibility of Emma failing to deliver acceptable designs on schedule. To ensure

its launch in time for the Golden Jubilee, each piece in the range had to be in retailers' hands by the preceding December at the latest. There was no room for failure, and Emma did not fail. She can now look back with considerable pride on the awesome success of her Golden Jubilee collection. At its peak, Moorcroft had more than twenty-five painters working on it, a design rated to be of sufficiently high quality for the Queen to grant permission to use the Royal Cipher on the base of each piece. The Lord Chamberlain's letter of consent was a real coup for the Design Studio.

From the outset, Emma's Golden Jubilee range continued to sell strongly all over the world. Early in 2002, Kim Thompson asked for a Golden Jubilee jug to consolidate that success. The reasoning behind her request was that Moorcroft jugs always sold well, and that to introduce one into Emma's

Golden Jubilee (2002). Height 15cm (6")   FACING: *Golden Jubilee (2002). Tallest vase 18cm (7")*

successful Golden Jubilee collection would enhance its appeal even further. Emma obliged, and between January and June 2002, 208 Golden Jubilee jugs were made and sold.

Happiness at work can bubble up for a multitude of reasons, but for the Design Studio one stands out. In his 2001 Open Weekend lecture delivered in the theatre at the Potteries' Museum and Art Gallery in Hanley, BBC Antiques Roadshow television celebrity David Battie explained how he had looked carefully at the work of the current Moorcroft designers. The spirit of William Morris was alive and well-represented in a number of them, but as far as he could see Emma Bossons above all others carried the mantel of William Moorcroft, the founding father of the art pottery. To make his point he showed on-screen Lily of the Valley, a vase made exclusively for the Low Pay Unit. Dedicated to the elimination of poverty in work as well as campaigning for the abolition of discrimination in all its insidious forms, the Low Pay Unit can claim success in its campaign for the introduction of the National Minimum Wage, the Working Families' Tax Credit and the Working Time Regulations – a fine record. Emma's design for the charity was, said Battie, in the best traditions of Moorcroft. Wholly organic in structure and colour, it emanated a delicious sense of movement.

In work as in life there must always be hope. The Low Pay Unit was a ray of hope in working lives that would otherwise have none at all. The Charity benefited financially from the sales of Lily of the Valley. All 500 vases sold out before the millennium year was little more than six months old. Hugh had vowed to himself that the exercise would be repeated. So shortly before the Christmas weekend in 2001, Hugh asked Emma for a second vase to help the Low Pay Unit. The result was Celandine which was launched in the Spring of 2002. Using the same shape, Emma chose to adopt the lesser celandine flower as her design theme. The name celandine means 'joy is to come'. One of the first of Britain's wild-flowers to bloom among the lush green grass of early spring, the lesser celandine, with its bright yellow flowers often enriched with delicate flushes of golden orange, carpets woodland and moist grass meadows. William Wordsworth so admired the flower, which grows in abundance in his beloved Lake District, that he wrote a poem about it, part of which reads:

There is a flower; the lesser celandine,
That shrinks, like many more, from cold and rain.
And, the first moment that the sun may shine,
Bright as the sun himself, 'tis out again!

As with Lily of the Valley, Celandine was limited to 500 pieces. Whether it was as good or even better than its predecessor will be for others to determine. As far as the Low Pay Unit was concerned, Celandine enabled a new researcher to be appointed to investigate poverty in work, ninety per cent of which is suffered by women.

Thirty-five years earlier when wealth and male gender ruled the day, a young, naïve and extremely poor Hugh Edwards had graduated in Law at University College, London. Six months later the same young man had passed his Solicitor's Final Examination. Before he could finally qualify as a solicitor it remained for him to sign up to articles of clerkship, or a training contract as it is known today. All attempts to identify a firm prepared to take him on as an articled clerk for the required two years had failed. In the law, that most exclusive of professions, nobody wanted the son of a music teacher. However hard Hugh knocked, every door remained firmly shut. More or less by chance he then learned that his parish priest, who was also Archdeacon at Worcester cathedral, had been a solicitor before his ordination. The country boy who lived at the end of Ryden Lane in the Worcestershire village of Charlton decided to ask the Right Reverend Peter Elliott whether he knew of a firm which might be willing take on an articled clerk who could not afford to pay a premium for the privilege. The going rate was three thousand pounds. In the mid-'60s you could buy a decent house for three thousand pounds, and Hugh had nothing to offer but an overdraft of five pounds. There was, the Archdeacon told him solemnly, little chance of him taking articles in his old firm of Kennedy, Ponsonby and Prideaux. From the name alone Hugh surmised that the Archdeacon was probably correct. However, the old priest intoned slowly, there was a slight possibility that Colonel Roy Harrison of Harrisons in Worcester might make room for Hugh.

Shortly afterwards, at three pounds a week without a premium, Hugh's career in the law moved forward, starting in Worcester and then on to the City of London for another thirty years. For the help that the Right Reverend Peter Elliott had given Hugh to launch himself into the Law, a debt had been incurred. Like all debts it should be repaid someday. That was a solemn promise he made to himself. Thirty years later, some fine artwork from a little known painter in the Moorcroft decorating shop caught his eye. What he saw were those same characteristics that had so

FACING: *A Tribute to Charles Rennie Mackintosh* (2004)
(top) Height 30cm (12") (bottom left) (2005). Tallest vase 25cm (10") (bottom right) (2001). Tallest vase 20cm (8")

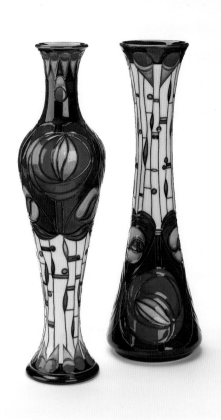

impressed David Battie during the 2001 Open Weekend. What David had said was true. Emma's work was organic in structure, showed an intense understanding of shape and colour and radiated a sense of movement and vitality. A naturally objective judge of quality, but with a totally subjective, even instinctive, understanding of what made a fine piece of Moorcroft pottery, Hugh looked regularly at Emma's work. Here was a young artist who had learned her basic skills in ceramic decoration at Wedgwood and at home with her parents. During her time at Wedgwood Emma acquired enough artistic skill to win a national watercolour contest sponsored by the Daily Mail. She had no degree or any other academic qualification to support her career as a designer, yet Hugh saw in her work qualities that told a story of perseverance, skill, an intuitive ability to harness colour and form and an indomitable will to succeed.

Initially, Emma was asked to design for Moorcroft in her own time. During the day she worked in the decorating shop as a painter. This was unsatisfactory for a number of reasons. As a painter Emma remained answerable to production director Keith Dawson, whereas designers were answerable to Hugh. In practice there was never any disagreement between the two men. Emma's work was patently too good to become the subject of petty territorial disputes, and it soon became clear that

Emma as a painter was a sheer waste of Emma as a designer. Hugh had been thinking along these lines for some time, but held back in case he offended Keith. However, in January 1999 the inevitable happened. Emma walked across the bridge from the world of production into the world of design, from Keith's world into Hugh's. From that moment she received salary cheques as well as a designer's commission on the sales of her work. Emma Bossons had become a full-time designer at Moorcroft. The thought gave Hugh much private happiness. He had fulfilled the promise he made to himself at the time he signed his Articles of Clerkship so many years earlier. The debt he owed to the old archdeacon had been repaid. Emma had been given the opportunity she deserved to pursue her career as a designer. In the fullness of time she would also have a debt to repay just as Hugh had done.

Inula (2001) Ltd.Edn.200
Height 15cm (6")

Once before Moorcroft had employed a totally unknown designer, Rachel Bishop, but in 1993 it had been different. Rachel was already well qualified to carry out design work at Moorcroft with a good degree to prove it. By 2001 she had been with Moorcroft for almost eight years, a long working relationship by any standard in the precarious world of design, and one which showed no sign of coming to an end. In her work the senior designer had made a huge contribution to the resurgence of the company's art and reputation. Rachel, as she still says to this day, was born to the job. From the time of her arrival as sole designer in 1993, sales of her work helped Moorcroft move onto a far more prestigious stage in the world of the applied arts. At Moorcroft, Rachel took charge of her own destiny and continually strove to move forward. Hugh believes that the post-1986 years will be seen as the art pottery's golden years. Much of the credit for this is down to Rachel. That is his unshakeable belief.

Some people have commented that Rachel's natural design style justifies a comparison between her work and that of William Morris. In many ways this is a view as narrow as it is unfair and naïve. Rachel is, and will always be, very much her own person. Some of her finest work is better than that of both William Morris and William Moorcroft, yet at times she can comfortably share a design style with either of them. That said, Prairie Summer, introduced as a range in 2002, owed precious little to the influence of William Morris and still less to that of William Moorcroft. Rachel had neither copied nor adapted the design. Prairie Summer reflects her own ceramic art rather than that of people who died decades earlier. Rachel has always been an original designer without any need or ambition to copy the art deco work of Clarice Cliff, the traditional flowers of Susie Cooper or indeed the work of any other designer, alive or dead.

An almost imperceptible shift in Rachel's design style had resulted in both Cymric Dream and Inula, designs commissioned exclusively by Liberty of London, the former in 2000 and the latter in 2001. Hugh admired both pieces equally. Each takes up certain features of Liberty's work over the preceding 125 years, but both were new in concept and innovative in approach. Liberty decided to launch Cymric Dream and Inula to coincide with their annual Arts and Crafts exhibition in two consecutive years. Both times success was instantaneous, but Rachel needed to move away from Liberty for a while and into pastures new. It was part of the Moorcroft philosophy of equality that prestige assignments should be shared around the Design Studio. This stopped designers becoming stereotyped or being regarded as the personal property of a particular retailer. Next in line for Liberty would be Emma Bossons.

As individuals, Emma and Rachel are very different people, even visually. With her raven-coloured hair tinted deep burgundy and with dark brown, almost black eyes, Rachel might well have Spanish or even Egyptian ancestry. On the other hand Emma, with her blonde hair and light blue eyes might well have ancestry dating to the Anglo Saxons. The more those who know them watch and listen, the more they are driven to the inescapable conclusion that Moorcroft is an extremely fortunate art pottery. Both designers are fiercely independent people who rely on instinct, intuitive skills and sheer imagination. Success follows both as a result.

Good fortune goes beyond two eminent designers. As if to emphasise the point, no sooner had the 2001 Open Weekend come to an end than Sian Leeper, a designer with an increasingly strong design style in exotic birds and animals, introduced her Leopard vase. Kim Thompson pounced on it immediately. It would be a special numbered edition to be sold exclusively during the month of June in the factory shop. Kim decided that Sian's reputation was in the ascendant. She was right. A healthy 140 Leopard vases were sold in a month.

Leopard (2001) Numbered Edition. Height 20cm (8")

NINE

Flowing Colours

The fennel plant, Rachel decided, would make a fine Moorcroft design. The leaves would challenge the tube-liners, those silent heroes of Moorcroft artistry whose work is always seen but never appreciated as much as it should be. The metallic oxide colours used at Moorcroft are mixed with water before being 'floated' onto the dry unfired surface of the pot. Were it not for the art of the tube-liners, the water-laden metallic oxide paint powders would drip down the body of the vase in lines of uncontrolled colour. This would result in unsightly colour runs like those often found on 'old' or 'antique' Moorcroft offered for sale on the secondary market. Such drips and colour runs would cause pots to be designated as imperfect today, although contemporary salerooms and secondary market dealers still manage to refer to them as 'flowing colours' or some similar euphemism.

Over the past fifteen years, the lines created by tube-liners have become progressively finer. The result has been a welcome improvement in the aesthetic quality of contemporary Moorcroft. The linework is now more than a mere aid to the application of colour, and for this Rachel can claim considerable credit. She has encouraged tube-liners to work with finer pipettes on their 'squeezy bags' as well as training them to work with coloured slip to enhance a particular design effect. For those Moorcroft collectors who take the time and trouble to pay a visit to the Works, the art of tube-lining is always a source of fascination. Far more difficult than it looks, the whole process is not unlike that of icing a cake. The tube-liner holds a rubber bag firmly in his or her hand. Attached to this 'squeezy bag' is a pipette, narrow at the mouth for fine tube-lining, with a wider one for thicker tube-lining. The rubber bag is filled with liquid clay, or 'slip' as it is sometimes called, and when the tube-liner squeezes the bag the slip runs down the pipette, out of the nozzle and onto the wet clay surface of the vase. These wet clay vases are known in the world of ceramics as 'greens'. By ensuring that the slip follows ink-pressed design lines on the surface of the 'green' vase, the tube-liner creates a full outline of the design, which looks at first like an intricate maze of self-contained surface areas. It is tube-lining which ensures that powdered metallic oxide colours mixed with water and floated onto the surface of the vase stay within these clearly-defined design limits.

By using fine tube-lining and coloured slip, Rachel had been able to use a plant like fennel to create a design theme. In the past this would have been difficult, if not impossible, but on this occasion it was the fennel plant itself and not the tube-lining that was causing problems for the senior designer. The slip had been dyed dark green to enhance the delicate qualities of the fennel leaves, but whichever way Rachel looked at her trials, the result was always the same. Fennel was a vegetable, and nothing Rachel did would overcome that fact. 'It's got to change. The whole thing's not working', she muttered in exasperation to Hugh in one of their sessions. What followed happened very quickly. As if by design magic Rachel contrived the disappearance of fennel and the simultaneous arrival of cosmos flowers. Set against a strong ground of golden yellow splashed with light brown, cosmos flowers paint-ed in shades of pink and mauve nodded and danced their way around the first trial. The continued presence of the original fennel leaves with their fine green lines had a cooling effect on a design which was alive with movement and warm colour. 'So what do you think?' Rachel asked, knowing full well what Hugh's answer would be. Her Cosmos range was ready to fly.

Never one to lose an opportunity, Rachel re-minded Hugh of her stylised design of coral-col-oured roses set against a rich burgundy ground. If her cosmos flowers had caused his tummy to turn a somersault, the first trial of her stylised rose de-sign had done little to stir Hugh's emotions as a collector. But then why should Hugh stand as both judge and jury in assessing the likely success of a designer's work? Moorcroft had an able design ap-proval committee, and it was for them to determine whether a design should go into production. His role as manager of the design process at Moorcroft was to encourage designers in their work and to en-sure that an adequate number of good designs were ready for appraisal at the right time.

There were times when he would imply that de-signers should be ready to back away from a design

Cosmos (2001). Tallest vase 20cm (8")

FACING: Cosmos (2001). Tallest vase 25cm (10")

if, for whatever reason, the design was not working. Nine times out of ten these principles worked well, but just occasionally a designer would take a stand with Hugh and request that more than one example of the same design should be presented to a design approval meeting. Emma had done this prior to the millennium with her sensitive plant, later called Fiji. The designer had preferred a distinctly green version of the vase, whereas Hugh had more confidence in a moss-coloured trial with a hint of mustard. In the event the design approval committee backed Emma's judgement, and Hugh had no doubt whatever that their decision was correct. Fiji sold more pieces during the millennium year than any other design in the Dateline Series. In no mood to quarrel with the senior designer, Hugh agreed to offer Rachel's coral rose design for approval at the next opportunity. It was accepted *nem con* and emerged carrying the name Masquerade Rose.

Before the arrival of the millennium summer, some especially good news emerged from the Design Studio. Nicola Slaney announced that she was pregnant and that her baby was due in early February 2001. The designer indicated that she would prefer to work 'up to the line' and then take her full statutory maternity leave. A sudden burst of pre-confinement activity witnessed the arrival of Albany, a design based on the Australian pincushion flower, as a range of twelve pieces; Trillium, with its stylised, almost geometric flower heads in shades of purple and green as a range of six pieces; and Waters of Time, her first prestige vase. In reserve, waiting for Open Weekend 2001, was Paradise Fruit. It was a grand finale for Nicky, but by January 2001 she had started her maternity leave.

Nicky's absence from the Design Studio created a worrying void, and Hugh found himself brooding over the matter with an intensity which surprised him. To see through all the designs required for the millennium had been difficult, but everything had eventually come together on time. Indeed, the great Moorcroft design tide actually flowed into the New Year with a design or two to spare. True to character, on her very last day before starting her maternity leave, Nicky had left a design with Hugh for 'safe keeping'. 'If nothing else, you can use it for the May Open Weekend', she had joked. Elise called it Kanzan Festival, but the design actually made its debut at Open Weekend 2002, not 2001. To this day no one knows how it was that Kanzan Festival failed to appear at the 2001 Open Weekend, but then Moorcroft is an art pottery, and the rules that apply in art potteries are seldom as precise as elsewhere.

Anxiety at Moorcroft is not uncommon. Emma had worried continuously about her Franjipani range, which first appeared in the millennium catalogue, with a discreet flush of light blue on most pieces. By the following year decisions had to be

FACING: *(top left) Masquerade Rose (2001). Tallest vase 18cm (7") (top right) Tallest vase 23cm (9")*
(below) Trillium (2001). Tallest vase 15cm (6")

Frangipani (2001). (Above) Tallest vase 23cm (9″) (below) Tallest vase 25cm (10″)

FACING: *Waters of Time (2001). Height 50cm (20″)*

Detail of Islay

made on Frangipani. She decided that the blue flush had to go. In its place another flush of colour appeared, this time a pale, creamy yellow. The new Frangipani cleared all its design hurdles on the same twelve shapes as those which had appeared in the millennium catalogue the year before.

In much the same way that Emma had worried about Franjipani, Rachel had growing doubts about her four Islay pieces, and these doubts increased by the day. Her decision to cull all four original shapes was made quickly and five new pieces took their place. Interestingly, Emma's Frangipani range in its revised colourway failed to reappear in 2002, but the five new Islay pieces survived for a further year.

Early on in the millennium year, Philip Gibson started work on a new design for release in the United States called Indian Paintbrush, and by the middle of the year the design was ready to meet its collecting public. At the time, Moorcroft collectors were joining the Club from all over America. Indian Paintbrush was very much an American design, and much to Phil's pleasure it was introduced in June as an exclusive range for the United States. It was not until 2001 that Indian Paintbrush made its debut in the Moorcroft catalogue.

Rarity can increase a collector's enthusiasm for a design, but at Moorcroft it is

Islay (2001). Height of jug 24cm (9.5")

Indian Paintbrush (2001). Tallest vase 25cm (10")

important to reflect that rarity generally has nothing to do with the quality of the design itself. Albany first appeared in the 2001 catalogue to considerable acclaim, but almost immediately ran into production difficulties. The first of these occurred when the chemical structure of a colour was changed by the supplier without notice. Initially Moorcroft was blissfully unaware of the problem, the only sign of which had been the arrival of a modest quantity of imperfect pieces. When the colour finally became unavailable, the outcome was inevitable. Albany was hurriedly discontinued. With some difficulty outstanding orders on all twelve pieces in the range were fulfilled from existing colour stock, leaving those Albany collectors lucky enough to own a piece sitting on an asset seen as rare in the secondary market.

Although Albany is undoubtedly rare, all four of Debbie Hancock's Seasons designs introduced in 2001 are even rarer. Early the following year, Moorcroft received a sharp letter from Portmeirion saying that the name 'Seasons' infringed a registered Portmeirion name. Unfortunately they were correct, and production of Spring, Summer, Autumn and Winter in the Seasons collection ceased out of legal necessity. Even though the design had already run for a year, Hugh had to grovel to an enraged Portmeirion. As a result, proposed design names are now checked out for availability. Lucky also are those collectors who own a Seasons vase! Luckier still are those who have a complete set of all four Seasons vases! Thoughts of this kind invariably make Hugh smile.

Indian Paintbrush (2001)
Height 20cm (8")

Sian Leeper's Belles Femmes provided a mischievous twist on the unfortunate Seasons affair. Sian's vase was massive, featuring ladies in swirling robes, with a distinctly Art Nouveau look. The surface of the vase was worked into four panels, and in each panel a robed lady stood in all her finery. There was a lady for Spring, Summer, Autumn and Winter. As a design Belles Femmes not only bore testimony to Sian's increasing maturity as a designer, but also to the ability of Moorcroft to design itself out of

Belles Femmes (2001). Height 63cm (25"). Spring, Summer, Autumn, Winter

Seasons (2001) Clockwise from top: Winter, Autumn, Spring and Summer. Height 8cm (3")

problems – something it would have to do again in 2003 with a vengeance. What Moorcroft lost in sales when Seasons was discontinued, it clawed back with the help of Sian's Belles Femmes. Had this been all, the Belles Femmes vases would still have made a significant contribution. What nobody had anticipated was that their arrival encouraged other designers to develop a liking for prestige work.

As if from nowhere Emma produced a massive Queens Choice bowl to enhance the impact of her two Queens Choice vases in the prestige collection. Much to the annoyance of Moorcroft retailers, examples of the bowl were tediously slow in coming through. Many of them had impatient customers waiting in the wings, and they grew tired of making excuses. The production team had found the bowl difficult to make, but however much they stamped their feet and tried to ignore the demand that was piling up, collectors' enthusiasm for prestige work stubbornly refused to go away. Debbie Hancock decided that Windrush would represent her in the prestige line-up, while Beverley Wilkes introduced a large version of her successful Odyssey design. Once again, the shape, linework and colour were exactly the same as her 2001 limited edition. Not a designer to be left out in the cold, Sian Leeper unveiled her Sophie range as a 2002 catalogue candidate. A year later Sian renamed her design Sophie Christina after her niece, and then added a handsome prestige version. By so doing, Sian had put her own mark on what was fast becoming a significant but unstructured medley of prestige pots.

At a meeting held during the late summer of 2002, Elise, Kim and Hugh took a long-overdue decision to rationalise the design and production of prestige work. There were, Elise reminded the others, not two but three kinds of prestige pots. The first was the annual catalogue piece itself, which took pride of place each year as a limited edition on the first page. That year Philip Gibson's Profusion had been accepted for this purpose. Then there were those pieces which were prestige versions of catalogue designs. Emma's Calla Lily introduced in 2002 and Shirley's Pheasants Eye both stood out as good examples. In the third category were those designs which did not feature in a catalogue as the year's lead piece or ex-catalogue as a prestige version of a catalogue design. Phil's famous Mediterranean Doves was an outstanding example. It was not difficult for those present to conclude that all three categories of prestige work should be kept separate in the future.

The production of prestige pieces, Kim reminded those present, was an idea first mooted on the basis that every piece other than the lead piece in the annual catalogue would be exclusive to the factory shop. Apart from the lead piece, it had never been intended that retailers should take prestige pieces into stock. That did not mean to say that whenever retailers had a special purchaser for a prestige item they would be denied the opportunity of requisitioning a piece at cost from the factory shop if one were available. To stock prestige pieces was asking retailers to make a heavy financial outlay. From the time the meeting closed, those present affirmed that whenever possible Moorcroft should revert to its original basic principle. The only exception would be the North American market, where a totally different attitude to prestige work prevailed. At the 2004 International Spring Fair in Birmingham, there were no prestige pieces of Moorcroft on display.

Indian Paintbrush (2001)
Diameter 10cm (4")

TEN

Interpretations

Moorcroft always looks on its relationship with Liberty of London with pride. The famous Regent Street store had been one of the first to show Moorcroft to its elite, avant-garde customers in 1901, or was it 1902? Hugh was unsure of the precise date. Despite a thorough search of all known archive material, so was Elise Adams. Even former journalist Neil Swindells, recently retired as night features editor of the London Evening Standard and erstwhile deputy editor of leisure and travel at the Daily Mail, had been forced to admit defeat. There were certain pegs on which to hang theories, as Paul Atterbury pointed out in his book Moorcroft Pottery, but as to the precise date of the arrival of the pots, everyone drew a blank. Only one fact was certain. There still exists a pot marked 'Made for Liberty' which bears the date 1902. Whatever else, Moorcroft had certainly arrived in Liberty by that time. If pottery had been delivered earlier, nobody involved in the Moorcroft story had found a shred of evidence to prove it.

Following the phenomenal success of her Golden Jubilee design, Emma was in the mood to produce something special for the store's Arts and Crafts show in May 2002. Liberty were totally frank. It was their undisguised ambition to consolidate on Emma's Golden Jubilee success. Well before her initial visit, Emma would have known that Rachel had adapted her Winds of Change design onto the JU3 shape for the millennium launch at Liberty of Fraser Street's new book *Moorcroft: Winds of Change*. The limited edition of 100 pieces had sold through well, but it had not provoked the volume of sales in other designs Liberty had hoped for. Special vases were important for Liberty and the speed of 'sell through' was monitored closely. Sales of Emma's Golden Jubilee collection were unprecedented, which was why the designer found herself on the receiving end of Liberty's special request.

To visit Liberty is always a daunting experience for a designer, but if Emma was nervous she showed no signs. Her invitation to travel down to London to meet the store's sales director Barbara King and buyer Rebecca Toone arrived at the Works early in 2002. To succeed, Emma had to show she had qualities which would prove

FACING: *Sweet Betsy (2001). Tallest vase 15cm (6″)*

Sweet Betsy (2001) Ltd.Edn.50
Height 40cm (16″)

as attractive to Liberty as Rachel's before her. Liberty had to be convinced. The welcome from Barbara and Rebecca was both warm and encouraging. Much less promising were the two Liberty pattern books which Rebecca produced to provide 'inspiration', the first dating from 1948 and the second from 1951, the year of the great exhibition in London. Emma opened the first book only to be confronted with an old Liberty design using ladders as its theme! Designs featuring ladders were not inspirational for a designer whose use of sensuous curves and vibrant colours were at the very heart of her style. Emma admitted later that the sight of ladders on the first page of the old pattern book had almost reduced her to tears. But she persevered, rejecting the traditionalism of the paisley patterns as well as the brash colours that would eventually mutate into a new design era of bold colour and abstract form known as the 'swinging sixties'.

While Emma struggled with a mass of unpromising design images from the Liberty archives, Hugh was revisiting the idea of the Regent Street store's hundredth anniversary as a retailing partner with Moorcroft. In 1913 it had been Liberty who had first funded William Moorcroft when he set up his new art pottery on Sandbach Road, Cobridge. In return for their cash Liberty secured a controlling stockholding, effectively turning Moorcroft into a subsidiary Liberty company. That continued until 1962 when the late Walter Moorcroft OBE bought out their stock. Whatever else, Liberty and Moorcroft agreed that by 2002 Moorcroft had sold its pottery through the store for more than a hundred years, a conclusion that made both Barbara and Rebecca smile. That hundred-year trading anniversary provided a one-off opportunity to consolidate the success of Emma's Golden Jubilee design. As a bonus it also added a celebratory dimension to the Liberty Arts and Crafts promotion in May. Barbara liked the idea, but from an abundance of caution she decided to check Liberty's archives as well as read Paul Atterbury's book on Moorcroft for herself. She had to be absolutely certain that Moorcroft really had been a Liberty supplier for more than a century. There was no room for mistakes.

For poor Emma the Liberty pattern books proved to be a miserable challenge, the more so when Hugh pointed out that Barbara and Rebecca had selected the years that approximated the date on which Queen Elizabeth II ascended to the throne. In the context of the Golden Jubilee that was hardly surprising, but after the end of the Second World War creative activity all over the world had been thin. Some designers had looked back to the years of Art Deco or even Art Nouveau to find inspiration. Others played with colour and more abstract design lines. Despite all these efforts, nothing of significance in design had been achieved in the United Kingdom or anywhere else. The war had simply lasted too long, and it was to be well over a decade before new ideas came along to challenge the traditions of the past. From the two large pattern books Emma found just twelve images she felt were vaguely helpful. After that, however many times she turned the pages the number never increased beyond twelve.

On the train back to Stoke-on-Trent Emma had little to say. At the end of four long hours at Liberty she emerged into damp, cold January air with twelve coloured images in her mind's eye. The originals arrived at the Works the next day as twelve colour prints. Hugh was disappointed. He hated designers being fed design ideas from the past. The notion was particularly inappropriate for someone like Emma, whose designs were invariably fresh, original, innovative and above all young and futuristic. From the Liberty experience it was becoming obvious that special retailer commissions had to be culled. The problem was that the traffic was not all one-way, particularly in the case of Liberty. Moorcroft still needed to highlight its hundred-year relationship with the store.

A little more than a week following the Liberty visit, Emma disclosed her thoughts on possible designs before initiating trials. These left Hugh uneasy on two counts. The first was the designer's proposed use of the 304 shape. For some reason

Winds of Change (2001) Ltd.Edn.100
Height 24cm (9.5″)

Calla Lily (2002). Tallest vase 25cm (10")

FACING: *Calla Lily (2002). Tallest vase 30cm (12")*

Calla Lily (2002)
Height 50cm (20")

unknown to Hugh, retailers tended to be wary of it. Those who know little about Moorcroft and its heritage prefer to ignore it in the nicest possible way, but for experienced Moorcroft collectors the converse is true. The appearance of the 304 tends to add gravitas to any range, accelerating sales to the collecting public as a result. Put simply, it had always been a difficult shape to get into retail premises, even though Emma had used it with great success back in 1999 for her memorable South African King Protea design.

The second cause of unease arose when the coloured sketch Emma produced radiated a strong sensation of yellow, an almost unavoidable consequence of looking at colour swatches taken from early 1950s fabric designs when yellow was a popular colour. Moorcroft had always worked on the theory that all human beings had inside their mind's eye one or other of the three primary colours: red, blue and yellow. Whichever primary colour a person had inside them had nothing whatever to do with their politics. It was the colour each individual enjoyed or felt most comfortable with. Clues are to be found in the colours of a favourite room, dress, shirt or sweater. For Moorcroft to produce only blue-based pieces following vociferous demand from the 'blues' would alienate the reds and the yellows, and so on. As time passed, however, it became more and more apparent to Moorcroft that while the blues and the reds split almost equally between approximately eighty per cent of the population, the yellows totalled probably little more than twenty per cent. If this theory is correct it explains why far fewer yellow-based pots sell than either reds or blues. Those involved in putting together the Moorcroft catalogue each year have to make sure that all three primary colours are represented in their correct proportions.

It would be an understatement to say Emma was disappointed at Hugh's unenthusiastic response. She had laboured hard on the design and was determined to have the vase trialed as drawn. 'Turn the yellow into clotted cream', Hugh suggested as she left the room. 'Create a piece which suggests the colours of heaven unseen with soft yellows, light blues and a dash of purple. It's good enough to become something like that'. If Emma had the slightest idea what he meant, she kept it to

Queens Choice (2001). Diameter 43cm (17″)

herself. The meeting with the young designer had not gone well, and in his reserved, almost abrupt way, Hugh knew he had done little to support Emma's first attempt to produce something spectacular for the Moorcroft/Liberty centenary celebrations.

Little more was said between Hugh and Emma until the following week when the designer asked for an appointment to see him. For designers to make a formal appointment is unusual. Mostly they use a 'can I see you?' in passing, followed by informal discussion over a mug of tea. If Emma's approach was different on this occasion, so too was the meeting itself. The designer produced from a medley of boxes and artist's cases not one but seven designs all derived from the Liberty samples. The original design was there just as Emma intended, but so too were six others any one of which had the potential to march through a design approval meeting with flying colours. Hugh was completely taken aback, and his obvious surprise made Emma laugh. Indeed, that laugh came as a relief to the Moorcroft chairman who could only guess how many long hours Emma had spent working up the designs from inspirational ideas.

It was not as Hugh expected, and still in a mild state of shock he authorised the first design trials

Calla Lily (2001). Height 20cm (8″)

to be made. In just over a week Hugh and Maureen would be heading to Malta for their first real holiday in two years. While they were away all seven designs would be trialled. The final instruction issued prior to departure was that Emma should be given all the support she required. Facilities would be made available for the designer to paint the trials herself, if she so wished. She would even be given freedom to nominate any of Moorcroft's leading painters to help her in her task. The decision was entirely down to Emma. On the day he returned from Malta, Hugh asked for a complete set of trials to be ready. His last phone call before he caught the plane to the Mediterranean was to Rebecca Toone at Liberty. Samples would be ready for approval immediately on his return, he told her voicemail.

For some days after the Liberty visit life had seemed to falter for the Moorcroft chairman. Emma was away working on her designs; the remainder of the Design Studio were preparing new work for the 2002 Spring Festival or Open Weekend; the sales team were either out on the road in the British Isles or away in North America; and the new February newsletter had already been posted to collectors' homes. Towards the end of the preceding year Elise had concluded that the number of newsletters each year should be increased from three to four. It was sound common sense. A three-monthly routine was more helpful to everyone than a four-monthly routine. It gave the writers continuity and collectors more frequent information. The net result was that everyone was busy at Moorcroft except Hugh, and when Hugh was idle his mood became reflective.

Before Blue Rhapsody had been identified as the Collectors' Club vase, other designs had been considered and then rejected for one reason or an-

Windrush (2001). Height 38cm (15″)
Sophie Christina (2001). Height 38cm (15″)

FACING: *Sophie Christina (2002) (above) Tallest vase 23cm (9″)*
(below) Tallest vase 33cm (13″)

Montana Cornflower (2001)
Left to right Ltd.Edn.300 and
Ltd.Edn.650. Tallest vase 28cm (11″)

other. One of these had been Rachel's Montana Cornflower, which first appeared for design approval as a Collectors' Club piece on the 92/6 shape. After an early rejection it was joined by a larger version carrying the same design. Both pieces eventually made a catalogue debut as limited editions. To keep the Montana Cornflower vases company, Jeanne McDougall's Topeka was also approved – a vase that had the classic ingredients of both colour and movement to commend it. A reworking of a familiar sunflower image, Topeka was destined to sell out quickly as a limited edition. Interestingly, it was not a design which involved an extravagant use of colour or intricate tube-lining, but one which added good humour and warmth to any collection. Significantly, Topeka was also a vase which focussed on the colour yellow!

The more reflective he became, the more Hugh's thought processes tended to dart at random from one place to another. He openly questioned Kim Thompson's wisdom in sowing seeds of doubt about the Montana Cornflower vases as catalogue limited editions on the ground that they involved a shape which was not retailer-friendly. They were collectors' shapes, he told her: sophisticated, elegant, beautiful. It was for Moorcroft to be the judge of quality of its work, and if the art pottery failed in that judgement the pots it made would not sell.

At this point Hugh's thoughts turned to Emma again. Calla Lily, as Emma called her design, had been adapted to fit a small blue plaque which made an unobtrusive entry into the 2001 Moorcroft collection. For some time Kim had reported that framed plaques were 'not right' for retailers, but Calla Lily was stubbornly working against the theory. Confirmation of its success came from Just Right, retailers in Denbigh, who passed on an interesting message to Kim. As soon as a Calla Lily plaque arrived in their shop, it walked out again almost immediately. Kim passed on the news to Hugh. Three months later, a range of ten pieces of Calla Lily lined

FACING: *Profusion (2002) Ltd.Edn.100. Height 40cm (16″)*

themselves up for the following year. It was Emma's response to collector enthusiasm. After seeing off an early challenge from Rachel's Prairie Summer, Calla Lily was destined to become the most successful Moorcroft design of its year, with the young designer's Queens Choice not far behind. Hugh did not have this information at the time of the Liberty visit. Had he done so, he would have added both designs to Emma's Golden Jubilee and Hepatica ranges as proven bestsellers.

The chairman's afternoon of reflection was interrupted by the delivery of Baby Ella's 'I've arrived' card. Everyone liked Ella's mother, designer Nicola Slaney. Elise's comment at the time Nicky started her maternity leave was well judged. 'You're going to miss her, Boss', she said. Hugh's eyes moved to the Wish Upon a Star ginger jar sitting on a shelf to the side of his desk. Nicky still had a great deal to contribute to Moorcroft, and he hoped she would see her way to resuming her career once her maternity leave ended.

Sweet Betsy was Emma's second contribution to the post-millennium era. Like Nicky's Trillium design, it was based on trillium flowers first seen at Ashwood Nurseries. There the similarity ended. Emma's Sweet Betsy trilliums were altogether different from Nicky's. Emma's had an overtly tropical look with a warm blue sky melting into a turquoise sea. On land there were trees of rainforest proportions, star-shaped blossom and a landscape of creeks sheltered by overhanging creepers, their leaves and flowers bending gently in graceful harmony. Nicky's work was a significant contrast. Her modernistic and distinctly geometric Trillium pieces might

well appeal to a younger generation, while Emma's Sweet Betsy was likely to attract those who liked the warmth, light and colour of exotic holidays. Nobody queried Sweet Betsy's acceptability, but as a safety measure the large vase in the group was turned into a limited edition. Two friends, two trillium designs, Hugh thought to himself. Elise was right. Nicola Slaney could be sorely missed.

Topeka (2001) Ltd.Edn.250. Height 15cm (6")

ELEVEN

Musical Art

Many people working in Stoke-on-Trent felt that Moorcroft had been fortunate to secure Ted Turner as finance director. He was a leading figure in the local establishment and one of the few accountants to have a designer as a daughter. Emma Turner worked for the John Lewis Partnership, while Ted was the son-in-law of Stoke-on-Trent's celebrated auctioneer, Peter Taylor. In October 1990, his career with chartered accountants KPMG had come to a climax when he was elected managing partner in their Stoke-on-Trent office. For Hugh, to catch Ted on the occasion of his retirement in 1998 and watch him immerse himself in his new role at Moorcroft was something of a coup. For the new finance director, the early months of 2001 remained a mild source of anxiety, albeit anxiety which had almost evaporated by the time spring turned into summer. The success of the first Moorcroft Spring Festival helped considerably, as did the May Open Weekend, a major triumph in terms of numbers, enjoyment and pure fun. Behind the scenes the Design Studio was flowing with ideas, its members now fully aware that hard work plus the courage of a handful of retailers had sheltered Moorcroft from the passing storm. As things moved forward, retailers began to notice James Macintyre's Star of Bethlehem and Connaught House's Cleome, more out of curiosity than envy. Virtually every retailer had survived a tough six months. It was unlikely that many would be prepared to take on the high financial risk associated with an exclusive design. Inevitably there were exceptions, and as a modest insurance against another autumnal dive in retail sales, Hugh called on Kim Thompson to identify five retailers trading as far apart geographically as possible. A week later their names appeared on Hugh's desk. Weavers from Saffron Walden, Just Right of Denbigh, Watsons from Salisbury, Watsons of Perth and Potburys of Sidmouth. With enough new designs in the cupboard to offer a very real choice, Kim called the retailers to a meeting where they would be free to select a design to be shared among them.

When it finally took place, the retailers' meeting was constructive. After a lively and often animated discussion they decided unanimously that Phil's Elfin Beck was

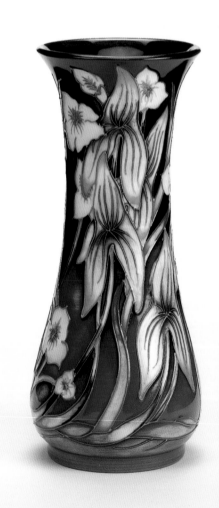

'right for us'. Each retailer agreed to take 50 pieces, but there was a sting in the tail. Phil was asked to make in-store appearances at all five shops, and this meant five days out of a designer's working life. It would be the same for the other designers, all of whom agreed to shoulder their responsibilities. Even so, each day in-store was a design day lost.

Not long afterwards, B & W Thornton in Stratford-upon-Avon started to make noises off-stage about the possibility of a second series of ginger jars, once again based on themes from William Shakespeare's plays. This was not unreasonable. The first series had been extremely popular, with examples of all five designs commanding up to a thousand pounds each in the secondary market. Barry Thornton's chosen play for the first ginger jar in the second series was The Tempest, and the indefatigable Philip Gibson took up the challenge. The resulting design weaves together common vetch, broom and vine with an intuitive sense of form and grace. The fruit and flowers that wrap themselves around the ginger jar are all mentioned:

> 'Now would I give a thousand furlongs of sea for
>   an acre of barren ground;
> ling, heath, broom, furze anything....'

Deft use of tube-lining around the base of the piece echoes the movement stirred up by the brewing storm. The Tempest is a fine piece of Moorcroft.

With two very different retailer commissions already on the Moorcroft order book, it came as a welcome surprise to learn that overseas retailers were also in the market. A.W. Hockridge in Toronto, Canada, asked if they could have a Nicola Slaney Trillium design to celebrate the store's hundred and first birthday. Bill Hockridge had made it known that Nicky's original Trillium was perfectly acceptable, provided the design came on a new shape and with a variation in the colourway. In a move that should never be mentioned in the context of modern employment law, Nicola Slaney was contacted in the middle of her maternity leave by one of her friends in the Design Studio. Shortly afterwards, a new Trillium vase appeared in a limited edition of 101 pieces with white flowers instead of red. Hugh

FACING: (top left) The Tempest (2001) Ltd.Edn.250. Height 15cm (6")
(top right) Trillium (2001) Ltd.Edn.101. Height 8cm (3")
(bottom left) Wenlock Edge (2001) Ltd.Edn.200. Height 15cm (6")
(bottom rignt) Elfin Beck (2001) Ltd.Edn.250. Height 20cm (8")

A Lark Ascending (2002) Ltd.Edn.350. Height 25cm (10")

From left to right: Allegria Orchid and Sesquipendale Orchid (2001). Both Ltd.Edn.200. Height 18cm (7")

concluded that baby Ella must have reworked her mother's original design, something which Nicky confirmed on her return! Encouraged by their success in 2001, A.W. Hockridge came back again the following year for another bite of the cherry. Their reward was a second exclusive Trillium vase, and like its predecessor every piece sold through comfortably to Canadian collectors.

For those who have never seen it, the Hockridge store is a collectors' paradise. Situated at the better end of Yonge Street, Toronto, the immediate impression is of a time warp. That first impression is, however, deceptive. The shop is lively, friendly and totally in tune with contemporary collectors' needs. A fifth generation of the Hockridge family in the form of Will and Rachel now preside, although grand old man Bill Hockridge is still a presence to be reckoned with. In period cabinets a few pieces of old Moorcroft mix healthily with the new. The shop hums with enthusiasm, while its care for collectors is a superb example of what a really effective Moorcroft retailer can do. The two Trillium designs were never destined to be the last to grace the Hockridge shelves, and sure enough in November 2003 a third limited edition appeared. Perhaps not surprisingly the edition number was 103, and once again it was Nicky Slaney who did the design honours.

Three special designs were enough for 2001, Hugh concluded. The timing of the launch of each one had to be carefully planned. There was little point in one limited edition competing with another, and the designers' own travelling schedules had to be synchronized. So much for the theory. In practice, other Moorcroft retailers sensed that something good was happening and were now in the mood to demand a slice of the action for themselves. More retailer specials were demanded of the hapless Design Studio. Emma was already out of the reckoning. Although her work on the Golden Jubilee collection was coming to a close, anything new had to wait until she took a long-overdue holiday. Just as things were beginning to look really awkward, Phil and Anji came to the rescue. Anji offered Dryandra, but promptly had it turned down as a retailer special. Moorcroft decided Dryandra would be more appropriate for Anji's Australian tour, scheduled to start in September that year. It was, after all, an Australian flower. Instead Moorcroft conceded a request from three leading retailers, The Posthorn, C.J. Beavis and Just Right to share an exclusive edition among them. Once again a selection of designs was offered to the group, with Anji Davenport's Scrambling Lily emerging as the winner.

At this point, design largesse in the form of special retailer commissions should have stopped there and then. Moorcroft was selling strongly worldwide, but by now its retailers sensed an opportunity to cash in. With a holiday behind her and the Golden Jubilee collection complete, Emma designed Fall for a special group of Canadian and American retailers. In shades of rich red, orange and black, the design featured a simple oak leaf and oak apple. North American collectors loved it, but not the thirty-one vases so badly painted they had to be smashed and remade. Slovenly work could never be tolerated. Moorcroft had survived for over one hundred years on its reputation for quality. Chinese copies and look-alikes were already appearing in some down-market shops, complete with ugly tube-lining and rough colours. Moorcroft had to avoid the world of sub-standard quality and stay permanently in the world of excellence. As a direct consequence, those who decorated Moorcroft pots subsequently designated as sub-standard on the grounds of poor painting or tube-lining would be the subject of disciplinary action. Chinese lookalikes were already an irritation. If Moorcroft produced bad artwork, those who pedalled Moorcroft lookalikes would be given the opportunity they craved for and become a menace.

Despite its small size, Moorcroft was a name growing in reputation all over the world. There were those who persistently told Hugh he was 'missing an opportunity to exploit the brand excellence of Moorcroft', or that 'Handmade in England' was a pleasant idea in artistic theory but an unprofitable one in practice. It would be best, they urged, to enhance profit margins by taking Moorcroft to China, making its pots in one of that country's mighty co-operatives, where labour was hired at seven hundred pounds a year or less. Hugh already had on file a letter from a Chinese factory offering to make Moorcroft at one-tenth of the cost. The result would be pots one-tenth of the quality, Hugh had snapped back angrily. Some English ceramic manufacturers had already slithered away to the Pacific Rim to take advantage of low pay, controlled labour and state-subsidised factories, plant and machinery. Hugh's conclusion was that those once-proud English companies would become mere distributors, although he doubted they would see themselves as such. Creaming the margins was the name of the game, they all howled at him. Losing control of your destiny, Hugh would retort. It was a word which Rachel noted in her diary.

Design, innovation and marketing were the three weapons Moorcroft had at its disposal to fight imitators and the copyist armies lining themselves up in the Far East. A wise collector might go further and say that combining superb quality with the potential for enhanced value was the way forward. Hugh was day-dreaming, but at that moment Emma unexpectedly popped her head round the door and interrupted his flow of thought. She had a clutch of new designs with her. One or two of these had existed for some months, during which time minor defects had been corrected. The young designer was now ready to push her work forward for formal design approval. One design, Illyarrie, had already grown from a single pot to a potential range of ten pieces. After discussion with its representative in Australia, Moorcroft eliminated two of the original ten pieces leaving eight modest shapes as a range for the Australian market. If nothing else, Illyarrie was a dramatic design in terms of colour. A warm, brownish-orange base had been used to symbolise the Australian outback, which played host to uncompromising red and yellow flowers from the eucalyptus family set against a bright turquoise sky. Ideas for Illyarrie had formed in the designer's mind when she toured Australia in 1999 to represent Moorcroft on television, radio and the printed media in all its forms. Both Emma and her travelling companion, Nicola Slaney, had been loyal and reliable Moorcroft ambassadors, with new designs continuing to flow from the experience long after their return. If Albany had been Nicky's contribution, Illyarrie was to become Emma's.

All Illyarrie design processes had been completed in time for Anji Davenport's tour of the Antipodes scheduled to start in September 2001. Dryandra had been earmarked to become Anji's personal design contribution. Moorcroft believed that the presence of Dryandra as a limited edition would be balanced by Illyarrie as a range. Hugh had little to say about Illyarrie. It was a striking design with colours almost alien to the conventional English eye. In contrast, for Australians it would suggest immediate familiarity. The reason was simple and straightforward. The uncompromising colours Emma used were an accepted part of everyday life in Australia, and familiarity is a pleasant sensation to release into a home.

High on the agenda for a September meeting between Hugh and Emma was the request for an exclusive design for Peter Jones China, whose retail business centred in Wakefield, Yorkshire. Many months earlier Peter Jones had been invited to a Design Studio meeting, the only retailer ever to attend. On a number of occasions Peter had asked Moorcroft to produce an exclusive Golden Jubilee design. A significant part of his reputation had been built on commemorative limited edition runs from various manufacturers, many produced by transfer prints.

FACING: *Illyarrie (2001). Tallest vase 25 cm (10")*

Peter arrived with a number of good ideas for a Golden Jubilee theme for the Design Studio to consider. One of these centred on the heraldic flowers of the United Kingdom. Unfortunately, as an idea it was already more than a twinkle in Emma Bossons' eye, but Peter had other ideas. White orchids and myrtle from the Queen's wedding bouquet, place settings for the wedding feast, corn and poppies from the Hartnell wedding train designed to set off Her Majesty's wedding dress to perfection. Whatever else, Peter Jones was not short on ideas. The problem for the designers was that once the idea had been put to them, it might then seem churlish to use

Scrambling Lily (2001) Ltd.Edn.250
Height 10cm (4″)

it for some other purpose. Because Emma's work on United Kingdom heraldic flowers was almost complete, Hugh was not in the mood to give a decision there and then. After telling the Moorcroft designers they were missing a trick in failing to have a commemorative edition waiting for the death of the Pope or the Queen Mother, Peter Jones left the room to an embarrassed ripple of laughter. 'You'd make a killing', he said to the assembled group. The designers struggled to smother their feelings.

Sometime after the Peter Jones meeting, Emma caught up with Hugh to say she had been thinking hard about the Wakefield retailer and his strongly articulated request for an exclusive design. She had concluded that Peter was fond of white orchids. More to the point, he had taken the Moorcroft decision not to offer his shops an exclusive Golden Jubilee design in good heart. An orchid or two from Emma would be good compensation. From her portfolio case the designer produced two orchid watercolours, the first showing the allegria orchid and the second the sesquipendale orchid. Both flowers were white with a faint flush of green set off with great simplicity by a subtle blue and green wash as the ground colour. Peter Jones liked what he saw, and it was he who later decided on the number of vases to be included in each limited edition.

While Emma busied herself refining work on a Wild Cyclamen design inspired by a visit to Ashwood Nurseries earlier in the year, Philip Gibson found himself sitting opposite Hugh without a watercolour in sight. Via his daughter Catherine, now company secretary at Moorcroft, Hugh had learned that Diane Tolley, an enthusiastic Moorcroft retailer, was eager to promote an exclusive design for her shop, the Wen-

FACING: (above) Dryandra (2001) Ltd.Edn.250. Height 15cm (6″) (below) Fall (2001) Ltd.Edn.250. Height 15cm (6″)

Trillium (2003) Ltd.Edn.103
Height 15cm (6")

lock Collection. Catherine had joined Moorcroft in January 2001. A qualified solicitor specialising in employment law, she was soon making her unique contribution to the art pottery. Before long she had become the in-house expert on intellectual property and design rights, both of which she set about registering and protecting with vigour. Diane had spoken to Catherine 'because your father is always so impossibly busy'. As manager of the Moorcroft design process, Hugh had called Phil to his office to ask him about the Wenlock Collection's request. As they spoke, Hugh watched Phil's eyes carefully. We have been asked for a theme, he told the designer, based on a famous poem which had inspired a piece of beautiful music. A.E. Houseman's poem 'A Shropshire Lad' contained verses about Wenlock Edge. In turn, the composer Ralph Vaughan-Williams had written his haunting ' On Wenlock Edge', which was very much a favourite of the Moorcroft chairman. Phil's eyes gave out a signal of concern, perhaps shock or even bewilderment. 'I'll think about it over the weekend' was all he would say.

The weekend came and went, as did the following Monday, but on Tuesday at 11am precisely, Phil returned to Hugh's office offering an apology. He had not intended to be rude, but the request had startled him. For over a month, Phil had been working on a design which he proposed to call The Lark Ascending, a name borrowed from George Meredith who had written a poem of that name. Years later, The Lark Ascending had also been set to music by Vaughan-Williams. Two poems, two pieces of music, two Moorcroft pots. Wenlock Edge was handed to the Wenlock Collection, while The Lark Ascending took its place in the 2002 catalogue.

Trillium (2002) Ltd.Edn.102
Diameter 13cm (5")

TWELVE

Chatsworth Weekend

Hugh enjoyed his holidays. Not only did they provide a welcome opportunity for rest, they also enabled him to re-acquaint himself with his wife of thirty-seven years standing. A lawyer in her own right, Maureen is editor of the Moorcroft Collectors' Club newsletters, the invisible guiding hand which ensured that her husband, Collectors' Club secretary Elise Adams, and the Edwards' daughter Catherine all conformed to the high standards required of them. Maureen is printer and publisher in the world of Moorcroft, as well as the long-suffering Mrs Street, a newsletter character renowned for her ability to control the worst collecting excesses of her husband, Fraser Street. For Hugh, Moorcroft is all about stories and dreams. Mrs Street, alias Maureen, is the cool reality of the world. She adopts the role of hapless mother who puts off buying new shoes for her children because a 'pot of exceptional quality' has appeared at just the wrong moment; the person whose eye for colour and readable prose has always been the backbone of Moorcroft newsletters, eyed with envy by other companies who want a Collectors' Club with panache, knowledge and an eye for history. The Moorcroft newsletters provide a source of entertainment, pleasure and information for all those who read them.

It was late summer 2002. Tucked away in the Sporades, a group of islands in the Aegean sea, lay Alonissos, its steep hillsides covered in fresh green pine trees, olives and perfumed herbs. Alonissos is an island paradise surrounded by a turquoise sea. The sun shone day after day, and with the wind whispering in the grass and trees you could almost hear the silence sing. Relaxing in a deck-chair,

Wild Cyclamen (2003). Ginger jar 15cm (6")

Wild Cyclamen (2003). Tallest vase 15cm (6″)

Hugh found himself talking to his wife about Emma's Wild Cyclamen design. Both had noticed on Alonissos the tiny cyclamen flowers already covering the ground in swathes of pink. A surprisingly wet summer had preceded the Edwards' arrival, causing the wild cyclamen to flower two months earlier than usual. What should have been a spectacular sight in November was already a spectacular sight at the end of September. There they were, delicate pink flowers climbing up from the red volcanic earth without foliage of any kind, just as Emma had drawn them. A genus found widely throughout Europe, wild cyclamen thrive as well in the gentle climate of the Mediterranean and Aegean, as they do on the snow-covered mountains of Turkey,

FACING: *Wild Cyclamen (2001). Lidded jar 13cm (5″)*

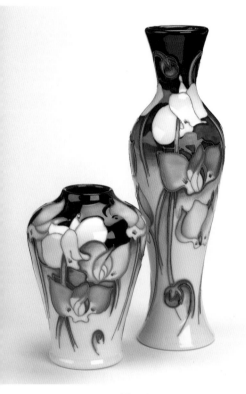

Wild Cyclamen (2005)
Tallest vase 20cm (8")

Afghanistan and Armenia. Emma's Wild Cyclamen had been designed to emerge from snow, whereas those Hugh and Maureen found on Alonissos grew on slender stems straight from the rock and soil. In both cases the flower heads reached upwards to an azure blue sky.

John Massey had been fortunate to have the exclusive opportunity to sell Wild Cyclamen from his famous Ashwood Nurseries for more than a year. Moorcroft had been equally fortunate to have John Massey as a source of horticultural information, as well as an independent judge of floral accuracy. The Wild Cyclamen range was released with five shapes via Ashwood Nurseries in August 2001. As a design, it delivered good value for collectors, and it was no coincidence that soon after the Edwards' return from the Aegean Moorcroft agreed with John that Emma's Wild Cyclamen would be released onto the world market. For Emma that was a pleasant surprise, and she responded by offering to redesign the whole range on totally new shapes. In that way pieces already sold by Ashwood Nurseries to their own collectors would remain special. Emma's work enabled a new Wild Cyclamen collection to line itself up and make an international debut in 2003. So great was the success of the range that two new vases emerged in 2005 to consolidate its appeal.

Holidays provided welcome relaxation. There were no telephones to intrude on daily life; endless opportunities for walks enabled limbs to be exercised that had been under-utilised longer than they should have been; the colours and fragrances of the countryside were there to be enjoyed. Most of all they provided endless opportunities to think about the future and reflect on the past. In Hugh's case this invariably meant thinking about Moorcroft. Seven out of eleven new ranges the following year would come from Emma, a remarkable and unprecedented contribution in Design Studio history. Much the same thing had happened outside the catalogue several times. Emma's Wood Sorrel appeared from nowhere; after warm praise the design was allocated to a group of seven independent retailers for inclusion in a Christmas catalogue they were assembling together.

FACING: *Wood Sorrel (2001). Tallest vase 15cm (6")*

Had Emma's contribution to Moorcroft art stopped dead in its tracks the moment 2003 arrived, it would still have been a remarkable year for her. It did not. The Spring Festival featured two mainstream limited edition designs from Emma, Ruffled Velvet and Bells of Spring. Ruffled Velvet was high quality ceramic art, which would have been popular either as a catalogue limited edition or as a range. It featured dark purple wild irises tinted with splashes of grey and yellow. In this way the design suggested a subtle touch of light on an otherwise sombre subject. Hugh is proud of number 91 painted by Wendy Mason. It sits serenely on a shelf in his lounge. Bells of Spring with its wild harebells turned into a personal disappointment for the Moorcroft chairman. The entire edition sold before the Spring Festival came to an end. There were simply no pieces left for him to buy.

The remainder of the Spring Festival that year had gone according to plan. A potential new designer at Moorcroft, Michelle Martin, had created Guenevere in her spare time. By day she was a Moorcroft painter, by night an ambitious designer. It was a design that had a distinct air of William Morris about it. Elegant in shape and subtle in colour, Michelle had used a restrained palette of blue to create bold, swirling poppies. Senior designer Rachel Bishop also made her presence felt. The slender, strap-handled jug was her chosen vehicle for Arctic Gold. Long after the limited edition had disappeared there were still collectors clamouring for more. 'He who hesitates is lost', runs the old adage. Arctic Gold with its cream and yellow daffodils vanished as if by magic. So too did Sian's Golden Artist, with its bright yellow and orange dwarf tulips. Something even more awkward was to follow.

(Above) Spring Collection (2003). Clockwise from top: Guenevere Ltd.Edn.75, Bells of Spring Ltd.Edn.50, Blossom Grove and Ruffled Velvet Ltd.Edn.100. Tallest vase 25cm (10") (below) Golden Artist (2001) Ltd.Edn.50. Height 15cm (6")

FACING: *Arctic Gold (2003) Ltd.Edn.250. Height 24cm (9.5")*

The final set of Blossom Grove eggcups escaped Elise entirely. As a result, no photographic record of the quaint collection was ever made. In his usual haphazard way, Hugh had purchased a set as a christening present and promptly forgotten them. Several years later Maureen found all six tucked away at the back of a kitchen cupboard! As a result, Elise was able to secure a photograph for posterity.

Emma was about to join Rachel on centre stage in design. Throughout her life Maureen had always been fair in giving credit where credit was due. While her husband was deeply committed to the design process, his responsibilities ended the moment Moorcroft decided on the purpose for which an approved design was to be used. That was the moment when new pots were costed and put into production. At the same time design images were prepared. This involves quality photographs and quality printing. Until the end of 2003, Gary Leggett had been the Moorcroft photographer. On his retirement, his former assistant Andrew Eeley took on the business. After photography, catalogues, newsletters and flyers would be passed on to Maureen for printing and publishing. She was meticulous. Bad photographs, or ones which fell short of her standards, were sent back to be retaken. Printers who printed badly, as opposed to printers working from poor source material, were politely asked to reprint at their own cost. Bell Press in Bishops Stortford were familiar with Maureen's work ethic, and errors were seldom made. They knew how to do their job, in much the same way they knew who authorised payment of their bills.

If Emma's contributions to Moorcroft dominated the summer of 2001, Philip Gibson's input was both significant and critical. Sinclairs, Moorcroft retailers owned by Christian Sinclair and managed by Margaret Grindrod, had joined the queue of retailers looking for limited editions of their own. Sinclairs had retail premises in Bakewell, Derbyshire, a mile or so from the Chatsworth home of the Duke and Duchess of Devonshire. Chatsworth had been the original choice for a special collectors' weekend. 'An away game', Elise Adams called it. Because of the outbreak of foot and mouth disease in Britain, Easter 2001 had been closed down as a window of opportunity for the Chatsworth event. Not until autumn was the great house ready to open its doors to visitors once more. Details of the event were agreed at a meeting with Chatsworth, represented by Her Grace the Duchess of Devonshire, and her estate manager John Oliver. Moorcroft ambassadors were Hugh, Elise, Kim Thompson and television personality Eric Knowles. From the outset the Moorcroft team had been surprised at the degree of energy and hands-on management shown by the Duchess herself, and the relationship was cemented the moment Her Grace learned that the Moorcroft chairman was almost as fond of chickens as she was herself!

FACING: *Chatsworth Collection (2001). From left to right: Chatsworth Ltd.Edn.350 and Cavendish Ltd.Edn.300. Vase 23cm (9")*

If Chatsworth were to become a reality, out of courtesy there was something Moorcroft had to do first. Hugh called for a meeting with Christian Sinclair and Margaret Grindrod. Among those on offer as potential designs for Sinclairs was Himalayan Orchid, a design by Phil drawn on the ever-popular strap-handled ewer. It was the perfect choice. Hugh presented Christian with one of only two pieces decorated with a cobalt ground as a present, and honour was satisfied all round. Himalayan Orchid sold out before Christmas, leaving those who say that Moorcroft events hurt retail sales whistling gently in the wind.

What Phil had not told Hugh was that the tableware used in the cafes and restaurant at Chatsworth had been one of his own designs from a past life. For this reason he asked to be considered as the designer with responsibility for two special pieces for the event. Designs should be relevant to the house, Phil suggested. It would be best not to put forward a design which had been inspired by something wholly unrelated and then allocated to Chatsworth for no better reason than it was available. Hugh concurred. It would also be fiendishly difficult for Elise or Hugh to write about a Chatsworth design, if the design inspiration had not come from Chatsworth itself.

For Phil, creating a design is part inspiration and part the outcome of thorough research. Chatsworth is renowned for its orchid house and camellias, the latter a favourite flower of the late Duke of Devonshire. It also has landscaped gardens designed by Capability Brown. To the north, rolling green hills provide a permanent reminder of the wild Derbyshire moorlands beyond. Phil eventually opted for an orchid and a camellia; but before his work was completed, Elise reminded Hugh that he had promised a selection of pots for Her Grace to choose from and not just two. At this point genuine unease set in. It had taken Phil almost three months to complete his design work, and yet there was a real risk that Her Grace might choose two other pieces and not Phil's. If she did, one or both might well have no design relevance to Chatsworth.

Fortunately a bright sunny day welcomed Hugh, Elise, Eric and Kim to Chatsworth, and the varied selection of pots which they carried with them. It turned out to be an occasion which required all the craft and skill the old lawyer could muster. The Duchess was clearly excited at the choice she had to make, jumping around from one bright window to another in an effort to see each piece to best advantage. At one point she even knelt down on the floor to peer closely at the camellia ginger jar. Hugh knelt down with her, moving the ginger jar slightly to the right to ensure that it caught the full power of the sun. In soft and what he hoped were persuasive tones, Hugh explained the relevance of camellias to Chatsworth, pointing out that the specimen used by Philip Gibson for his design was a rare variety and by repute much liked by Their Graces. The Duchess agreed. 'Such a charming shape', she murmured. 'I think we should have this one'. Quick to agree, Hugh moved the ginger jar away. One to go! For an awful moment it looked as if Emma's Honesty vase would be chosen. Once again Hugh intervened in the selection process. Despite its obvious charm and quality, Hugh intoned softly in his best Uriah Heap voice, honesty had little relevance to Chatsworth.

As soon as the word left his mouth he realised that an awful slight might be waiting to be felt. The Moorcroft chairman looked anxiously at Elise and Kim, hoping beyond hope that neither had noticed. How would he explain his comment that honesty had no relevance to the house? He had been referring to a design called Honesty, nothing more sinister. Fortunately the pair remained silent, and Hugh moved on quickly. Her Grace had picked up Emma's Wood Blewit vase. The wild, colourful fungi were almost certainly to be found somewhere on the Chatsworth estate, but this time it was Elise who chipped in and saved the day. The Wood Blewit design would never have the qualities which made it particularly special to Chatsworth or the family that owned it, she said. Very gently the Collectors' Club Secretary reminded Her Grace that a mushroom was regarded as a vegetable these days, hoping devoutly as she did so that the late William Moorcroft would not rise from his grave and accuse her of blasphemy.

Himalayan Orchid (2001) Ltd. Edn.250 Height 24cm (9.5")

'Quite so', replied the Duchess. 'We have orchids, and this orchid will do nicely don't you think?' Hugh nodded. So did Elise. It was the moment to remove both Phil's orchid vase and Emma's Wood Blewitt out of range before Her Grace changed her mind. Both were returned to their boxes and the comfort of the bubble wrap in which they had arrived. 'Names, your Grace, are the subject of a small favour'. Hugh could see that both Elise and Kim were breathing more easily. 'Would you mind if we called the orchid vase "Chatsworth" and the camellia ginger jar "Cavendish", His Grace's family name?' The Duchess' smile was the answer Hugh was looking for. 'Why not?' she said.

Friday 12th October 2001 dawned bright and clear. A cloudless blue sky, warm sun and a gentle breeze provided the perfect backcloth to what was to become one of the great days in the Moorcroft calendar. On Friday, Saturday and Sunday, into the sweeping lines of Chatsworth park came Moorcroft collectors in their thousands. More arrived than Chatsworth catering manager Philip Gates had anticipated, and there were certainly more than Elise Adams could have hoped for in her wildest dreams. Before long the John Pièrre café and the Orangery restaurant were busy with people still fresh from Eric Knowles' first lecture. Eric the television personality, Eric the author, Eric the director of Bonhams auction house, Eric the raconteur all made their contribution. His long-standing friendship with the Duchess helped, of course, just as it had facilitated the Chatsworth introduction to Moorcroft in the first place. The event turned into one of those occasions when Hugh found himself standing back to watch Moorcroft collectors enjoying themselves. It was as if he became detached, an invisible man almost apprehensive at the huge surge of enthusiasm so openly displayed for the pots he had loved all his life. Blenheim Palace next year, Hugh thought to himself. He could remember the big house with closed gates past which he had cycled both as a child and as a young man on his way to a date with the love of his life, Mrs Street, alias Maureen. Life at Moorcroft is about dreams, about looking into the future and about making something happen where previously there was nothing. The art pottery would travel to Blenheim Palace the following year.

With the excitement of Chatsworth breaking out all around her, Elise was fussing here, there and everywhere, like one of the Duchess' chickens Hugh thought to himself somewhat unkindly. For Elise, the Chatsworth event was turning into the huge success she had always hoped for and had worked so hard to bring about. Much of the credit was down to her. Deep inside himself Hugh reached the conclusion that Elise had an increasingly important role to play at Moorcroft, a role beyond that of Collectors' Club Secretary. To go out and meet collectors was a cornerstone of her personal philosophy, an idea still totally alien to many of those promoting ceramics in Stoke-on-Trent. People outside the city had long since learned that goodwill never hurls itself through the front door. It must be cultivated, promoted and gathered in. That was the way of the real world.

Letters from collectors landed on the Moorcroft chairman's desk for several weeks following Chatsworth, saying how much they had enjoyed the 'hunt the Moorcroft' competition, an idea offered by Kim. Carefully chosen pots from Moorcroft's Phoenix Years had been placed in rooms throughout the house to be 'found'. Collectors had to write down the name of the designer, the name of the design, and the approximate year in which each piece had been made. It was difficult to hide pots in rooms with a Poussin painting or a Michelangelo sculpture already in place, but Kim had done well. Some pieces proved to be exceptionally hard to find. First prize collectors were given a choice of high tea with the Duke and Duchess of Devonshire or a special Moorcroft pot. The winners on all three days selected the pot. That made Hugh smile, in much the same way as he smiled when the Duchess inscribed a copy of her book, Counting My Chickens with the words 'To Hugh, who also loves chickens'. Not nearly as much as Moorcroft, he thought to himself as he handed over to Her Grace signed copies of his books, *The Phoenix Years* and *Winds of Change*.

Hugh Edwards and designer Philip Gibson meet The Duchess of Devonshire at Moorcroft's Chatsworth event

THIRTEEN

Limitations and Liberty

If Elise Adams ever found herself exasperated at Moorcroft, the cause had little to do with design or production, the media, or even Collectors' Club management, but with limited editions. Everyone at Moorcroft knows that most limited editions are designs that work only to a particular shape. Designs that work well on a number of shapes generally become ranges. Emma's Savannah, Rachel's Meadow Star and Shirley Hayes' Bukhara might easily have been drawn up as ranges, but were used as limited editions in 2002. A regular cause of agitation for Elise was the sound of happy collectors ringing to say how pleased they were at finding a limited edition, as if they were invariably rare. Elise tells them, as patiently as possible, that limited editions in the world of Moorcroft can sometimes be more plentiful than pieces comprised in some Moorcroft ranges. A common and erroneous perception is that thousands of general range pieces are made at Moorcroft each year, in contrast to the 100/300 single pieces introduced as limited editions. This is simply not true. Even the famous Anemone Blue range, lovingly designed and nurtured by the late William Moorcroft and continued by his son Walter, sold around three hundred and fifty pieces a year throughout its entire sixty three year existence, and in some years considerably fewer.

What tends to make a piece rare, Elise will tell you, is not the number written on the base but the length of time a design has remained in production. Certainly a limited edition will never add up to more pieces than the number recorded on the base. Isle Royale was the lead catalogue piece in 2003. An excellent design, well-proportioned, wild, even eerie in colour and setting, it was also a limited edition of a hundred pieces—modest by any standard. In contrast, the number of pieces of Anemone Blue likely to have been made in sixty three years would have been 63x350, a little over twenty two thousand pieces altogether. In contrast, Anji Davenport's Coneflower range was introduced in 2002, reappeared in 2003 with three additional pieces and then vanished. It is doubtful whether more pieces of Coneflower were made over its two-year life span, than for example, the total of Sonoyta and Ranthambore limited editions, each of four hundred pieces.

FACING: *Albany (2001). Tallest vase 25cm (10")*

Albany (2001). Tallest vase 18cm (7")
Albany (2001). Jug 24cm (9.5")

An interesting example of the post-millennium rarity conundrum is a Nicola Slaney range of giftware and lamps. Because of production problems, Albany was discontinued very soon after its launch. As a result, every piece of Albany is rare, since only a few examples of each shape were made. It was much the same with Debbie Hancock's Windrush. Although first appearing in January 2001 as a range of eleven giftware pieces and four lamps, Windrush is by no means plentiful. The flag iris design theme was strong and the price good. Early 2001 saw Windrush move quickly from retailers' shelves; but after a few lively months, enthusiasm waned and then simple vanished. Despite its strengths, Windrush only survived in the giftware section of the catalogue until the end of the year. As lamps, however, the design remained in production until the end of 2002. Windrush is rare as a result.

Sian Leeper's Ranthambore was an unashamed favourite of the Collectors' Club secretary. Over its history, commentators had remarked that Moorcroft seemed incapable of creating images of birds or animals. Early attempts to design butterflies at the end of the nineteenth century resulted in insects with wings which looked so heavy they might have been made of concrete. Any lingering doubts had been laid to rest during the Phoenix Years. The arrival of Sian Leeper changed past thinking once and for all. On Ranthambore her tigers are stretched out by a lake in the sweltering humid heat of the midday sun, utterly relaxed. Collectors loved it. South Pacific, another of Sian's limited edition designs, followed suit. Shoals of colourful fish, turtles and crabs are just part of the magical mix of South Pacific. Those involved in the design process were pleased, doubly so because Sian preferred to work in the Nile Street

Windrush (2001). Height 30cm (12")

design studio rather than at home. Day in, day out she could be seen researching and working. When the mood took hold, she would even both paint and tube-line her own trials in the decorating shop on the ground floor. The success of South Pacific was repeated in 2006 with Sian's impressive new ten-inch ginger jar called Coral Reef. At Moorcroft, one design often becomes the herald of another.

There are times when total simplicity, soft colours and a sensitive use of shape make a welcome appearance. Tembusu, a Sian Leeper range featuring pink blossom and purple berries set against a rich cream ground comes into this category. Interestingly, Tembusu was one of the last designs to appear as both a collectable and a table lamp. The design was retired after just one year, leaving each piece sold in Elise's 'very rare' category. Indeed only thirty one clocks and forty two of the 87/6 vases were ever made. In contrast all three hundred and fifty pieces in Sian's exotic limited edition orchid design, Champerico, sold out well before the year's end. Put simply, in a tiny art pottery like Moorcroft, range pieces are often less plentiful than their limited edition counterparts.

The wise view offered by secondary market commentators is that the presence of a number underneath a piece of good pottery adds little to its immediate value, although it may cause the design to mature more quickly in the secondary market. This is why limited editions are especially popular with antique dealers, who happily assert a sale profit can arrive a year or two earlier than pieces in a range. As a celebrated Moorcroft expert once said, 'it can take up to five years for secondary market prices to increase, if they are to increase at all. Any shorter period tends to be largely accidental. Numbers underneath a pot make very little difference'.

Windrush (2001). Tallest vase 23cm (9″)
Windrush (2001). Tallest vase 25cm (10″)

FACING: *South Pacific (2002) Ltd.Edn.300. Height 35cm (14″)*

Over more than four decades of collecting Moorcroft, Hugh had decided that secondary market values were unreliable. Sitting at home one damp February day early in 2004, he was told by his daughter Karen, the unseen Moorcroft Webmaster, that a first edition of the Moorcroft Newsletter had sold on the Internet at a price in excess of £600. Somebody must have wanted that Newsletter very badly indeed to pay such a price, Hugh told her. At auction you only need two people who want something, plus the will and the finances to fight to the bitter end, and spectacular prices are guaranteed.

B & W Thornton's The Tempest designed by Philip Gibson in 2001 had defied all rules on secondary market price increases. Just three years after its launch at a retail price of £295, the price in the secondary market was more than £500. In 2002 James Macintyre & Co had secured another Philip Gibson design which was exclusive to their Leeds shop. Fountains Abbey sold out quickly with a retail price tag of £315. Those on-selling pieces on the Internet were able to secure prices in excess of £400 little over a year later. The problem is that a spectacular price on a particular day never guarantees the same price on another day. Fountains Abbey was a popular design with collectors. It was classic Moorcroft with just a hint of an abbey building, an abundance of white roses, and linework which suggested the presence of arched, abbey windows. An equally good design with a Yorkshire theme appeared in James Macintyre & Co the following year. Philip Gibson is a perfectionist, and to give him inspiration he read Emily Brontë's Wuthering Heights from cover to cover. The result was a design which featured visual elements described by the author—wild moorland, heather, harebells and the emperor moth. Like B & W Thornton, Macintyre's had cultivated a reputation for backing winners, but as Elisabeth Haldane, Macintyre's manager, so aptly puts it, 'that's all very well if owners sell, but Moorcroft owners seldom sell!'

The sheer joy of collecting Moorcroft has never been about how much profit an owner might make, but how much a vase, lamp, plate or bowl will enrich an owner's home by its presence. The more the Moorcroft designers strive to meet the requirement of enrichment, the more sacrosanct becomes the principle of quality. Those collectors who look at their collection and love the pieces for what they are worth look down the telescope from the wrong end. People should love their pots for what they are. In this way it is possible to enjoy a collection for a lifetime. Notions of value will inevitably creep into the equation. If a collector has taken care in putting together a Moorcroft collection over many years, it is perfectly normal to experience pleasure if pieces are eventually sold at a profit. Occasionally Hugh has to remind himself

FACING: (above left) Tembusu (2002). Jug 15cm (6")
(above right) Tembusu (2002). Tallest vase 18cm (7")
(below left) Wuthering Heights (2003). Ltd.Edn.250. Height 15cm (6")
(below right) Fountains Abbey (2002). Ltd Edn.250. Height 25cm (10")

*Open Weekend Collection (2002). Clockwise from top: Apeldoorn Ltd.Edn.50 (Emma Bossons),
Cockleshell Orchid Ltd.Edn.150 (Nicola Slaney), Queen's Bouquet (Sally Guy), The Hideaway Ltd.Edn.100
(Emma Bossons), Kanzan Festival Ltd.Edn.50 (Nicola Slaney), Montbretia Ltd.Edn.50 (Sian Leeper) and
Heaven Unseen Ltd.Edn.150 (Emma Bossons). Tallest vase 30cm (12")*

that if he had not sold his private collection of six hundred and twelve pieces of old
Moorcroft, mostly at a profit, the art pottery would not be alive today. As it is, he has
the pleasure of watching new Moorcroft designs arrive, a workforce enjoying their
jobs, and an occasional feeling of pure elation when something wonderful emerges
from the Moorcroft kilns in all its beauty. Even after almost twenty years of hands-on
involvement in making Moorcroft pots, Hugh still wants to own them all!

FACING: *Ranthambhore (2002) Ltd.Edn.400. Height 25cm (10")*

For Philip Gibson, 2002 turned into a vintage year. His prestige vase Profusion took lead position in the catalogue. It was a meticulous design based on blue hydrangeas, and it fitted its chosen shape like a glove. In real life, clusters of blue hydrangea flowers, sometimes lightly shaded with pink, produce delicate, cup-shaped fruit. In

Profusion, Philip used the hydrangea's familiar image before bending and twisting the colourful blue clusters of flowers into a less familiar but more artistic form. As a prestige vase, Profusion has great charm and beauty; it also shows an accomplished Moorcroft designer at his best.

With the cataclysmic events of 9/11 firmly in mind, Emma designed Spirit of Liberty. A double tile panel was also brought out. Availability of the tile panel, now called plaques, was strictly on request. As soon as Liberty became aware of the design, those in charge believed Emma's Spirit of Liberty was a tribute to their Regent Street store rather than the thousands of people who had been murdered in the inferno. This small misunderstanding was soon cleared up amicably, but it served to remind Hugh of the importance of Emma's designs scheduled for a launch at the famous London store in May.

The moment Hugh returned from his 2002 holiday in Malta, Emma was waiting with a number of promising trials to show Liberty. Her very first design on the 304 shape had not changed significantly, apart from colour. By using colour tones more akin to clotted cream than yellow custard, as Hugh had suggested, Emma had calmed down a potential explosion of imaginary yellow flowers. The remaining images on the vase had come from the depths of Emma's very vivid imagination. Something not dissimilar to peacock feather eyes moved around the base of the vase, before climbing up the stem towards cream-coloured flower heads on the neck and rim. It was a good design on a classic Moorcroft shape, but whether Liberty would accept it remained to be seen. The use of turquoise, shading to a reddish orange on some of the leaves, was a brave gesture in design terms, but Liberty had shown

Spirit of Liberty (2002)
Height 40cm (16")

FACING: *Spirit of Liberty (2002) Ltd.Edn.200. Height 35cm (14")*

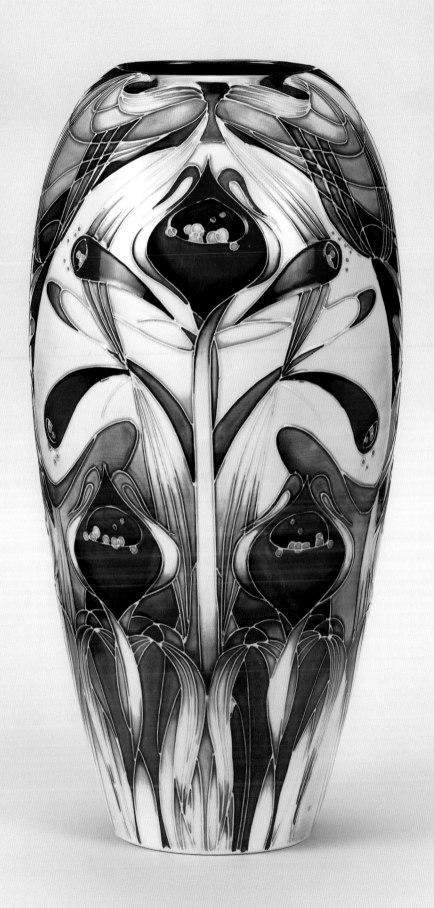

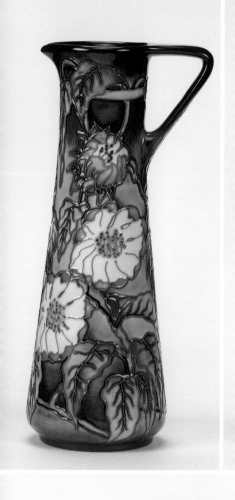

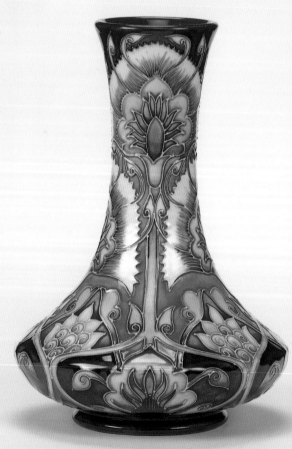

Fruit Thief (2002) Ltd.Edn.100. Height 20cm (8")

FACING: *(above from left to right) Sonoyta (2002) Ltd.Edn.400. Height 24cm (9.5")*
Champerico (2002) Ltd.Edn.350. Height 30cm (12"). Savannah (2002) Ltd.Edn.500. Height 23cm (9")
(Below) Meadow Star (2002) Ltd.Edn.300. Height 15cm (6")
Bukhara (2002). Ltd.Edn.250 Height 18cm (7")

itself to be adventurous on many occasions over the years. The Moorcroft chairman was optimistic.

A second vase with wicked birds hanging upside down pecking at rich, red and maroon berries against an unusual backcloth of what looked like stylised bamboo was particularly effective. A tulip design was also submitted for approval, as were two abstract pieces in shades of grey, blue and maroon. To crown a unique presentation, Emma adapted her work on the original 304 vase to create a round, lidded box. The lid was covered with peacock eye images and turquoise leaves identical to those of the vase. With a touch of pure genius, Emma tinted the leaves to enable them to fade from red to orange. It was a relatively small box, but when the time came for the Liberty presentation, Rebecca Toone and Barbara King were ecstatic. Hugh relaxed. For a single occasion Emma had produced five new designs. At the time it was unprecedented, but then Rachel's Reflections of a Decade collection for September 2003 was still to come!

The Centenarians (2002)
Both Ltd.Edn.100. Tallest vase 30cm (12")

After formal design approval, some of Emma's potential Liberty pieces took on different names. The classic vase itself became Heaven Unseen. Hugh had his way on that, but Liberty refused to take it. Instead it appeared at Open Weekend the same year. Six prestige versions of Heaven Unseen were also made and sold their way gently into the outside world via the Moorcroft factory shop. The tulip vase became Apeldoorn, and like Heaven Unseen made its debut at Open Weekend.

All three of the other designs were snapped up by the Regent Street store and launched at the opening of their Arts and Crafts exhibition two weeks before the May Open Weekend. The wicked birds became Fruit Thief, while both examples of Emma's more abstract design were dubbed The Centenarians. As for the lidded box – it turned out to be the star of the occasion. Called Jewel of M'dina, every piece had vanished before the Liberty event came to a close. It was a staggering result for a tiny art pottery based in Stoke-on-Trent.

Hugh still finds it difficult to look at the design work of Sally Guy in the Moorcroft

FACING: *Isle Royale (2003) Ltd.Edn.100. Height 40cm (16")*

Coneflower (2002). Tallest vase 35cm (14″)

FACING: *Coneflower (2002) Tallest vase 30cm (12″)*

Jewel of M'dina (2002) Ltd.Edn.100. Height 13cm (5″)

museum without being consumed with guilt. She had approached Moorcroft as a freelance designer in all innocence and tried hard to impress. Her Queens Bouquet design was a case in point. Originally Sally was asked to look at the Queen's wedding bouquet of pure white orchids, one of Her Majesty's favourite flowers. Sally did what was required of her, and trials were successfully completed. In what seemed an anticlimax at the time, Queens Bouquet made an appearance during the May 2002 Open Weekend, where it was instantly snapped up by collectors.

In all other respects the May 2002 Open Weekend was comfortable rather than dramatic. Drama is something that most people prefer to absorb in small doses. While Marie Penkethman's Trumpet Vine mug pleased her loyal Open Weekend fans, and with additional design contributions from Sian, Nicky and Alicia Amison, the occasion had a familiar feel about it. Some collectors were openly disappointed that Emma's Apeldoorn vase had been limited to only 50 pieces. A tiny bowl called Hideaway helped offset that disappointment, providing a little drama at the same time. Emma had struck an unusual note with a nest of baby mice! The Stoke-on-Trent traditionalists were outraged. Never had such a 'disgusting' design featured on North Staffordshire ceramics; yet Emma's spiders, snakes and caterpillars were still to arrive. Hugh was pleased to note that a Hideaway bowl suddenly appeared on the family sideboard: Maureen had shared his opinion.

Meadow Cranesbill (2002) Alicia Amison. Height 15 cm (6")

FOURTEEN

Trials and Tribulations

Since 1986, the Grade II listed building in Sandbach Road known as 'the Works' had received more love, care and cash than the factory was actually worth. A new roof had replaced its predecessor, rotten and riddled with holes; every brick had been re-pointed; walls throughout had been strengthened by an inner layer; doors had been replaced, windows realigned and re-glazed. The list was endless, but at last the Works and its famous bottle oven had both been lovingly restored. On its own it had always provided a worthwhile reason for collectors to pay a visit to Stoke-on-Trent. Hugh and Maureen had never taken a penny profit out of the business since they first joined Moorcroft in September 1986, preferring to put profits back into the company and for the restoration of its heritage buildings and creation of new jobs. For the first three years neither they nor their partners at the time sought re-imbursement of expenses, let alone to be paid a salary. It was not a hardship. They all loved the art pottery with a passion that sometimes surprised them. For Hugh and Maureen, to work for Moorcroft was a privilege and the beauty of its continuous outpouring of new pots was their reward.

The past hundred years had occasionally dealt some harsh blows. In a world of kiln truck collapses, flu epidemics, unreliable colour supply and cancelled orders, the additional burden of dealing with an historic building was something Moorcroft could well have done without. Making art pottery can be a volatile business, and if the winds of commerce blow cold it is never an option to sit and do nothing. The run-up to Christmas 2002 saw that now-familiar fall in orders, but retailers ordered strongly as soon as the new year arrived. To avoid recurring problems, Moorcroft had to grow in self-reliance and enhance its own retail sales. In Leeds' Victoria Quarter, just twenty paces from Harvey Nichols, James Macintyre and Co continued to trade profitably year on year. The store survives and thrives retailing Moorcroft alone. It is a happy place, run by collectors for collectors, with staff who clearly love their work. The Macintyre experience in Leeds suggested a possible way out. Like Macintyre's, Moorcroft would have to learn to rely on its own efforts. Driven by necessity, the fac-

FACING: *Anemone Tribute (2003). Tallest vase 25cm (10")*

Aquitaine (2003) Ltd.Edn.250
Height 20cm (8")

(Above right):
Open Weekend Collection (2003). Clockwise from
top: Lily of the Nile Ltd.Edn.50, Sweet Nectar
Ltd.Edn.75, Harwoods Lane Ltd.Edn.75, Little Gem
Ltd.Edn.150 and Silene Ltd.Edn.50
Tallest vase 35cm (14")

(Below right):
Lamp Designs as Vases (2003)
Clockwise from top: Nivalis,
Pirouette Breeze, Meadow Cranesbill, Nivalis,
Hibiscus Moon and Sumach Tree
Tallest vase 30cm (12")

tory shop became central to a long-term change in strategy. More than ever, Moorcroft had to enhance its visitor appeal and become a more attractive destination to that loyal army of collectors who have supported it through good times and bad.

In September 2002 a decision was taken to discontinue Juneberry, Cleopatra Blues, Masquerade Rose, Palmata, The Herb Collection, Trillium, Windrush, Trout, Indigo, Hellebore, Cosmos, Tembusu and, after a long fight for survival, Rachel's Islay design. For thirteen designs to pass into the secondary market was one thing, but the additional loss of Gypsy was a bitter pill to swallow. Retailers continued to turn their backs on it, despite the quality of the design with its rich heather and blue colours. Gypsy was one of the finest Moorcroft designs ever made. It was enough to make Hugh weep. Gypsy was cut adrift with a relatively small quantity of pieces sold. If anything was needed to convince Hugh that a reduced reliance on retailers was a necessity, Gypsy was it.

With almost fifty pages of design for collectors to digest, the 2002 catalogue was too large. No fewer than fifteen ranges bowed out during the year that followed, not taking into account the limited editions which automatically made their own exits as a matter of annual routine. It was a huge exercise in discontinuation, but it presented Moorcroft with a unique opportunity to reduce the number of pages in the new year's catalogue. What nobody had taken into account was an avalanche of new work from Emma Bossons. As a result, the 2003 catalogue appeared with forty-eight pages, much of it from Emma. First among many designs was Anemone Tribute which she introduced to commemorate the life and work of Walter Moorcroft OBE. A familiar

(Above) Anemone Tribute (2003). Tallest vase 23cm (9")
(below) Hellebore (2001). Jug 15cm (6")

Tigris (2003). Diameter 10cm (4")

figure at the Works right up to the time of his death, Walter was hugely liked and respected. He had died in September 2002 at the age of eighty-five, and had been something of a role model for Emma. It came as no surprise to her work colleagues that she should use anemones as her tribute, a fact not lost on Walter's widow Liz who took home the first Anemone Tribute trial vase.

At the same time as Rachel started to put together a raft of special pieces to celebrate her ten years as a Moorcroft designer, the remaining designers had to work as never before to complete a new catalogue full of vision, beauty and colour. It would have been easier for Rachel to stay out of the limelight while she worked on her Reflections of a Decade collection, but Rachel acknowledged that collectors had expectations. At a relaxed meeting with Hugh to which she brought chocolate biscuits as well as tea, the senior designer mentioned the 2003 Open Weekend. There had to be something special from her, she said. Collectors would expect it. After all she had accepted her employment contract on stage at The Potteries Museum and Art Gallery lecture theatre back in 1993. That something would have to be small, Hugh replied in what the senior designer usually describes as 'his practical tone of voice'.

A few days later a diminutive Tigris coaster appeared from nowhere. It was a thoughtful gesture from the designer to whom Moorcroft owed a great deal, but nobody anticipated the arrival of Rachel's magnificent Lily of the Nile on which flamboyant cream lilies dance and swirl from bottom to top. Hugh should have realised that a coaster, however significant, was too small to be a 'something' in the way Rachel looked at the world. While collectors were admiring Rachel's Lily of the Nile, her great friend Marie Penkethman chimed in with her Viola mug. Sian refused to stay out of the reckoning and proposed Silene, a design featuring an exotic, bright red flower. Paul Hilditch's Sweet Nectar and Claire Sneyd's Harwood's Lane completed a relatively modest Open Weekend Collection. Harwood's Lane used wild dog roses as its design theme, while Paul's Sweet Nectar came alive with an image of a hummingbird in flight.

The excitement Moorcroft generated at the 2003 International Spring Fair at Bir-

FACING: *Hartgring jardinere and stand (2003). Height 83cm (33")*

Ingleswood (2003). Tallest vase 30cm (12")

mingham was unprecedented. Ashwood Nurseries' collection of Wild Cyclamen had evolved into nine new pieces for the occasion, as if by magic. Emma had totally redrawn the range as she had promised. It was a sensitive approach, and retailers were quick to give the young designer credit. Less fortunate was Aquitaine, Emma's sole limited edition. From the word go, the colours used in Aquitaine refused to work together as the designer had intended. Painters became frustrated at their inability to perfect their art, and production of Aquitaine ground to an abrupt halt. Fortunately for Moorcroft such occasions are rare, but to own an Aquitaine vase today is to own a vase which is rather more rare than the number on each piece suggests!

(Left) Ingleswood (2003)
Tallest vase 20cm (8")

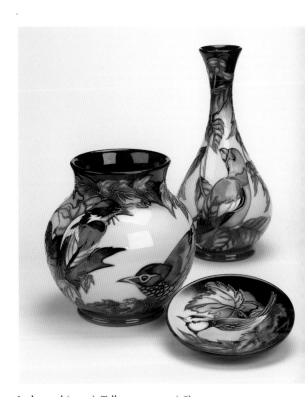

Ingleswood (2005). Tallest vase 23cm (9")

By the time Elise and Hugh met up together in the middle of February to plan the year ahead, the trade show at Birmingham had closed on a high note. It was touch and go as to whether Phil's Ingleswood collection or Emma's Hartgring range would turn out to be the best seller. Some collectors complained that Ingleswood was simply a collection of picture images and not a design at all. The line they took was that Moorcroft had survived for more that a century on design and not on pictures. Hugh was indifferent. He knew from Walter Moorcroft that neither his father William, nor Walter himself were all that competent at drawing animals and birds. This probably explained their virtual absence throughout the ninety years or so when father

and son were in sole charge of the design process at Moorcroft.

A brilliant and novel design, Hartgring was altogether different. Called after J.H. Hartgring, the celebrated Rozenberg designer, Hartgring appeared as a range of ten pieces. However, in early spring that year a mighty Hartgring jardinière and stand entered the prestige section of Moorcroft art. As a design, Hartgring was the first to introduce genuine creepy-crawlies into the images that Moorcroft introduced to the world – spiders and cobwebs, caterpillars, snails, ladybirds as well as some delicately coloured butterflies. As art, Hartgring moved Moorcroft forward, without assaulting the senses of those who admired progress in design but preferred it to be gentle.

The 2003 strategy meeting between Hugh, Elise and Kim was slow to start and took a long time to come to a close. Like all good meetings, none attending felt able to claim credit for any of the ideas noted down for action. April's Spring Festival and May Open Weekend would stay as they were. It was too late to introduce something new for March, but June was a different proposition. Those designs which had appeared in the Moorcroft catalogue as lamps would be made as vases, but only during the month of June. As an idea, it turned out to be a complete failure. Only seven 'lamps as vases' sold throughout the whole month! Collectors turned their back on the promotion, some preferring to spend their hard-earned money on the July sale while others took the view that it was probably best to retreat to the wings.

Nobody wished to change the length or the format of the July summer sale. It was a necessity of production life, a bi-annual opportunity to sell

FACING: (top) Hartgring (2003). Tallest vase 25cm (10″)
(bottom left) Hartgring (2003). Tallest vase 15cm (6″)
(bottom right) Hartgring (2005). Tallest vase 25cm (10″)

(Above) Florian Echo (2003). Tallest vase 15cm (6″)
(below) Florian Echo (2003) Ltd.Edn.25. Height 20cm (8″)

Chrysanthemum (2003) Ltd.Edn.25. Height 20cm (8")

blemished work. But August was altogether different. It was a time when many collectors were away on holiday and a new idea was required to give impetus to this
otherwise lack-lustre month. When it came it was simple. Carole Lovatt, a reliable
freelance designer, was asked to produce five special designs which Moorcroft could
produce using the blue-on-blue 'engobe' technique. Put simply, a dry but unfired
vase is dipped in blue slip (liquid clay). The moisture sinks into the dry body of the
vase leaving a light blue skin or 'slip' covering the surface. As soon as the piece has
dried out after tube-lining, the painters colour it using only cobalt blue in various
shades. The result has been a pot known to Moorcroft collectors for over a hundred
years as 'blue-on-blue'. Pieces made using this old technique are simple, organic in
form and unbelievably attractive.

FACING: *Chrysanthemum (2003). Tallest vase 25cm (10")*

As 2003 wound its way to a close, some of the planned activities for Collectors' Club members changed while others remained. Club members would be invited to Castle Howard in late September, while Kim's lamp promotion would add spice to October, a third lack-lustre month. To round off the year, Collectors' Christmas Weekend would be nudged forward a week in November to make room for the BBC's Children in Need charity auction. However, it was in December that most of the major changes occurred. Firm action had to be taken to counter-balance the annual pre-Christmas fall in sales. And the solution had to be long term.

It was Kim who suggested a postal sale in December. Others at the strategy meeting backed a novel plan to hold back the varied and often unique accumulation of trials and save them for a December exhibition. The occasion would open up an opportunity for Moorcroft trials to be sold as part of a focused release to those col-

Tazetta (2003) Tallest vase 15 cm (6")

FACING: *(above) Northern Star (2003) Ltd.Edn.50. Height 15 cm (6")*
(below) Northern Star (2003). Tallest vase 23 cm (9")

Tazetta (2003) Ltd.Edn.50
Height 20cm (8")

Leila (2003). Tallest vase 30cm (12")

lectors who made special trips to the Works in the hope of finding trial pieces for sale. With a trial exhibition in December, that hope would turn into a certainty.

Never before had so much been decided at Moorcroft on a single occasion. The important thing for Moorcroft was that the potential changes were totally applicable to every year-end at Moorcroft, not just the one under consideration. While this was all going on, Hugh found himself both puzzled and pleased: inexplicably he had started to lose weight. Nobody thought at the time he had cause for worry.

FACING: *Leila (2003) Ltd.Edn.25. Height 35cm (14")*

FIFTEEN

Reflections

Spring Collection (2002)
Clockwise from top: Springtime at Home,
Ella's Dream and Haarlem Gem
Tallest vase 20cm (8")

Whichever way it was viewed, Hugh's working relationship with Rachel Bishop had witnessed the arrival of some remarkable pots. Measured by the world of applied arts, it had been a long working relationship with no end in sight. The key was that each had learned how to respond to the other, how to measure mood swings and how to stay constant in the greater interest of Moorcroft. By the time 2003 arrived Rachel would have been designing for Moorcroft for ten years. Initially she had been sole designer, but after the formation of the Design Studio in April 1997, she assumed the role of senior designer. Ten years of service devoted to Moorcroft was cause for a real celebration; the question was what form that celebration should take. The low profile arrival in 2002 of Prairie Summer and Meadow Star had given rise to a number of conversations about the designer's ambitions for 2003. Hugh suggested that Rachel should hold back on all new work apart from her collection of celebratory pieces. By doing so Rachel would have time to plan ahead. It was all very logical, but what Hugh had not taken into account in making his opening pitch for a special collection was the imminent arrival of that year's Spring Festival. Collectors had expectations, the senior designer wisely reminded him, and one of those expectations was a daffodil design. Demands for something new in Rachel's world of daffodils had been continuous. The inaugural Spring Festival saw the arrival of Jonquilla, an instant sell-out. Memories of Jonquilla lingered. Collectors wanted more, and what Rachel gave them was Ode to Spring. Rachel had been right. Ode to Spring disappeared so quickly that poor Rachel had no chance to secure a vase for herself.

If Rachel's daffodils were becoming an annual fixture, so too was the Spring Festival. Working together at eggcup level once more, Anji, Emma, Nicky, Phil, Shirley

FACING: *Ode to Spring (2002) Ltd.Edn.150. Height 30cm (12")*

Narcissi (2002). Height 5cm (2")   *April Tulip (2002). Diameter 5cm (2")*

and Sian weighed in with Narcissi, a set of six new eggcups decorated with various types of daffodils and narcissi – one from each of them. Phil delivered Springtime at Home; Nicky, perhaps with some help from baby Ella, produced Ella's Dream; while Sian added Haarlem Gem to the festive mix. To round it all off, Emma turned in with a tiny vase called April Tulip. The arrival of April Tulip was greeted with a surge of enthusiasm by collectors that Easter, a surge suggesting a growing appetite for ceramic miniatures, a fact which Elise Adams registered with more than passing interest.

Soon after Easter, discussion between Hugh and Rachel started up again. In some alarm, the senior designer found herself agreeing to launch a special collection in September. It was a tight schedule, but after accepting the challenge with all the grace that befitted a senior designer, Rachel vanished. The agreement had centred on a collection which had to be ready for photography by July, for printing in August and for despatch to retailers starting on 1st September precisely. Rachel's collection would run until July 31st 2003. If anything Hugh had underestimated Rachel's determination to see the project through. Some weeks before the July deadline, trials started to arrive one after another. First was Owlpen Manor, a prestige vase inspired by a short break Rachel had taken at the famous house earlier that year. It would be a strong piece to lead her collection.

FACING: *Owlpen Manor (2002) Ltd.Edn.100. Height 50cm (20")*

Amberswood (2002) Numbered Edn. Height 24cm (9.5")

FACING: *Pavion (2002) Ltd.Edn.200. Height 28cm (11")*

After Owlpen Manor, designs flowed thick and fast. Pavion, an all-blue pot featuring delicate butterflies received rapid design approval. So far, so good. Two pieces were already in the bag. A peacock plaque, later called Juno's Gift, became the first-ever limited edition plaque to emerge from Moorcroft. Retailers loved it. Juno's Gift plaques were soon hard to find, with some enterprising collectors in the United Kingdom venturing across the Atlantic to secure an example. Sea Drift, an almost fragile design, and the legendary Amberswood jug both took their place in the line-up. Amberswood was to become something extra special. When the collection closed the following year, Moorcroft collectors from all over the world had purchased 1,260 Amberswood jugs!

Rachel said at the outset that if she designed her own collection she would revisit her 1994 Foxglove design and work it differently. It was a perceptive assessment of her own work by an experienced designer. Amberswood was a success almost without precedent, and jug number 1000 now lives in Rachel's own home. Because she had used her foxglove flowers in a different way, a possible name for her solo collection occurred to her. She asked for it to be called 'Reflections of a Decade'. As a celebratory collection it would be made up of ten pieces, one for each year with Moorcroft.

If anything about Reflections of a Decade disappointed Rachel, it was what she saw as the theft of her beloved Nivalis design on which she had been working for months as a fifteen-piece range.

Sea Drift (2002) Numbered Edn. Height 20cm (8")

To Rachel, it seemed as if Hugh had pushed Nivalis into Reflections of a Decade without taking her views sufficiently into account. By doing so she lost twelve out of fifteen beautiful pieces of Moorcroft. This left her feeling very unhappy. Only three Nivalis pieces were included in Reflections of a Decade. All attempts by Hugh to pacify Rachel were in vain. His offer to include Nivalis as lamps in the next annual catalogue seemed poor compensation for all the work she had done. However, on this occasion Rachel had underestimated her own

FACING: *(top left) Nivalis (2002). Tallest vase 15cm (6") (top right) Lilies of the Field (2002) Tallest vase 18cm (7") (bottom left) Arvensis (2003) Ltd.Edn.250. Height 13cm (5") (bottom right) Peace Lily (Sarah Cowan) (2002) Ltd.Edn.100. Height 25cm (10")*

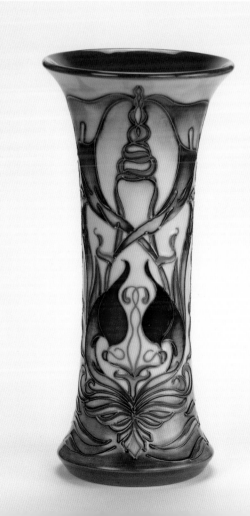

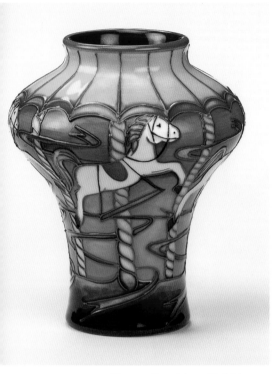

Merry-go-Round (2002) Ltd.Edn.350
Height 13cm (5")

ability. Hugh had not. The three small Nivalis pieces sold more successfully in terms of numbers and value than a good Moorcroft range in a catalogue collection, while Rachel's six Nivalis lamps became the best-selling Moorcroft lamps of all time.

Some might argue that by this time Rachel had done enough; but not Hugh. More than anything else, not least for Rachel herself, he wanted Reflections of a Decade to mirror the senior designer's huge contribution to Moorcroft. If she wanted a ten-piece collection, two further pieces were required, he told her cautiously. The look in her eyes was a mixture of resignation and tiredness, but she responded as he had hoped. The result was the re-appearance of one of her favourite flowers, the simple but elegant lily. Elise called them Lilies of the Field. Rachel agreed.

To be senior designer in an art pottery which has been in existence for more than a century is both a challenge and a responsibility. Reflections of a Decade saw Rachel take the lead and show designers how to plan and execute their art on centre stage. For Moorcroft, the September launch of her collection provided new work for the artists and craftspeople at Moorcroft at a time of year when orders became thin on the ground. It was an example for others to follow, and it left Hugh with very happy memories of Rachel's arrival at Moorcroft a decade earlier. If pushed, he would even admit to an emptiness at the thought of Moorcroft without her. There had been good times and bad times, but above all Rachel had ushered in an era of unparalleled beauty. Almost single-handedly, she had helped the art pottery clothe itself with colour. That would be her lasting legacy.

As Rachel was quick to point out, it later transpired she had worked up too many designs for Reflections of a Decade and not too few, as everyone had thought at first. One of these, Dream of a Dove, became the second Moorcroft 'locked room' piece on its website. A covered jar appeared a year later as Arvensis in Sinclairs, Moorcroft retailers in the north of England whose principal shop is in Hale. The Arvensis limited edition sold out within weeks of its launch, while Dream of a Dove still remains the best-selling Internet vase on the Moorcroft website.

FACING: *(above) Rag Dolly Anna (2003) Ltd.Edn.350. Height 13cm (5")*
(below) detail of alternative view of Rag Dolly Anna

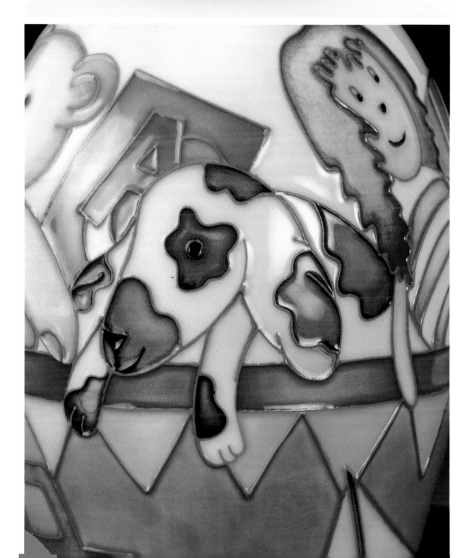

While Rachel was working on Reflections of a Decade, Emma remembered that August 2002 was the month Moorcroft needed to introduce a further nursery pot to follow Nicky's Wish upon a Star. Once again the proceeds of sale would be used to help subsidise the factory crèche. An unusual shape known as the 10/5 had caught the young designer's eye the moment master mould-maker, Trevor Critchlow, had finished modelling, blocking and casing it. From a relatively small base, the vase widened considerably around the shoulder before narrowing in at the neck in a tight flat trajectory. To Emma, the vase seemed to mutate into an old Victorian carousel before her eyes. Soon afterwards Merry-go-Round appeared, a design using bright yellows, blues and reds. The designer was astute enough to steer Hugh's mind away from the pervading yellow on which Merry-Go-Round relied for its overall effect by pointing out that her colours had been chosen for their 'nursery' appeal rather than adult idealism. A year later Sian Leeper applied the same logic to its successor, Rag Dolly Anna. Both pieces were seen as children's pieces, designed for what they are and to be enjoyed accordingly

As spring turned gently into a warm summer, Hugh suggested it was unnecessary for Rachel to make an appearance at Blenheim Palace. Reflections of a Decade, he reminded her, was an absolute priority. The following year she would be free to design for the next stately home, Castle Howard. As it happened, Rachel completed her work on Reflections of a Decade well before the date of the Blenheim Palace event. Rachel was free. Reflections of a Decade would be unveiled in all the splendour Blenheim Palace afforded, and the senior designer would be there to unveil it. She would attend Blenheim Palace with a celebrity appearance and would lead at Castle Howard with special designs the following year. Rachel had done all that had been asked of her. It was time for Hugh to back off. After more than ten years working with the senior designer, he had learned when to retreat and give her space. Apart from suggesting a possible Collectors' Club piece for 2003, he left Rachel to her own devices. It was time for the custodian of design to turn his urgent attention to Blenheim Palace itself, an event scheduled for September 2002. Special designs would be required to make it a success, but at that moment of time none existed.

Time was running out fast. Some Design Studio members were concentrating on the next catalogue. Sian was busy on Hibiscus Moon, a third limited edition for the Low Pay Unit charity scheduled for release in November. All in all, it was difficult to decide who should design for Blenheim Palace. Rachel had agreed to attend, but it would not be for her to introduce special designs. Eventually Hugh opted to approach Shirley Hayes and Kerry Goodwin, the latter a relative newcomer to Moorcroft with

FACING: *Scarlet Cloud (2003) Ltd.Edn.350. Height 35cm (14")*

long, natural ringlets that would have done credit to a Jane Austin heroine. Kerry had arrived at Moorcroft with a designer label on her CV, although she had chosen to learn the art of painting in the Moorcroft style before trying her hand at design. Kerry's first catalogue contribution made its debut in 2002. Called Sonoyta, it was inspired by creamy cup-shaped flowers with brownish orange shading on the underside of the petals. Sonoyta was likely to be more acceptable to traditional Moorcroft collectors, who would have appreciated its shaded blue ground colour. A suggestion from Hugh that she should design a vase for Blenheim Palace was a new challenge, and Kerry took it up with enthusiasm. The result was Woodstock, a colourful mix of wine coloured roses and purple lavender, both prominent features in the palace gardens. It was a design which helped identify Kerry Goodwin as a designer with a strong potential. This would be welcome news for Moorcroft retailers, Talents of Windsor. Earlier that year Talents had taken the brave step of commissioning Kerry, then an unknown designer, to bring forward an exclusive design for their shop. Their decision to call the vase Kerry was a nice touch.

Kerry's Woodstock was ultimately paired with Shirley Hayes's Sunderland, an attractive vase decorated with soft cream lilies flushed with a hint of pink. With the benefit of hindsight, Elise would have preferred to have seen Sunderland as a slightly smaller limited edition. Although more than forty pieces were left over at the close of the Blenheim Palace event, overseas Club members unable to attend snapped up every remaining piece of Sunderland, leaving the Club secretary pondering the possibility of a future allocation of stately home pieces to overseas club members.

With Reflections of a Decade behind her, Rachel started work on Scarlet Cloud, a design of which she was justifiably proud. Full blown, bright red and maroon poppies danced all over its surface in a vivid display of joyous movement. The poppy blooms were set off to perfection by a blue ground, the lighter tones of which might have come from a warm Mediterranean sky. Deep in his heart Hugh knew Scarlet Cloud had all the characteristics necessary for a range, but for some reason his ability to think clearly and positively seemed to be ebbing away. At the same time his weight continued to fall. Without Hugh pushing as hard as he would otherwise have done, Moorcroft opted to make Scarlet Cloud a limited edition. Any hope of a range failed to materialise.

By 2002, the great Moorcroft design plague had taken hold, with an almost continuous stream of requests for special pieces. This lead to an inevitable drain on design reserves. Canadian retailer Great Lake Lamp Parts entered the fray with a request for Algonquin Park. Their original request had been for an exclusive design

FACING: (top left) Woodstock (2002) Ltd.Edn.300. Height 13 cm (5")
(top right) Sunderland (2002) Ltd.Edn.350. Height 20cm (8") (bottom left) Kerry (2002) Ltd.Edn.300
Height 15cm (6") (bottom right) Love's Labour's Lost (2002) Ltd.Edn.250. Height 15cm (6")

based on the work of a group of painters known as The Group of Seven. It was not unreasonable. Sian Leeper was scheduled to make a personal visit to Canada in October, so she took up the challenge. A Canadian launch of Algonquin Park would coincide nicely with her visit.

It also would have been churlish to deny B & W Thornton their annual Shakespearian ginger jar before their second series closed in 2005. A brilliant tube-liner, Alicia Amison's famous 'Globe' vases still hold the record for auction prices achieved at a May Open Weekend. B & W Thornton's designated play for 2002 was Love's Labour's Lost. Barry Thornton had made his preferences clear, but to Hugh's delight the design offered by Alicia was clearly different from anything anticipated. Shades of blue and white gave the piece a soft, gentle appeal, with design images including wild columbine, lady-smock and lilies. Surprise mingled with delight. Those Moorcroft collectors so respected by B & W Thornton snapped up every piece of Love's Labour's Lost in no time at all. Like The Tempest before it, the design was a sell-out.

Hugh was less certain about Shirley Hayes' Scintilla. A second request for a special design had come from the group of independent retailers known as 'The Breakaway Guild'. It was a Moorcroft name for a number of leading retailers who had come together simply to promote the work of manufacturers in an up-market Christmas catalogue. Scintilla provoked sales, but it showed that the Design Studio was fast becoming unable to cope. On top of retailer requests, it would always have in-house events to consider. The mood at Moorcroft was changing. Whenever a retailer request arrived, the presumption would have to be a firm 'no' unless a very good case to the contrary was made.

FACING: (top left) Scintilla (2002). Tallest vase 20cm (8")
(top right) Christmas Collection (2002). Clockwise from Top:
Winter Wonderland (Anji Davenport), Christmas Cheer (Nicola Slaney),
Festive Lights Ltd.Edn.50 (Sian Leeper), Poinsettia (Sandra Dance),
Christmas Bounty (Kerry Goodwin), Woodland Trail (Philip Gibson) and
Christmas Bells (Emma Bossons) Height of loving cup 15cm (6")
(bottom left) Algonquin Park (2002) Ltd.Edn.250. Height 15cm (6")
(bottom right) Hibiscus Moon (2002) Ltd.Edn.250. Height 11cm (4.5")

SIXTEEN

Mixed Reactions

To this day, nobody is quite sure what happened to Philip Gibson's first Pasque Flower design trial. When it first came up for discussion in the early summer of 2001, there had been a series of inconclusive conversations between the designer and Hugh over colour. A deep burgundy wash with a hint of blue faded into a delicate cream at the neck of the 7/5 vase Phil had selected. Doubts had arisen about the ability of Moorcroft painters to cope with the colour combination Phil had chosen. Pasque Flower offered only a very small margin of error, and that margin gave rise to an unusually high risk of less than perfect pieces. At the first approval meeting held that summer, the initial Pasque Flower trial was passed over. It was neither accepted nor rejected. Phil had been considering several other shapes, including the 402/4, but for some inexplicable reason all activity around the design ground to a halt. It was as if Phil had decided Pasque Flower would never work properly and should be abandoned.

Autumn arrived. Hugh decided to take a walk around the factory shop, as was his habit in moments of boredom or during intervals between meetings. Those who noticed would speculate whether his purpose was a pocket full of sugar almonds from the shop's sweet bowl or a cup of coffee from the drinks machine tucked away in a corner behind his beloved bottle oven. Shortly before Hugh reached the drinks machine, two Pasque Flower trials caught his eye. Nobody knew how the 7/5 and the 402/4 trials had come into the shop; even if they did, those present were not prepared to admit the fact. Michele Nixon's face was an inscrutable blank, while Barbara Mountford suddenly found pots to polish and turned away. With one trial in each hand, Hugh returned to his room more puz-

FACING : *Pasque Flower (2002). Tallest vase 30cm (12") (above) Pasque Flower (2002). Tallest vase 10cm (4")*

Saadian (2002):
(top left) Diameter of lidded box 15cm (6″)
(top right) Tallest vase 13cm (5″)
(bottom left and right) Tallest vase 25cm (10″)

FACING : Saadian (2001). Height 45cm (18″)

Golden Jubilee (2002)
Diameter 10cm (4")

zled than he had been for some time. He decided to act, and what happened next happened quickly. Phil completed design work on another eight pieces, and at an approval meeting held less than four weeks later, a full ten-piece Pasque Flower range was passed for production.

At the same design approval meeting another unusual piece of work was accepted. Hugh had watched in fascination as Shirley Hayes' Saadian design evolved. It used both linework and colours more in tune with the work of William de Morgan than Moorcroft, but that was hardly surprising. Both de Morgan and Shirley Hayes had embraced the Islamic colour palette and design style. They had each created patterns and images more frequently found in traditional Arab plasterwork than English art pottery. As a person who had travelled extensively in the Middle East and North Africa, Hugh loved Saadian the moment he set eyes on it. He knew from the outset that retailers were more likely than not to ignore it, but the overall effect of Saadian was magnificent. If that opinion needed strengthening, it happened when the design finally appeared on a massive ginger jar modelled especially for the purpose. Fewer than ten prestige ginger jars carrying the Saadian design were made, but one of them stands in pride of place on an Arts and Crafts table in Hugh's home.

There was a general consensus at the Works that 2002 might well have been worse. If anything changed, then it changed almost imperceptibly and generally for the better. Elise introduced a special Golden Jubilee coaster for Open Weekend, a move appreciated by collectors. It also stood out as a year full of new ideas. Some worked and some did not. For the first time the catalogue featured table lamps carrying different designs from those used on giftware. In the past it had always been assumed that if a design appeared in the giftware section of the catalogue, it would automatically appear in the table lamp section. All of a sudden that assumption was no longer valid. In came lamps—Phil's Sumach Tree and a five-piece selection of Peony, Alicia Amison's Meadow Cranesbill and Emma's Pirouette Breeze. A small exception was made in the case of Meadow Cranesbill, where Alicia's lamps were joined by a specially adapted vase destined to become the Collectors' Day piece that

FACING: *(top) Pirouette Breeze (2002). Diameter of lamp base 20cm (8")*
(bottom left) Peony (2002). Height of lamp base 18cm (7") (bottom right) Sumach Tree (2002)
Height of lamp base 15cm (6")

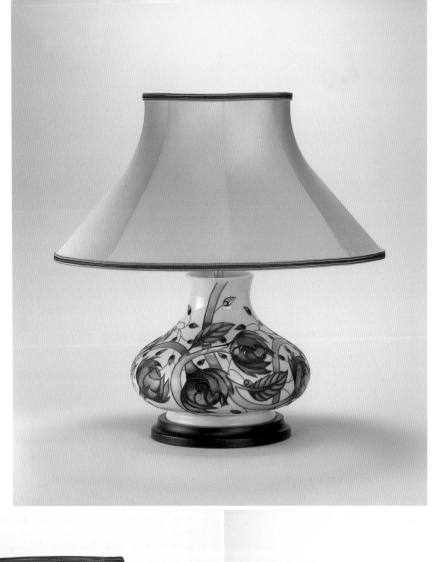

year. A new era for table lamps had dawned. Table lamps would now be specifically designed as lamps. By so doing the art pottery acknowledged lamps as furniture, belonging to a different marketplace from the one occupied by collectable ceramics. As furniture, lamps had to move in line with fashion changes, whereas collectables did not. What had once been an unwritten rule at Moorcroft had now become a fact of life.

Because Moorcroft designers are never told what to design, it is always a welcome surprise to see what arrives next. Almost out of the blue, two Moorcroft designers offered new prestige designs. First was Emma who unveiled The Gate Keepers, a ceramic masterpiece by any conventional definition. For Hugh, who had reached a point where very little surprised him, The Gate Keepers caused his stomach to turn a hundred somersaults. As a work of art, it was awe-inspiring. Stiff liar birds stood to attention protecting the truth, their vow to say nothing about the secrets they were hiding. Guards were in place to make sure no living being manipulated the facts: a circle of birds linked together like soldiers in colours of blue, green and orange. Emma's great liar birds were defiant, their vase epitomised strength of purpose. As a piece of ceramic art, The Gate Keepers radiated power.

Rachel's own contribution was in character. For inspiration she crossed the Atlantic to the most heavily forested of the Virginian barrier islands. The outcome was Parramore, a prestige landscape vase which took its name from the island and looked as if it were made with stained glass. It was the work of a world-class designer at her best, and for the second time in only a few days Hugh found himself thinking just how fortunate Moorcroft was to have both Rachel and Emma in the Design Studio. If the art pottery led by design, with Emma and Rachel on call it has the inspiration and skills to take on the world.

Complaints about the inadequacy of the first Moorcroft website were becoming more voluble. As Hugh is always happy to tell anyone, when he

(Above) Meadow Cranesbill (2002). Height 20cm (8"). FACING : The Gate Keepers (2002). Height 50cm (20")

first arrived at Moorcroft on 16th September 1986 bright-eyed and innocent, the art pottery had two telephones and a single manual typewriter with bars which leapt up and hit the notepaper each time the typist thumped the key. A museum piece today, that old typewriter epitomised the time warp in which Moorcroft existed in the mid-1980s. Since that time, every kind of modern computer aid has arrived. Moorcroft can boast state-of-the-art electronics for use with financial records, production, sales and stock, communication and the written word. Only in design are computers still absent, and that is by choice.

The first Moorcroft website had been delivered in a hurry, leaving staff to repent at leisure. However, by June 2002 a new, all-singing, all-dancing website had been designed and built under the watchful eye of Hugh's second daughter, veterinary surgeon Karen. When it went 'live' in June 2002 the reaction all over the world was encouraging. Elise Adams was delighted. So, too, was Karen, known as Kardy to her friends at Moorcroft, the person whose original ideas were behind the website. It had taken everyone involved almost a year to complete the main features, and it had been time well spent. During the day Kardy was a vet. By night she was the principal website strategist. She was later appointed the first Webmaster—that unseen person ensuring that everything in cyberspace works properly for Moorcroft. It was just as well. The first twelve months saw the new website receive over seventeen million hits. On the Internet today there are more than forty-five thousand entities extolling the virtues of Moorcroft, ranging from individual collector chat-rooms to quality retailers worldwide.

Among the features found on the Moorcroft website is a 'locked room' purchase facility which collectors can enter with their Collectors' Club user name and password. The first piece put up for sale in the locked room was Golden Net designed by Shirley Hayes. Elise then saw an alternative use for the design. The vase was immediately withdrawn, but not before just one solitary piece had been sold. If anyone is entitled to boast of uniqueness, it is the owner of the single Golden Net vase. It also stands

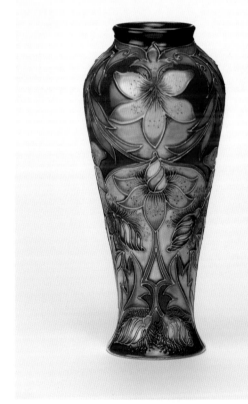

FACING : *Parramore (2002). Height 50cm (20")*

(Above) *Golden Net (2002). Height 20cm (8")*

as the first piece of Moorcroft ever sold using the Moorcroft website. After that things moved quickly. The moment Golden Net disappeared, Phil's Midnight Blue ginger jar took its place. For Elise, Midnight Blue was a perfect Internet design with its striking white flowers set against a dark blue ground. Internet images benefit from a clear contrast between the colours used.

Before long, Webmaster Kardy was able to report that other website features were working well. The auction pages had gone far beyond original estimates, enabling retailers to sell those pieces which they decided were 'not right' for them. Within six months, the number of registered bidders had risen to 2,500. A year later, in June 2003, registered bidders totalled more than 6,000, and by January 2006 the count had risen to 8,000. Some collectors started to ask Elise when they could use the auction facility themselves. As always, the Club Secretary was rational in her reply. Everything at Moorcroft takes time, and the company is not big enough to indulge

Atlantica (2002). Height 15cm (6″)

in the luxury of operating in the secondary market. Its primary duty is to sell the pots it makes for today, not the pots it made and sold yesterday. Even if that changed one day, the timing and the circumstances would have to be right.

The year the new website went live, Elise became heavily involved in the planning of two promotional trips to Canada and the United States. For the first, television personality Eric Knowles agreed to travel to Toronto with Elise and Donald Reid and fit in celebrity appearances for Moorcroft between filming sessions for the BBC's Canadian version of the Antiques Roadshow. For the second, Elise and Donald would travel with designer Sian Leeper. The North American trips were planned as the first serious export promotions by Moorcroft since the largely abortive tour Hugh had made at the time of the World Trade Center tragedy.

To accompany the travellers on each trip, Sian designed Atlantica, a patriotic design in shades of red, white and blue. When the trips came to an end, Atlantica was seen to have served its purpose. In Canada attendances had been good, but with a surprising emphasis on antiques rather than the more vibrant, joyous Moorcroft made today. Elise had always been reluctant to embrace older work, but she held no deep feelings against those who enjoyed doing so.

In the United States her perceptions changed. Americans were interested in history, but when they came to in-store promotions, they did so to enjoy the experience of Moorcroft today. For Moorcroft, the two tours were a brave experiment, but there was more work to be done. The 'antiques' mix was not working. Antique dealers and auction houses always have different agendas. Whatever else, the Moorcroft sales team would have to dedicate themselves to North America for many years and stay focused. There was no room for tantrums, for territorial jealousy or hierarchical manipulation. The future of North American exports called for supreme effort, single-minded hard work and an ability to show that the driving force at Moorcroft was an unshakeable love of the pots themselves.

(Left to right) Hartgring (2003), Sophie Christina (2002), Reverse of all name plaques. Length 18cm (7″)

SEVENTEEN

Succession

The sun shone through the great arched windows of Thaxted church in beams of pure golden light. Occasionally Hugh would slip inside the gracious building with its white stone pillars and incredible silence, often for no better reason than to think. The church had always had perfect acoustics, a lasting tribute to its medieval stonemasons, and one reason it had played host to some great soloists and orchestras. Violinist Yehudi Menuhin had made live recordings there. The Liverpool Philharmonic and the London Symphony orchestras had both performed under its massive, vaulted oak roof. Gustav Holst had been organist at Thaxted Church for fifteen years, composing The Planets and the music for the famous hymn 'Thaxted' with its immortal words 'I vow to thee my country' while he was there. In many ways the church was full of ghosts, much like the Moorcroft factory in Sandbach Road, and to Hugh it seemed only yesterday when the great church bells rang out to greet the arrival of the new year in 1997. When the sound of that mighty peal crashed into the night air, the first pottery to carry the Moorcroft name had become a hundred years old.

Around the church were a number of familiar plain white vases of considerable antiquity, all containing assortments of arranged flowers. Perhaps not surprisingly, Emma Bossons' Saffron Crocus vase made its debut a few months later. It was a vase of great quality, with purple crocus flowers. The whole of its sale proceeds flowed into church funds, enabling repair and renovation work to continue unabated and on schedule. In some strange way Moorcroft had attached itself to Thaxted church and the silence it afforded whenever its heavy wooden doors closed to shut out the sounds of the outside world. Silence was a commodity Hugh enjoyed. Not

(Above) Saffron Crocus (2003)
Ltd.Edn.150. Diameter 13cm (5")

FACING: Thaxted church

all his thoughts were coherent thoughts, but there was no better place to concentrate his mind in a wise way than the interior of one of the most well-known and beautiful churches in the United Kingdom. Indeed, Thaxted church enjoys many qualities of a cathedral.

For some time Hugh had found himself perplexed why it was that some painters seemed to have very little to do, even at times when the Moorcroft order-book was full. 'Close the crèche!' Ted Turner once told him, but Hugh had never seen the logic of the finance director's remark. At another time Ted suggested Hugh should 'close Cobridge Stoneware', a new Moorcroft subsidiary which made innovative stoneware. For the former commercial lawyer there was no obvious link between idle painters at busy times and the closure of a nursery facility fully utilised by Moorcroft mothers, or a new business which was not yet strong enough to stand on its own. Much more relevant in terms of financial logic was the pernicious system of 'average' incorpo-

Tulipa (2003) Ltd.Edn.150
Height 35cm (14")

rated into pay structures operating in some sectors of the ceramic industry, including Moorcroft. 'Average' pay rules had undoubtedly hurt Moorcroft financially for many years. Put simply, tube-liners and painters were paid on a piecework basis after an initial learning period during which they familiarised themselves with new designs. Piecework rates of pay were agreed by negotiation and implemented as soon as possible. By its very nature, piecework encourages speed. As soon as incoming trade orders declined, as they regularly did each autumn, painters and tube-liners would revert to a regular weekly wage, but one calculated on the piecework earnings of each employee 'averaged' over the preceding three months. Inevitably these three months reflected the time of optimum skill and optimum speed. Every year, weekly wage levels based on 'average' leapt upwards remorselessly with annual percentage rises in flat wage rates arriving on top of the 'average' increases rather like icing on a cake. In some years, rates of pay at Moorcroft had risen by more than 25%, and the more new designs the art pottery introduced, the greater were the incremental increases that 'average' delivered to the tube-liners and painters. In the old days, when designs seldom changed at Moorcroft, this cancer in the system lay undiagnosed. By the time it was finally cut out, the harm done to Moorcroft was huge. The financial surgeon who finally removed the 'average' cancer and introduced a conventional pay structure was David Holland, a young accountant who joined Moorcroft in 2004 to become finance director soon after Ted Turner retired.

Hugh sat in silence pondering these things for some time. As the afternoon drifted silently into evening, the rays of sunlight streaming through the church windows deepened to a shade of golden red. These colours were similar to Rachel's Royal Gold, a limited edition daffodil design which would be unveiled in 2006. At the time Hugh had no idea what the senior designer would introduce in 2006, but back in 2003 he had found himself reflecting on a year which had become a colourful mix of bits and pieces; a succession of designer 'freshen-ups' and curious one-

(Above) Sophie Christina (2003)
Tallest vase 15cm (6")
(Left) Orchid Garden (2003)
Height of lamp base 25cm (10")

(Top left) Hepatica (2003). Height of vase 13cm (5″) (top right) Woodside Farm (2003). Tallest vase 25cm (10″)
(bottom left) Coneflower (2003). Tallest vase 33cm (13″) (bottom right) Anna Lily (2003). Tallest vase 33cm (13″)

off pieces appearing from nowhere and then disappearing. Alicia Amison's Tulipa had been planned as an inaugural midsummer vase, and that was what it became. The vase came and went before anyone had time to blink, as did Emma's Orchid Garden lamp for Peter Jones.

To stretch his legs, Hugh wandered round the old church looking at the flower displays. Some of them were in need of freshening up themselves, but he had no new flowers to put in place of those that had died. Even so, he removed some shrivelled blooms and wrinkled leaves as gently as he could and threw them into a dustbin tucked conveniently behind a small door which lead out to the rear of the church-yard. It was just the same at Moorcroft, Hugh thought to himself. That year Sian had added a clock, vase and tray to her Sophie Christina range, while Emma introduced a small planter and vase to enhance the impact of Hepatica. Queens Choice had received the same treatment with three new vases, a planter and a plate, while Nicky's hugely successful Anna Lily was given a virtual makeover, with a clock and no fewer than six new vases. Not to be outdone, Anji Davenport moved two new vases into her Woodside Farm collection, while Lamia, that dowager lady of Moorcroft design, was rejuvenated by the arrival of six new pieces. Unwilling to stop the 'new look' stampede for 2003, Rachel also added four pieces to Prairie Summer, including a fourteen-inch charger. To round off the exercise, Shirley Hayes added four vases to Pheasants Eye, a design much favoured by the John Lewis Partnership.

It is sometimes thought that major Moorcroft retailers such as the John Lewis Partnership are impersonal, driven by accountants and devoid of aesthetic understanding. That is a far cry from the truth in the case of John Lewis. Their buyers have strong and accurate instincts as to what is good and bad in the applied arts. More importantly, those in-stincts guide them towards what is likely to sell and away from what will not. Much the same can be said of the Moorcroft design approval committee every time it sits in judgment on a new design. There is, however, one way in which JLP, as the Partnership

Queens Choice (2003)
Tallest vase 25cm (10")

is affectionately known, differs from other retailers. Part of its ethos is that there is no advertising of specific goods, no brand hierarchy, no labelling which puts one manufacturer above another. JLP customers are free to choose what they want to buy in an environment where goods are displayed side by side in parity. For that reason alone the Partnership is a vital Moorcroft retailer. When Moorcroft sells in a JLP store, it will have done so on its own, competing with other manufacturers on fair and equal terms. It therefore came as an exceptional pleasure when JLP asked Moorcroft to produce an exclusive limited edition for the Partnership, something it had never done before.

Emma was given the prestigious task of producing a JLP design. The result was Mystique. The slim, elegant shape Emma chose proved to be the perfect vehicle for a design of rich burgundy-centred orchids surrounded by delicate white petals and light green leaves, all set against a much stronger dark green ground. Around the rim of the vase the designer placed a stylised motif not unlike a white Fleur de Lys. Hugh is the proud owner of Mystique number 192/200, a prize that came to him very late in the day. Demand from collectors was strong from the outset. With promotion by Emma herself and television personality Eric Knowles, that was not surprising. What delighted everyone at Moorcroft was that JLP asked for Mystique in the first place. Collectors must have seen it that way, too. Despite his eagerness to buy, the Moorcroft chairman found himself at the back of a very long queue.

Mystique (2003) Ltd.Edn.200 Height 30cm (12")

By the time Hugh was ready to leave Thaxted church, the golden light of evening had turned into a lingering grey, tinged with red. It was the end of an afternoon of reflection in much the same way Mr John's retirement from Moorcroft in March 2003 was the end of an era. Younger son of William Moorcroft, the founding father of the art pottery, John Moorcroft had always been known as 'Mr John' at the Works. It was an old Stoke-on-Trent habit based on ancient principles of subservience.

FACING : *(top left) Lamia (2003). Tallest vase 30cm (12") (top right) Lamia (2003). Height of plaque 30cm (12") (bottom left) Prairie Summer (2003). Diameter of charger 35cm (14") (bottom right) Pheasants Eye (2003) Tallest vase 35cm (14")*

Everyone at the Works had called his father 'Mr Moorcroft' and the title 'Mr John' differentiated between father and son. Hugh called John by his Christian name without the 'Mr'. So did Rachel Bishop, but Elise Adams called him 'Mr John'. Kim Thompson addressed him in like manner, as indeed did almost everyone else at the Works. What particularly exercised Hugh's mind was the long drawn-out saga ultimately leading to John's retirement. At first John had confided in Hugh that he had wanted to 'see in the millennium'. Later he announced he wanted to 'see out the millennium', a statement which caused some minor embarrassment since a 'goodbye' party had been planned by everyone well in advance and was ready to proceed. All that had to be unscrambled. Mr John remained firmly in place at the close of the millennium, with Moorcroft staff and management back-pedalling on retirement parties. Inevitably it fell to Hugh to establish John's final intention. It turned out that his sixty-fifth birthday was the latest option favoured by the last Moorcroft to be employed at the Works.

Retirement vases presented to John Moorcroft (2003) Height 30cm (12")

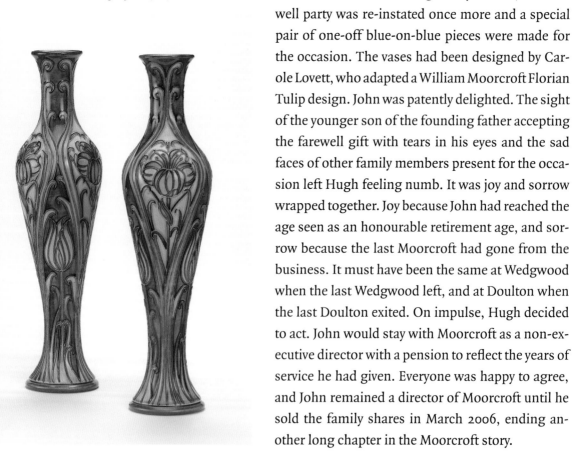

When 28th March 2003 finally arrived, the farewell party was re-instated once more and a special pair of one-off blue-on-blue pieces were made for the occasion. The vases had been designed by Carole Lovett, who adapted a William Moorcroft Florian Tulip design. John was patently delighted. The sight of the younger son of the founding father accepting the farewell gift with tears in his eyes and the sad faces of other family members present for the occasion left Hugh feeling numb. It was joy and sorrow wrapped together. Joy because John had reached the age seen as an honourable retirement age, and sorrow because the last Moorcroft had gone from the business. It must have been the same at Wedgwood when the last Wedgwood left, and at Doulton when the last Doulton exited. On impulse, Hugh decided to act. John would stay with Moorcroft as a non-executive director with a pension to reflect the years of service he had given. Everyone was happy to agree, and John remained a director of Moorcroft until he sold the family shares in March 2006, ending another long chapter in the Moorcroft story.

FACING: *Celtic Web (2003). Tallest vase 20cm (8")*

Celtic Web (2003). Height of clock 15cm (6")

As John bade farewell, Hugh found himself recalling a design approval meeting held at the end of 2002. A particular favourite of the younger son of the founding father to come up for consideration had been Celtic Web, with images inspired by Archibald Knox's work for Liberty during the early years of the last century. John's mother had been a Lazenby before her marriage to his father, William. The head of Liberty at the time had been Sir Arthur Lazenby Liberty, whose stewardship of the famous Regent Street store in London embraced the years when a young William Moorcroft was struggling to make his way in the world as an art potter. For not dissimilar reasons, and possibly out of deference to his father, John had given his bless-

FACING : *The Wanderer's Sky (2003). Tallest vase 30cm (12")*

ing to another Emma Bossons design, The Wanderer's Sky. Old-style trees and hills were the main features of an uncompromisingly colourful range, and it was easy to see how the design had a deep resonance for John stretching back to his father's era. As a result, he supported Emma's work. If anything, John had been a little unsure about the vibrant turquoise blue Emma had used for the sky. Interestingly, and perhaps entirely coincidentally, Emma changed the colours of The Wanderer's Sky the following year. Out went the strong turquoise and with its passing the range was re-named Evening Sky. The overall effect of the colour change was to bring Evening Sky much closer to Eventide, the famous William Moorcroft design that first made an appearance in the early 1920s. We shall never know if Emma had intuitively read John Moorcroft's mind, but his overt pleasure at the new look a year later was itself praise.

For weeks following John Moorcroft's retirement, Hugh had felt very much alone at Moorcroft. After all, John had been partly responsible for his arrival in September 1986. The Moorcroft chairman was younger than John by several years, but age was also creeping up on him. Succession at Moorcroft was a very real problem, but there were encouraging signs. Between them, Elise Adams and Kim Thompson had already shown a clear pointer to a future generation. Rachel Bishop was senior designer with her Design Studio to support her. When accountant David Holland arrived in 2004, the future was even more secure. Another generation had arrived to lead Moorcroft forward into a new dawn. It was just as well. Hugh's weight continued to plummet: by the end of 2003, he had shed well over two stone. He had no aches or pains; his pulse, breathing, blood-flow and temperature were all normal. As far as he could tell, Hugh had no cause to worry. Every conceivable medical test had been carried out. All had proved negative. Hugh relaxed.

An active fisherman, the Moorcroft chairman had been pleased at the arrival of Phil's Quiet Waters, doubly so when the designer produced a stunning prestige vase as a follow-up. Hugh had never contemplated catching Phil's shubunkins on rod and line, but fish as design themes had woven a clear thread throughout the fabric of Moorcroft history. Early Florian carp had been replaced by simpler images of fish in the late 1920s, while Sally Tuffin's carp design of the early 1990s had been a Moorcroft masterpiece. Phil's first fish design, Trout, had been expensive to produce, and some of the prices Moorcroft had to ask still make Elise wince. History would repeat itself in 2006 with Phil's brilliant Lagoon collection. Moorcroft had been waiting patiently for a truly excellent fish design for some years, and with Lagoon patience was rewarded. However, as the newly-appointed finance director

FACING : *Evening Sky (2004). Tallest vase 30cm (12")*

(Above) Miniature Collection (2006). Clockwise from Top: Grapes, Art Nouveau, Violet, Poppy Seeds, Dragonfly and Figaro. Height of each 3cm (2″)

FACING : Quiet Waters (2003). Height 38cm (15″)

David Holland pointed out, Lagoon would be expensive to make whichever way the figures were calculated. It was hard to tube-line and hard to paint. To change the design or weaken the colours would be sacrilege. Whatever else, Lagoon had a very high perceived value. To deal with the situation, the design was introduced as a novel collection of small limited editions. The 2006 experiment worked, but it was an experiment Moorcroft had never thought of using for Quiet Waters, a range that was quietly withdrawn after two years. The prestige version of Quiet Waters was available only during 2003. There are no records to suggest that any prestige pieces were made after the end of that year.

FACING : *Quiet Waters (2003) (top left) Height 25 cm (10″) (top right) Tallest vase 25 cm (10″)*
(bottom left) Diameter of charger 35 cm (14″) (bottom right) Tallest vase 35 cm (14″)

EIGHTEEN

DNA and Destiny

David Holland, a qualified accountant with an MBA from Henley and enough commercial experience on his shoulders to fit a man twice his age, eventually succeeded Ted Turner as finance director at Moorcroft. Ted resigned early in 2004, followed by a transitional ten weeks during which the two worked side by side. David grasped the financial reins in June, but after less than four weeks found himself perplexed. Although the system of average pay had been frozen at 2002 levels, it had not been eliminated. However, it was not that fact which troubled the new finance director. Somewhere in the sea of figures which he patiently fed into his slim white computer, something unpleasant lay hidden. Unable to identify the problem, let alone its solution, David picked up a copy of the 2003 Moorcroft catalogue, scanning its pages in an almost futile attempt to convert the images into figures. To succeed he would have to understand the complex issues of cost and perceived value that arose from design, linework and colour. For the latest member of the Moorcroft team, the task was proving difficult. Pricing ceramic art was not a concept David had ever had to embrace; but he persevered. On his right hand side, covered up to ensure fair play, he had a current Collectors' Guide to Retail Prices and on his left an open copy of the catalogue.

As designs, Sian's Chapada Toucan and Chapada Sun Conure were pleasing, but for the life of him David could see no logical reason why the price for each should have been the same. After a thorough examination, his conclusion as an accountant was that never could the same person paint two different designs in precisely the same time. In David's language it was like looking for two people with identical DNA, and the odds against finding them were about the same. If the two Chapada designs caused confusion, the next three designs he looked at were all on different shapes. That presented an even more serious challenge. Once again the accountant's calculation of price proved to be well over one hundred pounds adrift from the figures printed in the Collectors' Guide to Retail Prices.

At the same time, he was surprised at how much he felt drawn to what Hugh had

FACING : *Inset of Chapada Toucan vase (2003) Ltd.Edn.350*

FACING : *Chapada Toucan (2003) Ltd.Edn.350. Height 25cm (10")*
(above) Chapada Sun Conure (2003) Ltd.Edn.350. Height 25cm (10")

The Wild Highlanders (2003)
Ltd.Edn.350. Height 25cm (10")

described as 'pure design' rather than picture images. The first vase in the trio was Sandra Dance's Wild Highlanders. For David, the piece had a bleak, austere feel; but because of the frozen features of the landscape, he felt this must have been the designer's intention. More worryingly, the price he arrived at turned out to be one hundred and twenty pounds more than the figure in the Collectors' Price Guide. Aesthetically he found Phil's Flanders Moss vase and tile panel almost frightening to look at. For a man who had loved animals all his life, a frightened hare with staring eyes was not something he would have readily taken into his home. In point of fact, the eyes of the hare he was looking at had been badly painted, and the piece had been designated as a 'second'. Ironically, David's first stab at pricing the Flanders Moss pieces was much closer to the mark, a fact which surprised him. It was only when he ran a cross-check on Phil's 2004 Mountain Kingdom using the same formula that the accountant scored a bulls-eye. The figure he arrived at was almost identical to the one in the Guide.

At first David dismissed his success with Mountain Kingdom as a freak, one he was happy to put down to his love of birds in the wild. What had really happened was that David Holland had learned how to understand the complexities of an intuitive assessment of a pot and the almost black art of pricing them at levels which took a collector's perceived value into account. For the future, he decided to devise a Moorcroft pricing model to work out costs accurately. With that tick in the accounting box, the perceived value of a piece of Moorcroft to a collector would be a quest to be enjoyed. It was as good a starting point as any for his new job.

Sian Leeper's Katmai was to show a family of brown bears, one fishing in a river and the other looking after its cub. In the background, distant pine forests and high mountains suggested a vast expanse of spectacular wilderness. The first Katmai trial to emerge from the Moorcroft kiln was a total failure. The bear central to the design image looked as if it was being sick. Elise ordered the offending vase smashed

(Above) Katmai (2003) Ltd.Edn.200
Height 25cm (10")

(Top left) Flanders Moss (2003) Ltd.Edn.250
Height 20cm (8")
(centre left) Flanders Moss (2003)
Length of plaque 40cm (16")
(bottom left) Golden Oriole (2003) Ltd.Edn.750
Diameter 20cm (8")

Vale de Luna (2003) Ltd.Edn.400. Height 15cm (6")

and personally watched the shards disappear into the Moorcroft rubbish skip. After such an undeniably bad start, Sian re-drew Katmai and the offending linework was moved to one side. The wilderness took over, and in no time at all her Katmai vase was ready.

Vale de Luna proved even more troublesome at first. Throughout the summer of 2002 there had been endless conversations between Hugh and Nicky, not over the merits of the design itself but over the combination of colours. These simply refused to work together. From the outset Hugh noticed that Vale de Luna was another design with echoes from the era of William Moorcroft – a design that the founding father would have recognised and embraced had he been alive to see it. What Hugh saw in Vale de Luna as a collector was that dark green trees in the traditional Moorcroft style would be far more attractive to collectors if they had a splash of burgundy about them, but the more he and Nicky sought to bring out a burgundy splash, the more stubbornly it refused to percolate to the surface of the vase after its second firing. After eleven unsuccessful trials, both agreed to abandon Vale de Luna if the twelfth trial failed. Changes were made to the colours, shading was modified and moved around, two shadows and a tree disappeared. Then as if by magic, the design suddenly worked. Right on cue and in exactly the correct places the burgundy splashes which first made an appearance on Hazledene pieces in 1914 shone through. Vale de Luna was ready for production.

The saga of the Vale de Luna vase left a long-lasting impression on Hugh, and at Open Weekend 2005 he produced his first and only Moorcroft design. Requiem for Trees sold at auction on four consecutive days at an average price in excess of eight hundred pounds. Although each piece was admittedly one of only four ever made, the prices were a vindication of his enthusiastic use of dark green mixed with a splash of burgundy. In a landscape of dark green trees which some described as 'austere', the burgundy splashes provided gentle relief. Requiem for Trees was later to become a best-selling greetings card.

Deep in the intelligent mind of designer Nicola Slaney, the colours on Vale de Luna drifted into other patterns. Initially it had been Snowberry, which used burgundy and subtle shades of green on a pure white body. This colour combination was so successful that it re-appeared under another design guise as Duet in 2005. For its part, Snowberry eased its way unobtrusively into the 2003 collection as a modest range of eight pieces, including an exceptionally fine coaster. That great Moorcroft army of coaster collectors seized on the Snowberry version with a surge of enthusiasm so strong Club secretary Elise Adams felt obliged to follow it up with the arrival of Panache, the first Collectors' Club membership renewal coaster. In 2005 Panache was followed by Rachel's even more successful renewal coaster, Triple Choice. A year later the senior designer consolidated that success with her New Forest coaster, completing a neat trio of unusual coasters.

Nicky's original Snowberry design was also the catalyst for another of Elise's thoughts. The Club secretary had taken note of John Moorcroft's fulsome praise of Celtic Web when it received design approval. Special praise had been reserved for the diminutive 32/2 shape, which turned out to be exceptionally popular. Much the same thing had happened the year before with Rachel's Nivalis and Sian's Tembusu. By the time Nicky's 32/2 Snowberry had turned itself into a runaway success, Elise realised there was an enthusiasm for a particular aspect of shape, namely its size. Miniatures, usually defined by leading auction houses as being two inches or less in height, had become hot property among Moorcroft collectors. Senior designer Rachel Bishop added a 32/2 to her Prairie Summer range in 2003, followed shortly afterwards by Little Gem, a vase which appeared at Open Weekend in May on the same shape as a limited edition. Elise decided to act. She would campaign to bring

forward other miniature shapes to keep the popular 32/2 company. In this way one of the simplest and yet most innovative ideas to emerge from Moorcroft for some time began. The result was an inaugural collection of six miniatures, handsomely boxed as a set and launched to the world in January 2006.

Picking up her Snowberry colour threads of burgundy, green and white once more, Nicky proceeded to design Alpine Meadow, scheduled to appear in the 2004 Spring Festival. Kim decided Alpine Meadow was 'not right for her', and the Moorcroft shop team agreed. Just as with Snowberry, one of the striking features of Alpine Meadow was the designer's use of a pure white clay body. In the ordinary course, Moorcroft is made with ivory coloured clay, which has a slightly creamy overtone. Pure white means precisely that – as white as snow. 'Maximum edition size of fifty for Alpine Meadow', chanted Kim and the shop team. 'Much too small for a great design', Hugh and Elise sang back in unison. In the end, the edition was fixed at 150 pieces, against a commitment by Hugh to buy a hundred pieces personally. There are times when the Moorcroft chairman can be accurately described as stubborn, arrogant and reckless. In the case of Alpine Meadow, it was just as well he combined all three characteristics. Every piece in the Alpine Meadow edition sold in two days, leaving Hugh fighting hard to secure two vases – one for himself and one for Maureen.

David Holland was not the only person with philosophical problems over Moorcroft pictures, as opposed to Moorcroft designs. An ardent Club member seriously upset Hugh when she remonstrated in strong terms at the 'comic strip' direction into which she felt Moorcroft was drifting. Design had enabled Moorcroft to survive for over a hundred years, she tiraded, and why was it necessary to

Clockwise from Top:
Triple Choice (2005), New Forest
(2006) and Panache (2004)
Diameter of each 10cm (4")

abandon design and put comic strips in its place? The principal object of her criticism was Phil's Ingleswood Collection, which had first appeared in 2003 and was 'refreshed' from time to time thereafter. The year after its launch witnessed not only the arrival of three new pieces for Ingleswood but also a double tile panel. Whatever

FACING : *Snowberry (2003). Tallest vase 18cm (7")*

design purists wished to believe, Ingleswood was selling strongly all over the world. Because strong sales supported jobs, Hugh disagreed with the collector, albeit in measured terms. Moorcroft birds were birds with a Moorcroft look about them, entwined with make-believe leaves, branches, bushes, fruit and berries, he had said. In this way the final result would always be a design in the Moorcroft style rather than a picture. An option was to decorate pots with lifelike birds by using transfer prints. Other ceramic manufacturers did this very successfully, but birds at Moorcroft were different. They were very definitely designed birds and not pictures. Even as he spoke, an image of the 2003 year plate Golden Oriole flashed across Hugh's mind. Certainly the bird was reasonably realistic, but its habitat was stylised. The colours were bolder and more imaginative than real life. Yet despite his passionate defence of Phoenix Years' images, the collector's criticism provided food for thought.

Elounda from Alicia Amison and River of Dreams designed by Sarah Cowan were both derived from graphic images, but nobody could seriously assert the two carried pictures rather than designs. A design, Elise suggested, was something which stirred the brain and the senses to levels of appreciation far beyond the image itself. It enabled the senses to react in a totally uninhibited way. Picture images never

Ingleswood (2004)
Diameter of charger
35cm (14")

FACING : *Alpine Meadow (2004) Ltd.Edn.150. Height 20cm (8")*

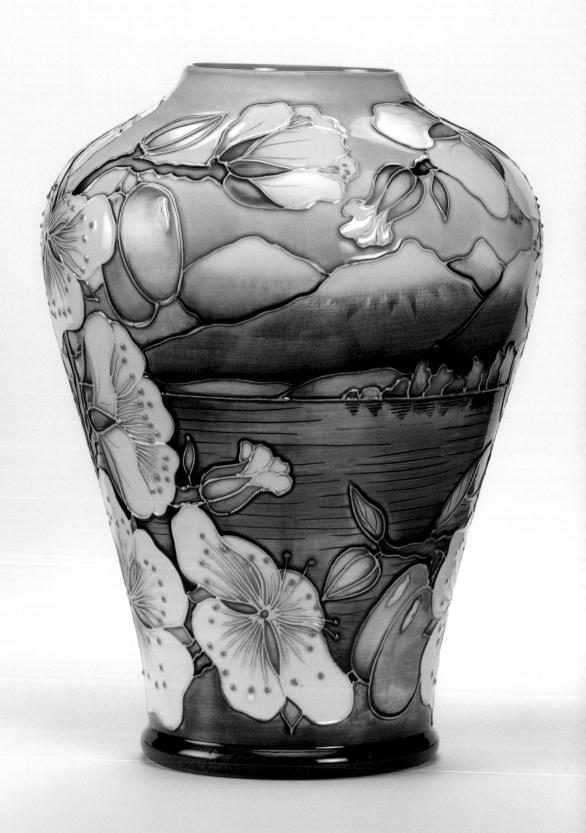

seriously aroused aesthetic emotions. That was both their strength and weakness. 'Worcester-style images' as Elise called them, were pretty, well-crafted and nice to look at. On their own they often stir sentiment, but seldom the senses.

Sitting in his room at the Works drinking tea, Hugh took the opportunity to tell Rachel how well her Destiny vase had been received. The senior designer was smiling. She and Hugh had shared over ten years working together, and the famous partnership showed no sign of ebbing. For both, Destiny was the finest design Rachel had ever produced, and Hugh had been the first to say so. It was the lead piece in the Innovation by Design collection, put together to celebrate the five-year anniversary of the Moorcroft Design Studio over which Rachel presided. Why should she not receive a Destiny vase for herself, Rachel enquired with an unconvincing look of innocence on her face. It was Hugh's turn to smile. His 'it will come in time' response cut little ice – rightly as it turned out. Every single piece of Destiny was to sell out, and it was not until 2006 that a special Destiny vase was handed to Rachel, appropriately marked 'Designer's Piece'.

One characteristic shared by Hugh and Rachel was that both were opportunists. Hugh had promised the 2003 Castle Howard event to Rachel as a suitable climax to the senior designer's exhilarating and successful ten-year anniversary celebrations at Moorcroft, and at their 'Destiny' meeting Rachel reminded him of the fact. Rachel was ready to take centre stage at Castle Howard, the prestige event scheduled for the end of September. Her designs were also ready. What collectors found waiting for them at the stately home made famous by the television saga 'Brideshead Revisited' was Fanfare, and Lady Cecilia. Although he liked Lady Cecilia with its coral roses drifting in abundance round the contour of a small, round vase, Fanfare totally captured Hugh's heart.

With real peacocks at Castle Howard, the temptation to use peacock feathers as a design theme proved irresistible. Rachel chose a slim, elegant ewer with a small strap handle for Fanfare. A Rachel Bishop peacock feather design guaranteed the success of Fanfare. With the event in full swing, Hugh stood watching Rachel sign Fanfare ewers one after another with a gold pen. The sight of collectors crowding around her made it seem like the old times of the mid-1990s when there were only the two of them to sustain design, tell stories and recall dreams at Moorcroft. The designer turned, caught Hugh's eye, read his thoughts and smiled. There was still much for them to do, more to complete and a few things to change. The first of these was the seemingly endless stream of requests for exclusive limited editions, now acknowledged to be a threat to Moorcroft design capacity. It was also fodder for the

FACING: *Elounda (2003) Ltd.Edn.350. Height 23cm (9")*

River of Dreams (2003) Ltd.Edn.350. Height 35cm (14″)

FACING : *Destiny (2003) Ltd.Edn.150. Height 40cm (16″)*

pay system which was hurting Moorcroft so badly.

The latter part of 2003 had become open season for special designs for those privileged retail customers who had the resource and willingness to risk a serious capital outlay on funding them. The art pottery already knew that none of these limited editions had a guarantee of success attached to them. As in everything else, success depended on the quality of the design, the size of each retailer's customer base and the enthusiasm of the retailer's own sales team to engage with collectors. Geoff Taylor in Reigate had been a quality Moorcroft retailer for many years, with customers who not only enjoyed attending the special events he put on at Denbies Wine Estate, but who also had a shrewd eye for good designs. Emma was not surprised to receive Geoff Taylor's request for a small version of her prestigious Montagnac design. She always enjoyed working on designs featuring grapes, and worked assiduously on the Geoff Taylor commission using what she called 'mini-Montagnac prin-

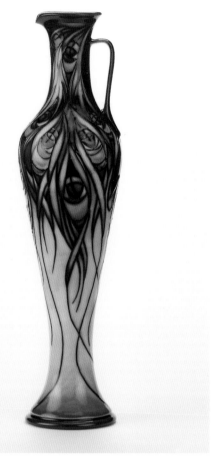

Fanfare (2003) Ltd.Edn.300
Height 30cm (12")

Carillon Blue (2003) Ltd.Edn.250
Diameter 13cm (5")

ciples'. The first trial of Mountain Vineyard had lush purple grapes and a vibrant blue sky presiding majestically over a landscape filled with rows of grapevines fading into distant hills. It was vintage Emma Bossons, but Geoff Taylor asked for changes. The lush purple grapes became green grapes of the kind found at Denbies Wine Estate, while the vibrant blue sky clouded over to a distinctly English grey. The retailer was delighted with the alterations. Emma was not. Mountain Vineyard was launched from Denbies Wine Estate regardless.

Carillon Blue was selected after intense but affable discussion between Weavers of Saffron Walden and the William Sissons Gallery. The design was Sian Leeper at her best, with a chosen colourway that would leave traditionalists happy wherever they lived. Every time Hugh looked at it, small details shone through and highlighted themselves, and it was these tiny close-ups which turned it into an attractive work of art.

Shortly after Carillon Blue appeared, Connaught

Mountain Vineyard (2003)
Ltd.Edn.150. Height 18cm (7")

Lady Cecelia (2003)
Ltd.Edn.200. Height 10cm (4")

House in Nottingham and Collectables in Newcastle-upon-Tyne each successfully commissioned exclusive designs for themselves. Philip Gibson did the honours for Connaught House with Shirewood and its vaguely familiar 'Sherwood Forest' theme, while Sandra Dance's Petunia vases displayed purple petunia flowers on two traditional Moorcroft vases. The design had a sombre, albeit slightly regal feel about it. In contrast, Shirewood conjured up images of chestnut and oak trees. The former was a feast for the eye, the latter a feast for the imagination; either way, both Shirewood and Petunia were destined to make their way into the Moorcroft history books as designs rather than pictures.

(Top left) Shirewood (2003) Ltd.Edn.150. Height 25 cm (10")
(bottom left) Shirewood Watercolour Showing Reverse Side of Vase
(top right) Petunia (2003). Both Ltd.Edn.150. Tallest vase 20 cm (8")

NINETEEN

Downward Spiral

As each year progressed, the assortment of trial pots in Hugh's room at the Works grew and grew. Elise never doubted that any attempt to tidy up would be met with a grumpy rebuff. To clear the room would be to risk a reaction. In the curious world of collecting, the longer a pot lives in a room the greater the risk that a person either falls more in love with it or out of love. Most collectors will have experienced this strange phenomenon. Those pieces which fail the test of time either tend to become family gifts or are discreetly sold. As a collector, Hugh had always accepted this rather quaint truism, and as each day rolled by pots tended to shift up and down the chairman's popularity scale, some surging forward, others sliding backwards, much like human beings in her husband's life, Maureen once shrewdly observed. Fortunately for Hugh, the Collectors' Club secretary eventually discovered the secret for herself. From that moment there were two subscribers to the barometer theory at Moorcroft which reads, 'I still really like that pot' at the top of the scale to 'It appeals to me less these days' at the bottom.

Phil's Blue Rhapsody had cruised through the design approval process before either Hugh or Elise had time for second thoughts, but it was not the same for Queen of the Night which emerged as the strongest contender for the 2002 Collectors' Club slot. At one time or another the hapless vase had stood on shelves, vanished inside desks, and was once found upside down in the cupboard which housed Hugh's mini-fridge and lunchtime sandwiches. The 152/5 shape had always been a favourite ever since a much younger Hugh rescued a severely cracked New Florian vase from a junk stall in London's Portobello Road antiques market. By the time of its release, Elise had also started to worry about Anji's Queen of the Night, but they were transient anxieties. The bold, white-flowered vase with its dark blue-green ground shading almost to black at the base and rim sold happily. Queen of the Night was seen by Moorcroft collectors to be as beautiful as the flower from which the design takes its name.

(Above) Queen of the Night (2002). Height 13cm (5")
Below) Anatolia (2003). Height 23cm (9"). FACING : Anatolia detail

Both 2003 and 2005 turned out to be good years for Rachel in the world of the Moorcroft Collectors' Club. The choice of a Rachel Bishop design as the Club piece in 2003 was not unexpected. It was the year which marked the tenth anniversary of the senior designer's arrival at Moorcroft, and Anatolia was the vase she brought forward to celebrate the occasion. With its tightly structured design of heart-shaped frames, tiny red and blue flowers and yellowish-orange leaves, Anatolia was a masterpiece of intricate design. It was also a vase of considerable substance with an appropriate price to match. Hugh had watched its introduction nervously, but his fears turned out to be unfounded. Anatolia joined the ranks of successful Moorcroft designs the moment it became available.

Centaurea made its debut as the Collectors' Club vase in 2005. Of all the vast library of Moorcroft shapes, the 70 shape was almost certainly Hugh's favourite. In the early 1970s he had acquired the original blue-on-blue double-gourd Florian Carp vase designed by William Moorcroft, which later assumed the role of lead piece in the Moorcroft centenary museum exhibitions of 1997. As a result, the Florian Carp vase had been on public display both in the Potteries Museum and Art Gallery in Stoke-on-Trent and Saffron Walden Museum for almost a year. Eventually Hugh decided to have the double gourd shape recreated. Elise seized the opportunity to commandeer the new vase for the Collectors' Club and passed it to Rachel to see what she could do. The double gourd vase is a challenging shape for a designer, whatever the circumstances. To be asked to use it as a Club vase made it even more so. As far as anyone could establish, the double gourd shape first appeared approximately a hundred years earlier. Centaurea seemed as good a name as any for Rachel's new Club design in the circumstances.

Emma had designed Symphony a year earlier. Like the double gourd vase, the bonbonnière and cover was also a shape not seen for almost a hundred years. Emma's design showed burgundy and cream flowers wrapping their way gently around the stem of the bonbonnière, while purple berries clung to it in a way which tempted the viewer to reach out and pick them. 'Those berries are good enough to eat, Boss', enthused Elise, and she was right. The rich colours, attractive lid and flowing line-work all contributed to yet another in a growing line of successes for Emma. The only doubt he had ever had about Symphony, Hugh would confide to those collectors interested in trials, concerned the original lid. The tip of the knob on the very first lid had been coloured somewhere between Cornish cream and yellow mustard. 'It looked', Hugh says, 'like a boil about to burst'. An embarrassed Emma had agreed immediately, and her colour modification enabled the lid to become a fitting crown for a sensational piece of Moorcroft.

Centaurea (2005). Height 23cm (9″)

Since the launch of the Star Award pieces in 2001, designs introduced exclusively for the Collectors' Club had developed something of a cult status. The interest and enthusiasm their arrival provoked was particularly rewarding for Elise. Sweet Thief had become the most successful, but there were more Club members in the One Star membership bracket. A tacit understanding developed in design circles that Rachel should lead the Star Award pieces second time around. Rain Daisy appeared first in much the same way as Sweet Thief had done. It was small, affordable and well designed from top to bottom. Shirley Hayes' Two Star Red Ribbons jug was bold, colourful and significantly larger, while Emma's Three Star Accolade attracted a strong following. It was vintage Emma, and the name 'Accolade' was particularly appropriate. To the surprise and delight of everyone at Moorcroft, in 2002 the De-

*(Above) Symphony (2004). Height 20cm (8"). FACING : Second Star Awards Collection (2004-2006)
Clockwise from top: Cuckoo Song, Red Ribbons, Accolade, Rain Daisy and Oriental Poppy*

sign Studio found itself as having among its members the youngest elected Fellow of the Royal Society of Arts. Elise's christening of the modest cherry blossom vase 'Accolade' was a nice touch.

With all Moorcroft designers very much 'on a roll', Phil and Anji completed the second Star Award line-up with the Four Star Oriental Poppy and the Five Star Cuckoo Song respectively. Anji's Cuckoo Song was available only to members who had been in the Collectors' Club for more than fifteen years. Over the inevitable cup of tea in Hugh's room, the chairman and Club secretary speculated on whether sales of Cuckoo Song would accelerate before 2006 came to a close. If they failed to do so, the vase would remain in the 'exceedingly rare' category, as had Sarah Brummell-Bailey's Honeysuckle ginger jar almost three years earlier.

For a novel reason, Sian Leeper had every reason to be pleased when 2006 arrived. Her Apollo butterfly design became an overnight bestseller with the double gourd version voted by those who work at Moorcroft as 'vase of the year'. From whichever angle you looked at it, the conclusion was the same. The Apollo double gourd vase was the perfect marriage of design and shape. Similar compliments were offered to Sian for her Collectors' Club ginger jar, Arctic Tundra. Sweeping arctic terns framed three central images of a family of polar bears in an arctic landscape. The technique was the same as that Sian had used so successfully in Apollo, a ten-piece range with graphic images of apollo butterflies framed by daisies as a secondary design feature. Simple but effective, Hugh had told her. Only the snowflakes on Arctic Tundra had presented problems, but after a series of late but successful tests, the new Collectors' Club ginger jar was ready for launch.

In contrast to the exciting but fragmented activity that was the hallmark of 2003, the appearance of Emma's Orchid Arabesque was low-key in the extreme. The design was admired by Maureen, once a ballet dancer herself. She had been impressed with the fluid movement apparent on every piece, and Orchid Arabesque was an appropriate name. The problem with the design was that retailer reticence once again cast a cloud. The design was far too subtle for most trade buyers, who described it as being 'not for us'. The inevitable happened. Just as the same reluctance to buy killed off Rachel's glorious Gypsy design, Emma's Orchid Arabesque suffered the same fate. As a result Moorcroft quietly retired the range in the same year it was introduced. Only a relatively small number of pieces were made. Somewhat perversely, retailer timidity seems to have a knack of rebounding positively in secondary market values. A classic example is William Moorcroft's Persian Pattern, dismissed at the time of its introduction just before the First World War as being too foreign!

Arctic Tundra (2006). Height 15cm (6")

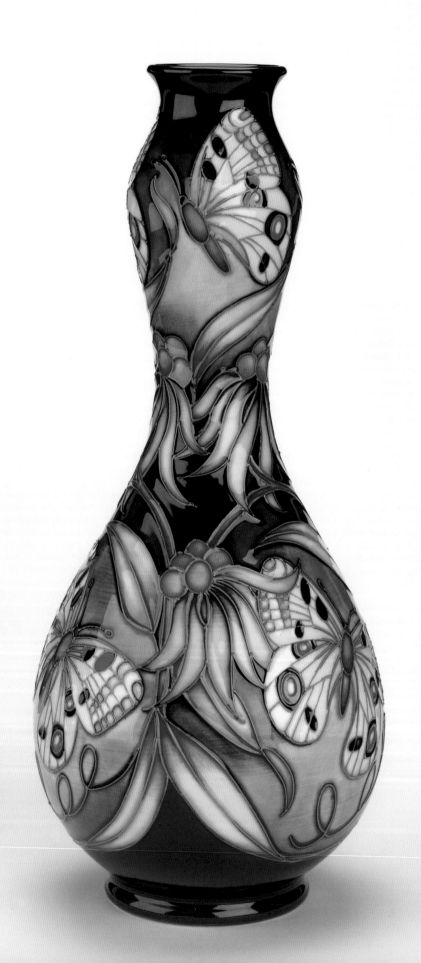

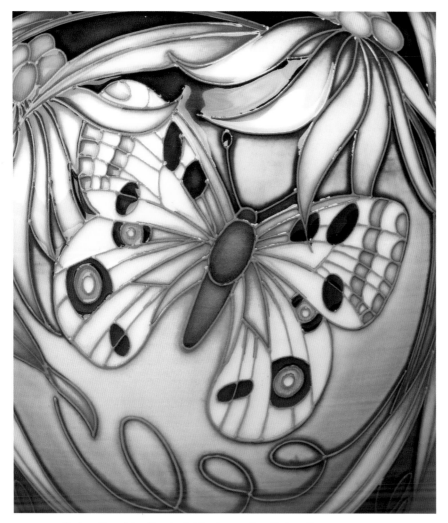

FACING : *Apollo (2006). Height 28cm (11″) (above) Inset of Apollo (2006)*

In some ways Delonix, Pheasants Eye and Palmata all had a style firmly liked by some, but not others. There was nothing about the three designs which suggested compromise. Shirley Hayes had used strong colours and tight linework, a technique providing very little room for the three designs to breathe. As a result they were all expensive to make. Some thought they lacked the high perceived value to attract collectors and become bestsellers. The rich mix of purple, maroon and grey of Delonix was as strong as the colour combination Shirley had used in Palmata, with its rich vibrant red flowers set against a jet black ground. Both designs also translated into handsome limited edition prestige pieces, Palmata in 2001 and Delonix in 2004. As the late Susie Cooper said, 'the spaces created by a design are as important as the design itself', but in the final analysis it did not matter. Out in the wide world were a good number of very perceptive Moorcroft Collectors who secured examples of Pheasants Eye, Palmata and Delonix for their homes.

It had become increasingly worrying that Moorcroft seemed unable to produce prestige pieces. Designers had all become experienced in prestige work, but the number of prestige pieces coming through the production process fell to a mere trickle. With a large pile of unfulfilled orders, Hugh added pain to misfortune by authorising an April release of a further three large pieces, two from Emma and one from Rachel. Admittedly Emma's Hartgring jardinière and stand was a rework of her successful range, but Garden of Eden was a totally new work. With a serpent slithering through dark undergrowth, Emma's design was further evidence the art

(Above and FACING*) Orchid Arabesque (2003). Tallest vase 30cm (12″)*

pottery had started to break new ground in its imagery. Rachel was working hard to enhance her ten-year celebrations, and the appearance of a prestige version of Anatolia was a shrewd move by a designer who had studied the habits of collectors more closely than most. All three prestige pieces sold well, but the Moorcroft production team failed to make any significant inroad into the orders received. 'We'll get there, you'll see', was a frequent response to Hugh's increasingly irritable questions. Something was wrong, but however hard Hugh looked, the cause of his worry continued to elude him. Finance director Ted Turner shrugged his shoulders and suggested Hugh pull the plug on further design work for prestige pieces. There was something frighteningly logical about Ted's remark. What was the point of selling prestige pots, if the prestige pots themselves could not be made? It was an unpleasant thought.

Ironically, the moment Emma started working on Garden of Eden, Sian completed Paradise Lost, a complex design on a huge vase more than twenty-five inches high. It was classic Sian Leeper: colourful parrots, tropical flowers and an abundance of rainforest greenery. A strict limit was placed on the number of pieces, and as a result only a handful of the huge Paradise Lost vases were ever made. The self-imposed limit on sales came as a considerable disappointment to the Moorcroft sales team. Many more pieces of Paradise Lost could have been sold, but however hard Hugh pushed the affable, friendly and perpetually relaxed Moorcroft production director Keith Dawson, prestige pieces continued to come through at little more than a trickle. Worse still, however hard Hugh stamped his feet, the pace of production of orders on the sales book showed no sign of accelerating. The final straw turned out to be the April arrival of Emma's Gate Keepers and Rachel's Parramore prestige pieces. Hugh was finally stirred into action. The size of the prestige order mountain had to be reduced, but first of all the cause of its failure to shrink had to be diagnosed.

To cast a prestige vase is a highly-skilled task. Because each piece is heavy, special pulleys lift the moulds to prevent injury or strain. All pieces are turned on a vertical lathe, not a horizontal one as is normally the case. Even more important is the fact that prestige pots, once tube-lined, take an age to dry out. More than three weeks 'standby' is required for the largest. Forced drying is not an option. Pots that are dried in a 'hot' room tend to crack, wasting all the tube-liners' work. The Sandbach Road decorating shop has wide, high shelves or 'stillages' as they are known in the Potteries, on which prestige pots will dry naturally over a number of weeks. When he started to investigate in earnest, the first thing that Hugh discovered was that

FACING : *Delonix (2003) Tallest vase 25cm (10″)*

Paradise Lost (2003): (top left) Third panel with Emperor Tamarin Monkeys. Height 63cm (25")
(top right) Second panel with Rainbow Macaws. Height 63cm (25")

very few large pieces were standing on the stillages to dry. Lack of 'green' tube-lined clayware suggested the tube-liners had not been given prestige pieces to decorate. It was necessary to find out why.

Keith Dawson's answer was straightforward and honest. He did not have a sufficient number of tube-liners to supply work to prestige painters as well as mainstream production painters. The news came as a terrible shock, and the only obvious solution was long-term. Keith had already trained some of the Moorcroft painters and

FACING : *Paradise Lost (2003): First panel with Jaguar. Height 63cm (25")*

tube-liners to become dual-skilled. In addition to their original skill, they learned the art of another. It was a start, but nowhere near enough to become a solution. In the circumstances, nobody would want a trained tube-liner to paint. Only by increasing the number of qualified tube-liners would the number of idle painters fall. It takes up to eighteen months to retrain a painter as a tube-liner, and that time was not available. It was desperate. The awful fact was that Moorcroft had a significant number of redundant painters on its books.

Even at this juncture the sheer size of the problem still eluded Hugh. For Ted, production problems were production problems, and if the production director was unable to sort them out, it was for Hugh to sort them out as Chief Executive Officer. The final months of 2003 were slipping away. To please Hugh, and in an attempt to halt his daily criticism, Keith moved senior tube-liners onto prestige work. The moment that happened, lack of work among painters previously working on general catalogue ranges and limited editions became even more obvious. With heavy use of overtime among tube-liners, the situation eased somewhat. Keith somehow managed to cope with the additional burden of Sian's Tea Rose Collectors' Days vases plus the six designs required for the 2003 Spring Festival Collection. Overtime again helped, but the pile of prestige orders stubbornly refused to shrink.

The trouble was that it was not simply a problem relating to prestige pots, but part of a wider crisis, which came to a head early in 2004. Ted Turner was approaching sixty and advised Hugh that he wished to retire as finance director. David Holland was appointed as his replacement shortly thereafter. While all of this was going on Hugh's health began to deteriorate. Maureen decided something had to be done. Her plan was a June walking holiday on Exmoor, but somewhere in the higher reaches of the Doone Valley, Hugh felt a dull pain near the base of his spine. Shortly afterwards David Holland telephoned the Edwards on holiday with an urgent request to return to the Works.

Just as Hugh had done, David had discovered that the balance between tube-liners and painters at Moorcroft had gone badly awry. Put simply, one tube-liner can 'feed' work forward and keep approximately two painters busy and in work. The problem facing Moorcroft was that each tube-liner was fighting a losing battle trying to keep more than three painters fully occupied, not two as should have been the case. It was an impossible task. Keith had done what he thought was best, but after David Holland's clinical financial analysis, the real reason for idle painters became painfully obvious. Moorcroft had insufficient tube-liners to pass work through to every painter it employed. It was not a question of 'not enough tube-liners to do

FACING: *Garden of Eden (2003). Height 50cm (20")*

Tea Rose (2003). Height 18 cm (7")

prestige work'. It was a question of not enough tube-liners, full stop. For months, if not years, Moorcroft had been paying painters with not enough work to do. By paying redundant painters, Moorcroft was haemorrhaging cash. For this reason the new finance director decided to ask Hugh and Maureen to break their holiday.

On their return the outcome was inevitable. The redundant painters lost their jobs, and almost overnight Maureen Edwards' beloved crèche was closed to save costs. To continue, the crèche would have had to become self-financing. No longer could it be heavily subsidised as had been the case. In a final attempt to preserve the facility, Maureen devised a scheme where at least part of the crèche could be retained if ten qualifying mothers agreed to pay a reasonable charge for their children's places. In the event, only seven mothers were prepared to give the commitment required, and the crèche closed. The Chancellor of the Exchequer, Gordon Brown M.P., had already legislated to provide free nursery places for three and four-year-old children. The pioneering Moorcroft crèche facility had served its purpose.

What came through the 2004 restructuring exercise was a slimmer, fitter and more efficient Moorcroft. All action necessary had been taken, and there was more time now available to think through remaining issues and deal with them wisely. While all this was going on, the pains at the base of Hugh's spine gradually worsened, spreading round to his abdomen as they did so. He felt as if his whole body was on fire.

(Left) Birds of Paradise (2003) Ltd.Edn.200. Height of plaque 40cm (16″)
(right) Juno's Gift (2002) Ltd.Edn.200. Height of plaque 30cm (12″)

TWENTY

Regeneration and Recovery

On the table in front of him lay a Lamia plaque with its swooping dragonfly, bulrushes, water and waterlilies. By the time 2005 arrived Rachel's Lamia design would have graced retailers' shelves for ten years, a fact that only Hugh and a handful of others at the Works had a memory long enough to recall. The plaque epitomised peace. Whichever way you looked at it, Lamia was a gentle, restful design. Hugh made a mental note that when the time came, its tenth birthday would be celebrated in style. But as he stared at it, the plaque also stirred something much deeper. Work on tiles had become a fact of life at Moorcroft. Emma's Birds of Paradise plaque formed part of the Innovation by Design Collection introduced to celebrate the fifth anniversary of the Moorcroft Design Studio. It was a runaway success, just as Rachel's Juno's Gift plaque had been the previous year.

Still smarting from the 'comic strip' criticism, Hugh concluded that tiles really were pictures to hang on walls, and it mattered not whether the images were based on reality or designs. Twelve-by-eight-inch plaques had already been used for some years to create the seasonal images Maureen used as raw material for Christmas cards. A logical step would be to use those same plaques to create greetings cards. The supply chain manager at Moorcroft, David Johnson, had worked at Carlton Cards for nine years before joining Moorcroft. The inevitable happened. In 2005, after an approach by Anne Crowther and Chris Griffiths, long-standing Collectors' Club members, Moorcroft signed an agreement with their company, Little Acorn Designs Limited, which published greetings cards. Among the first to appear was the tranquil image on Rachel's Lamia plaque.

In the complex world of the applied arts one thing often leads to another. The first series of ginger jars made for B & W Thornton in Stratford-upon-Avon had been hugely successful. A second series started in 2001. It had been agreed that ginger jars in the second series would continue to be based on themes taken from Shakespeare's plays. Some of these, such as A Midsummer Night's Dream, had an abundance of design imagery, while others, including King Lear, had very little. In 2003, Rachel was asked by B & W Thornton to consider Romeo and Juliet. To carry out the

work she opted to use rose trees as her central design theme, with belladonna, rosemary and angelica as secondary images. Rachel would say that the Romeo and Juliet imagery fell somewhere between feast and famine, as did her Othello commission destined to appear in November 2005 as the final piece in the second series. Othello was a sombre pot, as befitted the Shakespearean tragedy out of which the senior designer's inspiration came. Rachel chose to use figs and roses to bring Othello to life. The year before, Emma Bossons had designed Twelfth Night, the penultimate piece in the second series. To this day Hugh can remember very little about the arrival of Twelfth Night, a light, airy design of pale pink English roses and small, delicate violets in shades of purple, violet, mauve and burgundy. By November 2004 he had succumbed totally to the illness which almost took his life. Ellenberg's Syndrome, Professor Stephen O'Rahilly at Addenbrook's hospital in Cambridge called it. That month Elise took over Hugh's design responsibilities, allowing her colleague to fight for his life.

Whenever he looked back, 2003 was a year in which loose ends were tied up, a number of successful designs given a new look and designs for lamps re-assessed. Emma's new lamp added cheer to the Queens Choice lighting presentation. At the other end of the scale, Sian introduced a new set of five Hibiscus Moon lamps with its medley of large, almost white hibiscus blooms. It was the same design that Sian had used for her limited edition jug designed for the Low Pay Unit. The original jug was good, traditional Moorcroft. When the five lamps arrived, everyone realised the colours had a warm feeling about them. Their colours would co-ordinate with most home furnishing schemes.

Anji's tour of Australia in September had been preceded by a limited edition designed for Victoria's leading Moorcroft retailer, Dalbry Antiques. The release of Flannel Flower proved to be both popular and timely. It was a curious design using an even more curious combination of colours. Grey, fading to blue and brown was not a mix normally associated with Moorcroft, but for Dalbry and their customers the design worked well. This led to the inevitable request for another exclusive piece the following year. The result was Red Hairy Heath, a vase covered with flowers of the same name which 'had to be as pink as thick lipstick', Dalbry's owners Bill Bryant and Brian Dalglish had chorused together. Emma Bossons obliged, and Red Hairy Heath appeared on two shapes, one a larger version of the other.

Anji closed her Australian tour in style. A competition mounted for the occasion had a handsome Rainbow Bee Eater vase as a prize, one of only two pieces made. One was presented to the Australian Channel 7 show viewer, Mrs Gray, who had

FACING : (top) Romeo and Juliet (2003) Ltd.Edn.250. Height 15cm (6″)
(bottom left) Othello (2005) Ltd. Edn.250. Height 15cm (6″)
(bottom right) Twelfth Night (2004) Lrd.Edn.250. Height 15cm (6″)

suggested a design which used the native Australian bird in the first place. The second was auctioned among Collectors' Club members. The highest bid came from a Tasmanian collector. In keeping with the spirit of the occasion, Moorcroft donated the proceeds to an Australian charity.

Over the water in New Zealand, retailers and collectors had become much more lively. By 2004, the success of Phil's initial New Zealand Collection and its subsequent additions had become part of Moorcroft folklore. Barbara Redmond, owner of The China Shop in Ashburton, had noticed the change and requested an exclusive design of her own. Phil had developed an almost cult status as 'the New Zealand designer'. What he created for The China Shop was Manuka. Barbara was delighted, and so were New Zealand collectors. In terms of world availability, Manuka was a very small edition, and examples are already highly sought after in the secondary market.

Back at home, regeneration of Burslem, the mother town of the Potteries, was forging ahead. The dereliction and decay that had resulted from decades of neglect were being slowly and steadily reversed. The old Town Hall had been given a sensitive 'makeover', its huge interior converted into a visitor attraction with inter-active ceramic activities for children and adults alike. On show, day in and day out, was the work of factories still making china and pottery in Burslem. In the thick of it all were Hugh and Kim. While Kim set about devising ways to keep five million tourists happy each year, Hugh helped guide the process of renovation of the Wedgwood Institute, the Victorian indoor market and the construction of over a thousand new, quality homes around the centre of Burslem itself. As a recognised world name, Moorcroft had taken its rightful place alongside Dudson, Steelite, Wade and others. None of these were small companies like Moorcroft. Hugh liked to remind himself occasionally that if Dudson, Steelite and Wade were pushed together, they would employ more people today than Doulton had done twenty years ago. It is a popular myth that the Potteries are in decline. They are not. For those with the time and the energy to look, the sub-region boasts of more ceramic companies and factory shops than any other part of the world of equivalent size.

In words that were almost visionary, the planners decreed Ceramica would be a 'shrine to the work of the living, and not the high altar of sepia-tinted work of dead men'. In Hugh's vision for the future of Burslem, every one of the thousand new homes would be built: streets closed to traffic, pavement areas taken over by cafés, shops with 'Burslem style' fascias, new schools, medical centres and shops would all follow. This path to the future was set out in the Burslem Master Plan

FACING : (top left) Manuka (2004) Ltd.Edn.150. Height 15cm (6") (top right) Flannel Flower (2003) Ltd.Edn.200 Height 20cm (8") (bottom left) Rainbow Bee Eater (2003). Height 35cm (14") (bottom right) Red Hairy Heath (2004). From Left to Right: Ltd.Edn.75 and Ltd.En.150. Tallest vase 30cm (12")

commissioned by the Burslem Regeneration Company, which Hugh had caused to be formed and which he chaired. Jobs in Burslem would be supported by the five million tourists who visit the Potteries each year. It was now clear that these tourists still come because of the pots made by living ceramic companies, not pots from the past lying in junk shops. It was central to the whole scheme that the ceramic industry remain alive. Hugh had introduced Kim Thompson to the tourism arm of Burslem regeneration, and the Burslem Regeneration Company chairman was happy to watch her create her own waves on the stagnant waters of neglect. Kim asked for an exclusive Moorcroft collection to be sold in Burslem's Ceramica shop, a

(Above) Traveller's Joy (2003). Tallest vase 25cm (10")
FACING: Liberty Collection (2003). Left to right: Rachel (green) Ltd.Edn.50, Rachel (red) Ltd.Edn.50 and Jasmine Ltd.Edn.150. Tallest vase 30cm (12")

modern appendage to the sedate Burslem town hall. The result was Traveller's Joy, a five-piece Sian Leeper range, each carrying images of summer-flowering clematis in shades of pink.

Another significant piece of real estate situated a hundred and fifty miles away in Regent Street, London, was Liberty. Already retail partners with Moorcroft for more than a century, Liberty had been delighted at the financial contribution Emma Bossons had made to their coffers with her Jewel of M'dina, Fruit Thief and The Centenarians. Rachel followed Emma in 2003 with Jasmine on the 138/12, her favourite Moorcroft shape. It was a memorable design showing pink and white jasmine blossom and light green leaves curling around the contours of the vase. To display her jasmine to best effect, Rachel used an oatmeal-coloured panel as a backcloth. Cleverly, the designer had allowed the leaves themselves to flow out of the oatmeal panel and onto a dark blue panel, giving the design a powerful presence.

A second vase with sprays of imaginary flowers reaching up to the rim provided a welcome and dramatic contrast to Jasmine. The only problem was that Rachel had designed the second vase in two alternative colourways. One version carried a rich burgundy ground, the other a dark blue/green ground. The choice Rachel asked Liberty to make was not something they had expected, so Liberty director Barbara King opted to use both colourways. It was a masterstroke, but nobody could think of a suitable name. 'Why not Rachel?' Barbara asked. The thought was considerate. Hugh could think of no more fitting tribute to perhaps the finest Moorcroft designer of all time than to call a classic example of her work by her Christian name.

The success of the slim Jasmine vase and the two Rachel pieces had a dramatic effect on the senior designer the following year. Shortly before the Edwards left for their Exmoor holiday in June, Liberty launched Rachel's Ophir and Solomon designs. Once again the launch coincided with the opening of the Liberty Arts and Crafts festival in mid-May. For the first time since the millennium, a large crowd of excited collectors were all struggling to buy Rachel's work in one of the most famous stores in the world. Rachel herself looked animated and happy, and she had every reason to be. Solomon was a structured design which would have enhanced the reputation of William Moorcroft himself. Stylised tulip flowers with stamens drawn like feathers leapt to the rim of the vase or curved elegantly around the lower body. The colours were also unusual. Greyish green leaves worked in unison with bold orange blooms, subtly fading to maroon. The design was set against a rich, purple ground shading to dark blue at the rim. Solomon's companion, Ophir, used a not dissimilar colour palette with burgundy, orange, oatmeal, a subtle mix of grey and green, and deep

FACING : *Liberty Collection (2004). Left to Right: Ophir Ltd.Edn.100. and Solomon Ltd.Edn.150*
Tallest vase 25cm (10")

blue. The flowers themselves hailed directly from the depths of Rachel's imagination, each framed against a dark blue ground with serrated, greyish green leaves. The feature that marked out Ophir was the introduction of finely tubed chain work as part of the design image. Rachel had successfully used tube-lined chain work on Cymric Dream several years earlier. In production terms, Ophir took the Moorcroft tube-liners an age to produce at a time when tube-lining capacity at the Works was at a premium.

Whatever else, the Moorcroft chairman could claim no credit whatever for the Liberty presentation in 2005. Almost a year later Hugh's health had improved sufficiently for him to travel to Liberty, albeit with the aid of a walking stick. Recovery had been a long, slow process, but drugs now kept the pain at bay. Liberty found a chair for a very thin Moorcroft chairman to sit on, and both Rachel and Kerry Goodwin gave him a big hug. The senior designer was smiling more broadly than she had done for some time. As soon as the Liberty doors opened, crowds of collectors surged in. It was an incredible sight. Rachel's Lazenby and Tudric Dream both sold out quickly, the latter carrying a name bestowed on it by Rachel to mirror her millennium vase, Cymric Dream.

Kerry Goodwin was still a relative newcomer to the Moorcroft Design Studio. At her best, Kerry's work was innovative, even inspired, but at other times Kerry could be too complicated. Elise had worked hard on the innovative side of Kerry Goodwin, coaxing her away from her more intricate design style towards something less challenging to the eye. The result was Dasara, lead piece in the 2005 collection. Close behind Dasara came another

(Above) Tudric Dream Watercolour. (Below) Lasenby Watercolour
FACING: *Liberty Collection (2005). Left to Right: Tudric Dream Ltd.Edn.50, Lasenby Ltd.Edn.50 and Liberty Tribute Ltd.Edn.75 Tallest vase 35cm (14")*

striking example of how effective Moorcroft bonbonnières can be if they carry the right design. Every piece of Kerry's Liberty Tribute disappeared into purple Liberty bags. Kerry must have known things were going well. There was a queue in front of her desk fast approaching Rachel's queue in size. For both designers the Liberty event had been an overwhelming triumph.

On the strength of Rachel and Kerry's performance at Liberty, Iain Renwick, the store's chief executive, invited Hugh out to lunch a few weeks later. It was an almost surreal occasion. Two former lawyers talked in an animated fashion for well over two hours about design and the applied arts without a single designer in sight!

Liberty Tribute Watercolour

FACING : *Dasara (2005) Ltd.Edn.200. Height 35cm (14")*

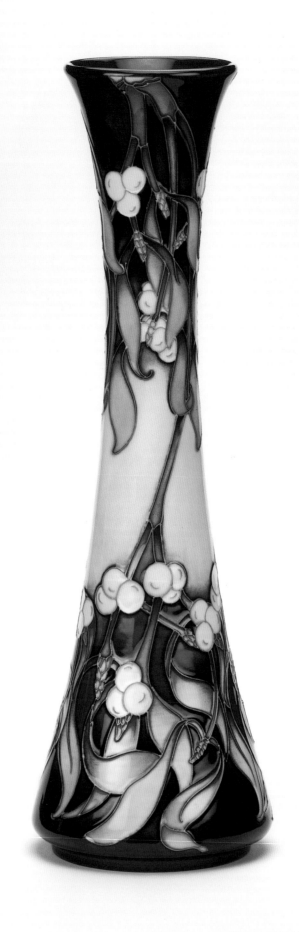

TWENTY-ONE

Thoughts of Connoisseurs

Christmas 2004 was a festive season which passed Hugh by almost unnoticed. Virtually the only contact he had with the art pottery were the almost daily text messages from Rachel on his mobile phone. Sometimes Hugh found himself wondering how the senior designer gathered so much news to pass on, but her messages were strong medicine for a very ill man. He could not sit because of pain, he could not walk because his muscles had wasted away, and he could not stand without support. Occasionally he would pass out altogether. The only real option left open was to lie down, and this he chose to do on a sofa in the room which housed his collection of Moorcroft. All around him were pots that would never even have existed had he not become involved in the art pottery back in 1986. Hugh often felt that the only part of him working properly was his brain, and even that failed from time to time because of the cocktail of drugs entering his system daily. Without the use of his hands he could barely read a book, let alone write one or reply to Rachel's text messages.

With Christmas decorations on the walls and cards placed everywhere to cheer up the room, Maureen had done more than any human being could ever have. She had to help him up when he fainted, feed and cloth him day in and day out, and do what she could to keep him in touch with a world which had suddenly erupted into a storm of get well cards. Not surprisingly, Christmas Weekend 2004 seemed as if it were shrouded in mist. Hugh could not see through that mist. He could only imagine what was going on at the Works. Rachel sent a text message to say that collectors had enjoyed Christmas Weekend. It was a message which made Hugh smile, and when he smiled it seemed as if the pain eased a little. He found himself recalling Christmas Weekend in the millennium year. Everything was less complicated in those days. A set of Anji's Woodside Farm eggcups sat in a neat group on a shelf near to the sofa on which Hugh was lying. For some reason the eggcups mesmerised him, but he had no idea why. Life had become confusing.

Early in 2003 Sian Leeper suggested that retailers at large should become more involved with Moorcroft at Christmas. To show that she meant what she said, Winter Harvest made a sudden appearance. The pieces used were relatively small but each

FACING : *Christmas Kiss from the Christmas Collection (2003) Ltd.Edn. 250*
Designer Rachel Bishop. Height 30cm (12")

Winter Harvest (2003)
Height of ginger jar 10cm (4")

showed Sian's vibrant red and black design off to perfection. Deliveries of Winter Harvest continued right up to the time the Works closed for Christmas, and calls from happy retailers suggesting that Winter Harvest was 'right for us' added to a mood of good humour.

With Hugh away, Elise was finding life increasingly difficult at the Works. Administration of the Collectors' Club took up a great deal of time. Assuming responsibility for design in Hugh's absence took up even more. One problem for Elise was that she had no idea whether her additional responsibilities would be temporary or permanent. A huge amount of work was required to complete the new catalogue collection for 2005, and Elise was already one of the busiest people at Moorcroft. Moorcroft was all about design. It was both the heart and soul of the art pottery's business. Initiative, ideas and understanding were essential parts of the design process. Over the years Elise had watched Hugh and knew how he went about his work.

In June 2004 Hugh had supervised the introduction of the Connoisseur Collection. Ideas were always the precursor of design inspiration. Within Moorcroft were a number of artists of a very high standard. No serious collector of Moorcroft could fail to remember the name of legendary painter Wendy Mason, but there were others, including Sharon Austin, Julie Dolan, Heather Honeyfield, Vicky Lovatt, Hayley Moore, Joanne Mountford, Sue Pointon and Bev Wilkes. Among the tube-liners were Alison Benson, Gill Johnson and Marie Penkethman as everyone would expect, but to their names should be added Sandra Hartshorne, Caroline Hulme, Karen Potts and Clare Sneyd. The concept behind the Connoisseur Collection was that the best artists that Moorcroft had would bring life and substance to an unusual collection; where basic linework enriched with fine tube-lining and a myriad of colours would transform a relatively straightforward design into something magnificent.

For the Connoisseur Collection, colour was provided by the painters themselves. Admittedly Kerry Goodwin designed and coloured Medora. It was her own work, but

FACING : (top) Christmas Collection (2003). Clockwise from Top:
Guiding Light Ltd.Edn.50 (Michelle Martin), Partridge in a Pear Tree. Ltd.Edn.100 (Rachel Bishop),
Holly Ltd.Edn.150 (Sandra Dance) and Festive Fruit. Ltd.Edn.20 (Anji Davenport). Tallest vase 15cm (6")
(bottom left) Medora (2004) Blue and Grey. Tallest vase 23cm (9") (bottom right) Medora (2004)
Orange and Red. Tallest vase 23cm (9")

then Kerry had been schooled in the art of painting Moorcroft before she became a designer. Elise had particularly liked Kerry's grey and blue version of Medora, which introduced a wholly novel colour combination. The other designs - Chrysanthemum, Eustoma and Portelet Bay - all came from Carole Lovett. Hugh's firm favourite had been Jo Mountford's pink and red version of Portelet Bay. The Edwardian vase, as he called it, was rated as one of the finest pieces of Moorcroft to emerge from the Phoenix Years. The natural rarity and colourful fragility of the cymbidium orchid were good reasons to secure examples of the wine and cream, pink and red, and pink and orange versions of Portelet Bay, while the pink and yellow Eustoma pieces told their own story in vibrant colour. Although the blue/grey and red/orange Medora vases

FACING : *Chrysanthemum (2004) (top left) Red and Ivory. Tallest vase 23cm (9")*
(top right) Pink and Green. Tallest vase 23cm (9") (bottom left) Pink and Blue. Tallest vase 23cm (9")
(bottom right) Eustoma (2004) Pink and Cream. Tallest vase 30cm (12")
(Above) Eustoma (2004) Yellow and Green. Tallest vase 30cm (12")

(Above) Orange and Pink. Tallest vase 30cm (12") FACING: Portelet Bay (2004) (above) Wine and
Cream. Tallest vase 30cm (12") (below) Pink and Red Tallest vase 30cm (12")

had both colour and quality, it was the chrysanthemum flowers which seemed to
charm collectors. For everyone involved, the Connoisseur Collection had been an
experiment; but it left in its wake an indelible mark on Moorcroft. In terms of colour
it also acted as a signpost which showed the way to the very heart of the art pottery.

If the Connoisseur Collection was a test of pure artistic skill, the Midsummer
Surprise blue-on-blue collection which arrived for retailers at the same time was
an exercise in unabashed craftsmanship. The designs used in the Midsummer Surprise collection had all been seen before and were known to be successful. Their
proven track record made them attractive to Moorcroft retailers, most of whom

subscribe devoutly to the word 'cautious'. On this occasion Elise had a vested interest in the outcome of the design approval process. One of the pieces up for consideration was her own Muscari, which earlier made a successful debut as an auction piece during the 2004 May Open Weekend. If retailers occasionally made Hugh cross, their reaction to the Midsummer Surprise collection actually made him happy. It surged into the market place both at home and overseas. Moorcroft had demonstrated it could still make pots in the same style, using the same technique and with the same successful outcome as it had done a century earlier.

Ashwood Nurseries have quietly supported Moorcroft over the years with private access to their propagation glasshouses, books, pictures and unlimited advice on horticultural detail. Whenever its designers chose to pay a visit, they were always given a warm welcome. By 2004, Ashwood had the distinction of winning no fewer than 42 consecutive gold medals at the Royal Horticultural Society's annual show. It is a world-class nursery and a jewel in the United Kingdom's horticultural crown. Emma has a profound respect for John Massey, the driving force behind Ashwood, and her Ashwood Gold ginger jar reflected this admiration. Featuring hellebores, hepatica and wild cyclamen in three separate panels, Ashwood Gold was so successful that the Royal Horticultural Society made a friendly approach to Moorcroft to ask for a special vase for themselves. An encore for Ashwood Nurseries was inevitable. The following year Emma's Lenten Rose made its appearance. Around the vase cream and pink hellebores danced happily in a glorious mixture of pink and cream. The cream colour Emma used was flecked with a slight hint of black which

FACING : *Midsummer Surprise Collection (2004):*
Clockwise from Top: Ragged Poppy (Nicola Slaney), Midnight Blue and Peony (Philip Gibson), Muscari (Elise Adams), Coneflower (Anji Davenport), Windrush (Debbie Hancock) and Rachel (Rachel Bishop), Tallest vase 35cm (14")

(Above) *Ashwood Gold (2004)*
Ltd.Edn.200. Height 15cm (6")
(below) *Lenten Rose (2005)*
Ltd.Edn.150. Height 18cm (7")

increased its attraction in the most subtle way possible. 'To make it work you need to love what you are doing', Emma had said. Lenten Rose worked.

The design approval meeting at the end of 2004 seemed almost surreal to Elise. The faces around the table were all familiar, but Hugh and Maureen were missing. In some ways she had not focused her mind on the prolonged illness of 'the Boss' as she affectionately called Hugh. The unexpected imposition of design duties at the peak of the design season had turned out to be a huge challenge. Those sitting in judgment on the Design Studio work for the 2005 catalogue were generally good-natured and sympathetic. Elise handled the meeting as she always had done. She arrived well prepared and fully conscious of the overriding needs of Moorcroft.

Emma's Knypersley was a twenty-first century rendition of the engobe pottery technique, with gentle shades of green added to the blue-on-blue features of an open landscape. Knypersley is an area of open countryside among the hills in which Emma spent her childhood. Once again she had proved herself to be an innovative designer. Her work was not a copy of William Moorcroft's original engobe work. Instead Emma moved on, and with Knypersley her memories of past days proved to be very much a springboard into the future. Collectors loved it.

Also up for approval was a large new shape carrying Rachel's famous Lamia design. The vase was a significant piece of ceramic art and its arrival provoked animated discussion around the table. Lamia was one of the most enduring Moorcroft designs of all time, and it had reached its tenth birthday. To celebrate the anniversary, Rachel decided to bring out a second prestige Lamia vase as a successor to her original one. In 1995, the prestige Lamia vase became the herald of a full Lamia range. At Elise's meeting a smaller piece also made a welcome appearance as an additional treat for Lamia fans. As always, Rachel's presentation was neither too much nor too little.

The senior designer's Florian Dream and Tribute to William Morris were both safe bets. With Florian Dream the senior designer was on home territory, while her Tribute to William Morris followed naturally from a deep-rooted admiration for his work. A large version of the Tribute to William Morris design had been launched at the Burghley House event in mid-October. Built among the Lincolnshire wolds, Burghley House is truly magnificent. It took thirty-two years to complete and has gardens designed by Capability Brown. Hugh had made a surprise appearance at Burghley House. He could hardly walk, and his complexion was the colour of a candle on a church altar. Hugh knew nothing of Sian Leeper's three Burghley House pots, still less of the imminent arrival of Rachel's Tribute to William Morris. Sian had doubts about her Burghley vase while the Lady Victoria and Cecil vases were

FACING: *Lamia (2005). From Left to Right: Ltd.Edn.150 and Ltd.Edn.50. Tallest vase 45cm (18")*

(Top left) Burghley House Collection (2004)
Clockwise from Top: Burghley Ltd.Edn.150,
Cecil Ltd.Edn.100 and Lady Victoria Ltd.Edn.150
Tallest vase 18cm (7")
(top right) Tribute to William Morris (2004)
Tallest vase 18cm (7")
(bottom left) William Morris Collection (2004)
Clockwise from top: Isabella Ltd.Edn.250,
Alpina Ltd.Edn.150 and Serotina Ltd.Edn.50
Tallest vase 25cm (10")

FACING: *Tribute to William Morris (2004)*
Ltd.Edn.50. Height 40cm (16")

(Above) Florian Dream (2005). Tallest vase 23cm (9")
FACING: Tribute to William Morris (2005). Tallest vase 23cm (9")

surrounded by a host of question marks. In the applied arts it is fortunate that everyone sees beauty differently. For Elise, a guaranteed prescription for chaos and hell would be a world where all human beings enjoyed the same images and colours. All three of Sian's designs sold well. Her anxieties proved unfounded.

William Morris proved totally different. The great designer-cum-poet-cum-everything worked his magic through Sian's Isabella, Serotina from Emma and the first pieces to comprise Rachel's own Tribute to William Morris. The latter was made up of two vases, a coaster and a large vase. Burghley House was the first occasion at which the large vase had been displayed. To this day Elise is unsure where Alicia Amison's Alpina came from, but it was accepted as being vaguely 'in the style of William Morris'. More importantly for Moorcroft, Alpina sold out. It was one of those quirks at which the ghost of William Morris would have probably smiled, just as he would had he seen the look of relief on Sian's face when Elise told her the last Isabella vase had been sold to a visiting collector shortly before Christmas. As for

Mayfly (2006). Height 28cm (11")

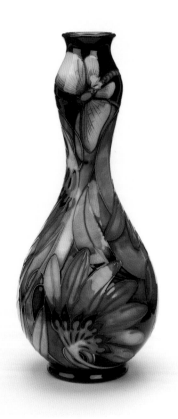

Serotina, all fifty pieces vanished almost overnight. Elise was pleased, doubly so when she learned that an example had found its way into Hugh's personal collection soon after the close of the Burghley House event.

The Collectors' Club secretary had always found it a sobering experience to sit in judgment on another person's work. At the design approval meeting there was no Hugh to catch her eye, just a sea of faces thinking their own thoughts. Florian Dream passed the test much as Elise had anticipated. It was a modern rendering of an early William Moorcroft design technique, in much the same way as Rachel's Tribute to William Morris reflected that other great man's style and imagery. Collectors' initial reaction at Burghley House suggested A Tribute to William Morris was more than acceptable. Mayfly from Emma and Loch Hope from Phil also received the seal of approval, but not before warning shots were fired which suggested that Loch Hope might prove an expensive design to produce. The new finance director David Holland had started to make

FACING : *Mayfly (2005). Tallest vase 28cm (11")*

(Above) Minuet (2005). Tallest vase 30cm (12")
FACING: Loch Hope (2005). Tallest vase 25cm (10")

his presence felt. With ten pieces in the Loch Hope range, the price agreed would make the design vulnerable to poor sales unless it was seen to have the added bonus of high perceived value. Design quality and perceived value won the day, and Loch Hope completed its first year as a bestseller. As if to emphasise the point, it reappeared the following year.

Mayfly also survived, much to Emma's relief. The annual name plaque slipped away, but the range itself moved forward into the new year with the sole addition of an attractive double gourd vase. Elise started to relax, and by the time Nicola Slaney's delicate Minuet joined her nine-piece Duet on the 'approved list', she was happy. At the same time she was desperate to pass on the news to Hugh, but how could she? Elise made up her mind. She would deliver the mountain to Mohammed. The pots would all be packed away in her car and taken to Hugh's home.

Burghley House

FACING: Duet (2005). Tallest vase 30cm (12")

(Left) Kali Zoe (2005) Ltd.Edn.300. Height 35cm (14") (right) Ragged Robin (2005) Ltd.Edn.200. Height 23cm (9")

TWENTY-TWO

Cost of Tears

After a tense design approval meeting, Elise lost little time in packing her car to the roof with every piece of Moorcroft that had been approved or rejected by her colleagues. She would tell Hugh about the meeting, pass on all the news since his last visit to the Works, tell him all about the October lighting promotion on which she had worked so hard with Kim. Elise had been particularly proud of the Silk Flower lamps designed by Anji. There were five in all, and their presence had provided a good boost to the 'lamp show' as Kim had called it. There were so many things she wanted to tell the Boss. When she arrived, Maureen was waiting for her looking tired. Even so, she helped the Club secretary unload her car and lift the carrycare trays through to the lounge where Hugh was lying.

What she saw shocked Elise. The Boss seemed to have wasted away. Clearly in agony, his skin was deathly pale, while Sam, his old black Labrador, lay close to the sofa as she had done week after week. David Holland had told Elise to brace herself, but never in her worst nightmares had she expected anything like it. A week earlier David had managed to show Hugh key financial paperwork by kneeling on the floor and holding each sheet above his head one by one. Elise decided to do the same with the pots. Emma's Kali Zoe raised a smile, while Rachel's Ragged Robin remained suspended for some time. Elise could not have known that Hugh was thinking hard. Suddenly he moved, moaning with pain. A drop of water had fallen on his face. There must have been water in the Ragged Robin vase. Hugh turned to look at Elise. She was crying silently. The drop of water had been a tear.

Silk Flower (2004)
Diameter of Lamp Base 20cm (8")

(Left) Hope (2005) Ltd.Edn.400. Diameter 20cm (8") (right) Harlequinade (2005). Tallest vase 18cm (7")

Ironically, Sian's Hope year plate appeared next, and the name provoked a wistful smile. The design had been rejected. Looking at Hugh, Elise realised this might prove ominous. She made a huge effort and pulled three new Harlequinade pieces from their bubblewrap. Harlequinade had provoked great enthusiasm when Emma's range first arrived for design approval a year earlier. Its colours made it very different from anything Moorcroft had ever produced, apart from a few black and white Florianware pieces designed by William Moorcroft in the early 1900s. By a twist of misfortune, however, Harlequinade made its 2004 catalogue debut next to Sian's sweet pea design, Daydream. Both ranges were unusually dark in appearance, but to place them side by side in a catalogue somehow turned a dark look into a sombre one. Even so, Harlequinade was seen as innovative, while Daydream had emerged as one of Hugh's favourites that year. As with Harlequinade, the arrival of a Daydream jug raised another smile. Things had started to work out better, and Elise pressed on.

FACING: *Harlequinade (2004). Tallest vase 30cm (12")*

Daydream (2005). Height 24cm (9.5")

Queens Choice had been on the receiving end of four new pieces, while Anna Lily actually boasted six! Hugh moved his arm slightly, indicating that there was no need to remove either the Queens Choice pieces or Nicky's Anna Lily additions from their respective carrycare trays. The new Lamia arrivals and a substantial 365/12 Prairie Summer vase were both given careful scrutiny. After a minute or two all were given a firm 'thumbs up'. Rachel's Windflower lamps seemed to have been well liked, particularly the 4/8 version. They were alive with movement and sympathetically dressed with colour. 'She's got it right', Hugh whispered. Elise nodded in agreement. Rachel's Windflower lamps were powerful designs.

Emma's White Rose vase and plaque attracted lingering attention. The style was different from everything else on offer. The design had echoes reaching back to the nine-piece April Tulip range which Emma brought forward in 2003. Elise had not the slightest idea why Sian's Amber Glow had almost been rejected, and she was encouraged to see that the Boss liked it. The 7/10 vase was a substantial pot, but size on its own contributes nothing to the quality of a vase. Hugh had always told Elise that perceived value should be the guiding factor.

Hugh was becoming tired. Ararauna was discussed pleasantly but quickly. With a slight movement of his hand Hugh indicated that he liked it. It was classic Sian Leeper. In the same way Renaissance, Solomon's Seal and Sweet Harmony were classic designs from Rachel Bishop. The old collector's eyes had closed. Elise decided that Kerry's Golden Crown lamps and Phil's Provence lamps should be talked through with Maureen in the kitchen over a cup of tea. As she left the room, Hugh indicated that Phil's Elderberry limited edition vase should stay with him for a while, The more he looked at it, the more he realised that Phil had pulled away from the 'picture' brink. Elderberry was a design of substance on a vase that cried out to be enjoyed. It became the first piece to arrive as an addition to Hugh's personal collection in 2005.

FACING: *Daydream (2004). Tallest vase 30cm (12")*

(Top left) Queens Choice (2005). Tallest vase 25cm (8") (top right) Anna Lily (2005). Tallest vase 25cm (10")
(bottom left) Lamia (2005). Tallest vase 40cm (16") (bottom right) Lamia (2004). Height 30cm (12")
FACING: *April Tulip (2003). Tallest vase 15cm (6")*

White Rose (2005). From Left to Right: Ltd.Edn.300 and Ltd.Edn.250. Height of vase 23cm (9")

FACING: *(top left) Prairie Summer (2005). Height 30cm (12") (top right) Amber Glow (2005) Ltd.Edn.150. Height 25cm (10") (bottom left) Solomon's Seal (2005) Ltd.Edn.200. Height 25cm (10") (bottom right) Sweet Harmony (2005) Ltd.Edn.150. Height 40cm (16")*

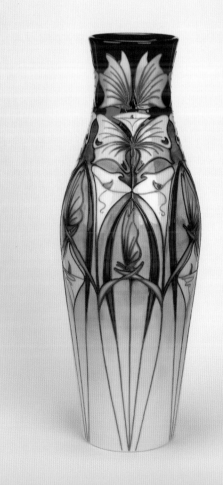

Ararauna (2005) Ltd.Edn.50. Height 50cm (20")
FACING: *(top left) Renaissance (2005) Ltd.Edn.200. Height 28cm (11") (top right) Elderberry (2005) Ltd.Edn.250 Height 20cm (8") (bottom left) Cheetahs (2004) Ltd.Edn.150. Height 20cm (8") (bottom right) Star of Mikan (2004) Ltd.Edn.200. Height 35cm (14")*

The old sofa had been Hugh's resting place for weeks. With his dog at his feet, thoughts about Moorcroft were churning away inside his brain. Elise had done well, and the sight of new work had boosted his morale. Memories of Harlequinade lingered as his thoughts drifted away to Crete and the tiny village of Plevriana. Plevriana had become the name for a new Rachel Bishop range. The village was a favourite holiday destination for the Edwards. Two years earlier Rachel had asked Hugh to come back with photographs of pomegranate trees, a task which turned out to be harder to perform than the initial request was to make. The Edwards' hire car must have travelled well over a hundred miles before Hugh eventually tracked down a pomegranate tree with all the right qualities. Unfortunately he found it back in Plevriana itself, which was mildly irritating. The fact that the tree was in a chicken run full of pecking chickens had made it even more so. While Hugh was being pecked to pieces, a large Cretan lady wearing a black dress had watched the antics of a strange man in shorts dancing in her chicken run from the door of her white house. Hugh had told Emma the story of the black dress, the white house and the chickens. Harlequinade had been the result. Rachel had been the first to learn that Hugh had danced for her pomegranate photographs in front of a large Cretan lady in a black dress. There was still reddish orange blossom on the odd twig or two at the time, and the pomegranates were very under-ripe and green. Even so, the pictures were good enough for Rachel's purpose, and Plevriana made its debut as a range in 2004, with Harlequinade for company. It was a happy thought, and with it Hugh fell asleep.

(Above) Golden Crown (2005)
Height of Lamp Base 18cm (7")
(below) Plevriana (2004)
Tallest vase 18cm (7")

FACING: *Knypersley (2004). Tallest vase 30cm (12")*

(Left) Plevriana (2004). Tallest vase 15cm (6")
(below) Sonoma (2005). Tallest vase 18cm (7")

Back in the Edwards' kitchen, a light lunch followed Elise's cup of tea. The Boss had shown little interest in the three 'freshen-ups' Rachel had designed for her Californian grapes design, Sonoma, but what had really surprised Elise was his apparent indifference to Emma's bonbonnière designed for her Isis range. Maureen came to her rescue and reminded the Club secretary that her husband was already familiar with the Isis bonbonnière, which had been taken out of the Isis range shortly before its release in the 2004 catalogue. Elise was cross with herself. That particular decision had been her own. The Isis bonbonnière had been delayed for a year to give Emma's other bonbonnière, Symphony, a clear run as the 2004 Collectors' Club piece. Looking at the Isis bonbonnière a year later seemed strange. It would have made a perfectly good Collectors' Club piece in its own right. It was not to be. The bonbonnière became the lead Isis piece in 2005 and justice was done.

FACING: *Sonoma (2004). Tallest vase 20cm (8")*

(Below) Isis (2005). Height 20cm (8")
(right) Ragged Poppy (2004) Ltd.Edn.350
Height 25cm (10")

When he first joined Moorcroft early in 2004, David Holland had no concerns about the job he had taken on. Finance director Ted Turner, avuncular and friendly, was still around part-time. Designs released at the International Spring Fair in Birmingham were selling well, and Elise's Collectors' Club was thriving. Financial spreadsheets told him that Nicola Slaney's Ragged Poppy limited edition sold out before the end of March. Anji's Cheetahs and Emma's Allegro Flame and Swan Orchid followed suit in April. Despite the success, some complaints had been made. David's conclusion was that retailers were the same the whole world over. If something sold out, then the edition was too small and bread taken from their mouths. If the edition failed to sell through, it was too big and 'not right for us'.

FACING: *Isis (2004). Tallest vase 30cm (12")*

Allegro Flame (2004) Ltd.Edn.150. Height 38cm (15")
FACING: *(top left) Swan Orchid (2004) Ltd.Edn.400. Diameter 20cm (8") (top right) Jewel (2004)*
Ltd.Edn.200. Height 30cm (12") (bottom left) Siberian Iris (2004) Ltd.Edn.250. Height 23cm (9")
(bottom right) Aphrodite (2004) Ltd.Edn.300. Height 13cm (5")

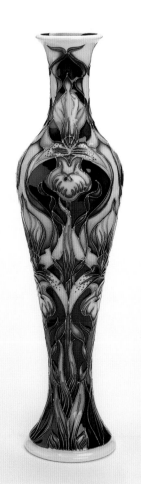

Rachel's Jewel and Sian's Siberian Iris fell into the category of limited editions which retailers told the Moorcroft sales team should have been smaller. Jewel was a sophisticated piece of work and ignored by most of them. Siberian iris also deserved better treatment. For those involved in the design process, it showed the first traces of a new Sian with its dramatic use of trellis-work to portray Siberian Iris in an almost three-dimensional way. For a designer better known for lions, tigers, giraffes and other exotic animals, Sian's siberian iris flowers gave out a clear message that the designer was moving on. Collectors instinctively realised this was so, and their enthusiasm made good reading on the accountant's computer screen.

Although they took almost two years to make, every piece in Rachel's prestige Caravan edition sold through to collectors. Several years earlier, over the inevitable cup of tea, Hugh told Rachel about The Caravan, a hotel in Isfahan, Iran, at one time listed as one of the top ten hotels in the world. Everything in The Caravan had been hand-made: wrought iron staircases, Islamic plasterwork, carpets in best quality silk, cutlery, china and ornaments. Outside in the hotel grounds among almond, lemon and rose trees, caged nightingales sang strongly in the warm, night air. It had been like paradise back in the late 1970s, when Hugh and Maureen had stayed there. Some time later Islamic purists had apparently demolished it all. It was not for Moorcroft to query their decision. It had no right to do so, but Rachel took the story to heart, and used it for inspiration. On a smaller scale, Sian's Star of Mikan also had a distinctly oriental feel about it, while Shirley Hayes' Aphrodite was designed to please romantics the whole world over.

In a brief conversation, David learned of Ted's fondness for Anji's Desert Ivory, a classic Moorcroft design which was a dream for those who enjoyed good, solid traditionalism and pleasing colours. First time round, Phil's Moonlight probably topped David's 'must take home' list, but Hugh had persistently maintained his overt enthusiasm for Jewel and Siberian Iris. The trouble was that every pot David tried to price, his calculations still turned out wide of the mark. This was not a failing he wanted anyone to see. What use was an accountant in charge of an art pottery's finances if he had no idea how to assess the price of the pots it made? His conclusion was that production cost analysis could only constitute one half of the equation. There had to be something else as well. Hugh had urged him to take perceived value into account. The only problem was how to define perceived value. 'Just forget your figures for once', Hugh told him. 'Let yourself go and see what emotions the pot stirs inside you. In Moorcroft emotions have value. If you were a collector, you would understand what I mean. When you follow your emotions, perceived value, or lack

FACING: *The Caravan* (2004) Ltd.Edn.100. Height 40cm (16")

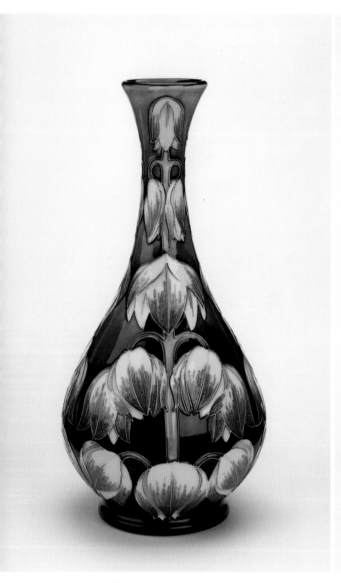

(Left) Desert Ivory (2004) Ltd.Edn.300. Height 30cm (12")
(Right) Moonlight (2004) Ltd.Edn.250. Height 30cm (12")

of it, will make itself known to you. If your emotions fail to add value to the cost of making the pot, it should be abandoned. If you are unable to see any perceived value, as a collector you would decide against buying the pot. It's as simple as that.'

On a number of occasions when nobody was looking, David tried to master the 'perceived value' conundrum; each time he found himself acutely embarrassed. 'Relax', Hugh had said, 'and let your emotions take over. They must override everything.' David finally succeeded in doing so, and no one was more surprised at the out-

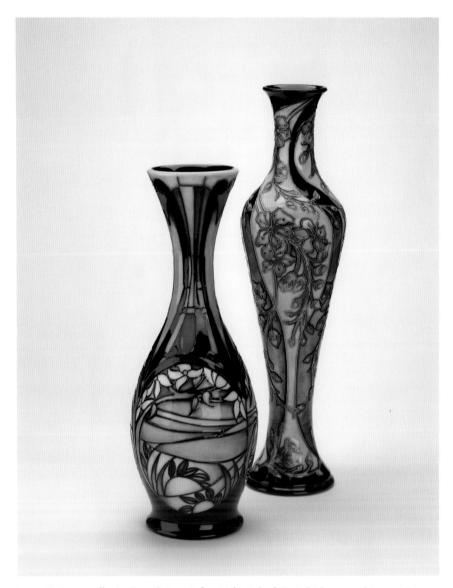

James Macintyre Collection (2004). From Left to Right: Vale of Aire Ltd.Edn.150 and Autumn Sunset Ltd.Edn.100. Tallest vase 30cm (12")

come than he was. Cloths of Heaven designed by Nicky made its appearance at the May Open Weekend that year. 'Perceived value?' David asked himself after a ten-minute reverie, during which he let his emotions race ahead of his brain. 'Fantastic!' Cloths of Heaven became the first piece of Moorcroft the man of figures was to buy for his own home. David Holland had become a Moorcroft collector.

David was a Yorkshireman from Leeds. What surprised him was that although Emma's Vale of Aire had strong nostalgic attractions, he was quick to notice that

Crimson Nectar (2005) Ltd.Edn.50. Height 20cm (8")
FACING: *Mountain Kingdom (2004) Ltd.Edn.100. Height 40cm (16")*

Hugh favoured Rachel's Autumn Sunset, a second limited edition also earmarked for the Leeds retailer, James Macintyre & Co. Both pieces had been launched at the same time. The size of the Autumn Sunset edition must have had something to do with Hugh's choice, David concluded. In point of fact he was wrong. Autumn Sunset had been a very emotional choice for Hugh. Limited edition numbers had nothing whatever to do with it. With Ellenberg's Syndrome taking hold, the Moorcroft chairman had taken into account his own potential Autumn sunset.

While Hugh was away, that all too familiar plague of retailer specials had broken out again. Somehow he managed to take a new year telephone call from Elise, only to learn that American retailer, Ed Pascoe, had secured Crimson Nectar, a Philip Gibson design featuring red hibiscus flowers and humming birds. Admittedly Crimson Nectar was a substantial pot, but the edition size was a mean 50 pieces. Hugh had known Ed Pascoe for over twenty-five years. He was a fine retailer schooled in the art of Doulton, and until Doulton started to fade out of Ed's life the American had shown little interest in Moorcroft. A prerequisite to survival in any walk of life is an ability to change, and above all else Ed Pascoe wanted his business to survive. To do

so he had to change, and part of that process was a willingness to focus his considerable ability on Moorcroft. Although Crimson Nectar had been first in line, more was to follow. In October that same year, Ed indicated that he would like another small limited edition. Hugh was back at work by this time, and he agreed to Ed's request. It was still a very lame Hugh, and a Hugh with spasms of occasional pain, but Professor O'Rahilly had said the illness had gone. Rachel Bishop's Celeste is an unusual combination of line and colour on a slim, attractive shape. Everyone at the Works commented on how lucky Ed Pascoe had been to receive it. That comment turned out to be prophetic. Celeste was to become the last in a long line of retailer commissions. Shortly after its release, a decision was made to refuse all further retailer requests for the time being and to seriously prune the number of special pieces available at Moorcroft events. Even B & W Thornton and James Macintyre & Co. were embraced by the change.

Celeste (2005) Ltd.Edn.50
Height 30cm (12")

TWENTY-THREE

Daffodils

In hindsight, it was ironic that Rachel's new lamp range that year should have been called Sweet Eternity. Rachel's career at Moorcroft continued to break new ground, and Sweet Eternity helped prove her theory that Moorcroft should be timeless. Everybody liked the four Sweet Eternity lamps with their light and dark pink, almost mauve, petals and grey/green leaves with a discreet flush of burgundy. All of them proved popular.

The year 2004 started life in an almost haphazard way, and it was to end on a sombre note. Elise was deep in thought, but she moved away from Rachel's line of

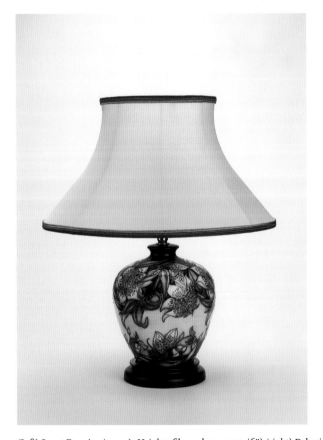

(Left) Sweet Eternity (2004). Height of lamp base 15cm (6") (right) Delonix (2004). Height 20cm (8")

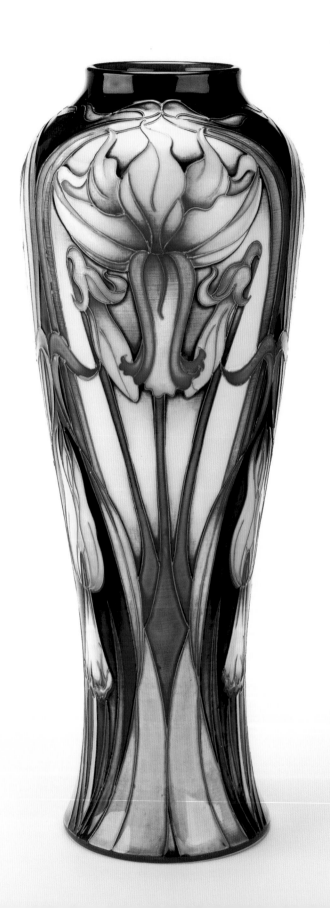

lamps across to her computer. Always a perfectionist, the Club secretary hated mistakes. As a result she would fastidiously check and re-check the decisions of the design approval committee, as well as scrutinise past issues of the newsletter and catalogue to see if anything had been left out. On this occasion she discovered that Shirley Hayes had refreshed her Delonix range with the addition of a modest eight-inch vase. According to her records the piece had never been shown to the design approval committee, but there it was tucked away in the catalogue as large as life. It had been Hugh's fault. He had pressurised her into bringing out her approval list early, and a small mistake had been made. Somehow she would make sure that Hugh received an identical Delonix vase with her special compliments, just to remind him that pressure can be counter-productive.

Almost exactly a year later, the object of her Delonix thoughts was said to have 'stabilised', whatever that meant in medical terms. One bright winter's morning with frost clinging to the trees and a sprinkling of fine snow across the landscape, Hugh saw dark green daffodil shoots at the bottom of his garden. He had known for two or three weeks that things were improving, and a sure sign this was so was a powerful resolve to walk down to the daffodils and pick the first flowers the moment they came into bloom. Maureen encouraged the thought. Although he continued to recite Christina Rossetti's poems one after another, he had turned the corner. His wife always told him to think positively. It was due solely to her unbelievable love and care, that the memory of months lying flat on his back had started to fade. Maureen still had to help him up and down the stairs, lifting his legs one after another, to dress, even to feed him, but with the imminent appearance of the first daffodils of spring, his own strength of purpose started to re-assert itself. The two of them had known each other since they were little more than children, and throughout their life together daffodils had always been at the top of Hugh's list of favourite flowers. There could not have been a more appropriate moment to grasp hold of life and stay alive. Maureen knew that when the daffodils emerged in carpets of yellow and white, the memory of a long, bleak winter and terrible pain would fade.

It had become almost a matter of routine that Rachel should design a daffodil vase for the Spring Festival. Rachel dislikes routine as much as she dislikes being told what to design. Despite this, whenever she feels collectors have expectations, she always does what she can to meet them. For the senior designer there is always a danger that routine may take away the sense of achievement provoked by a successful piece of work. Long before she became involved with the art pottery, Rachel always looked forward to spring with a mixture of pleasure and anticipation. She

FACING: *March Gold (2005) Ltd.Edn.75. Height 35cm (14″)*

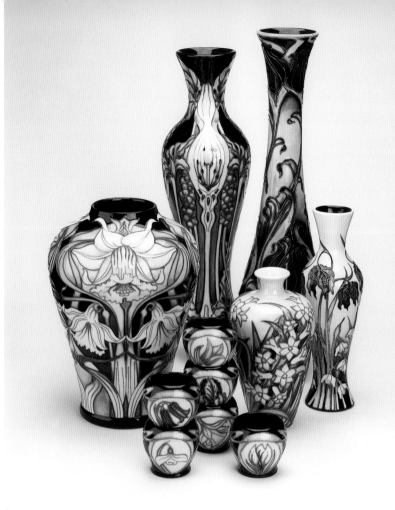

knew that Hugh shared those emotions and that daffodils were his favourite flower.

As early as February, Hugh and Rachel had managed to talk on the telephone for the first time in months. 'Guess what?' she said. 'I've done another daff pot'. 'Guess what?' had been the reply, 'I'm going to pick the first daff that comes out this year'. Their conversation made Hugh laugh. 'My pot's too good for you', Rachel quipped. 'I'll pick my daff before your pot even comes out', Hugh retorted. It was a close call. By the time the Spring Festival arrived, design work on Rachel's March Gold was complete, and every pot made. Hugh had also picked his first daffodil of spring.

The year before Hugh's illness Rachel had introduced Wordsworth for the Spring Festival. Although it might have seemed obvious to call the vase Wordsworth, it was a nice touch. That year Rachel's Wordsworth had Nicky's Alpine Meadow for company, four other pots and yet another set of egg cups, this time designed by Sian Leeper. Elise called the egg cups Parisian Dream. So popular had Moorcroft egg cups become that Emma designed Spring Medley for 2005, which arrived as an unusual limited edition of 50 sets of six.

A text message from Rachel suggested that she had gone into overdrive for the Spring Festival: '4

Rosalinde (2005) Ltd.Edn.100
Height 20cm (8")

designs 4 SF 2005'. In addition to March Gold, Rachel had also designed Elegance, Ostara and Distinction. Phil's Spring Pearl vase and plaque rounded off the Spring Festival presentation at the Works. Thoughtfully, Elise added Carole Lovatt's Rosalinde for Moorcroft retailers. The success of the small limited edition ensured that those bastions of the china and glass trades were all happily chirping that Rosalinde was 'right for us'. The previous year there had been no special limited edition for retailers. For the Spring Festival, Emma delivered La Tulipe Noire, and Sian offered Hyacinth and her Parisian Dream eggcups. When the Spring Festival opened on the 1st April, a central topic of conversation centred around Kerry Goodwin's Cuckoo

FACING: (above) Spring Collection (2004). Clockwise from Top: La Tulipe Noire Ltd.Edn.100, Alpine Meadow Ltd.Edn.150, Hyacinth Ltd.Edn.50, Parisian Dream eggcups, Wordsworth Ltd.Edn.150 and Cuckoo Pint Ltd.Edn.50. Tallest vase 30cm (12") (below) Spring Collection (2005). Clockwise from Top: Spring Pearl plaque Numbered Edn, Ostara Ltd.Edn.100, Spring Medley eggcups Ltd.Edn.50, Elegance Numbered Edn., Distinction Numbered Edn. and Spring Pearl Numbered Edn. Tallest vase 20cm (8")

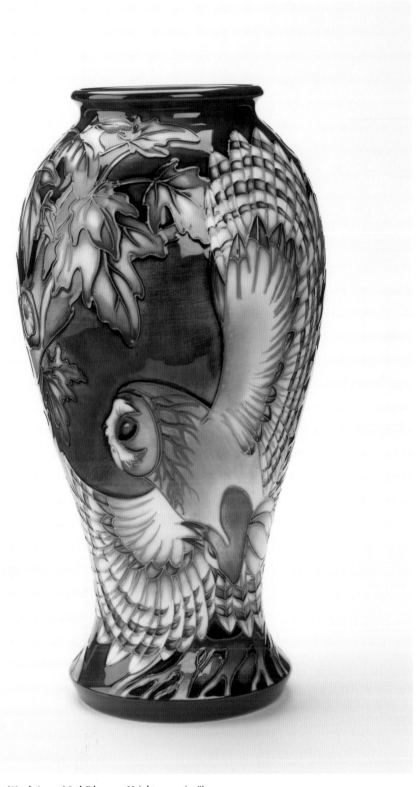

FACING: *Night Watch (2004) Ltd.Edn.100. Height 30cm (12″)*
(above) Reverse Side

Remembrance (2004) Ltd.Edn.250
Diameter of lidded box 10cm (4")

Pint. Certainly the shape of the vase had been used for early William Moorcroft Aurelianware at the end of the nineteenth century. Aurelianware pieces were decorated with transfer prints, a fact which seriously restricts their value in the secondary market today. Even so, the Edwardian shape, as it is known at the Works, had always been seen as attractive, even elegant. The subject matter of the design also had a proven track record. The late Walter Moorcroft had used cuckoo pints as a source of inspiration on at least two occasions. After slight hesitation, these factors caused Kerry's Cuckoo Pint vases to disappear well before summer arrived.

Hugh always enjoyed involvement in special editions for charity. For Moorcroft to design for charity had started partly as a result of the two Low Pay Unit vases and partly as a result of the Thaxted Crocus vase introduced in November 2003. On another occasion Elise had responded positively to a request from the Douglas Macmillan Hospice. The result was Remembrance, a Sian Leeper design featuring forget-me-nots. The use of an attractive box and cover with a sensuous outline was an inspired choice. Tiny blue flowers with golden centres moved around the lid of the box in small waves. The Douglas Macmillan Hospice had every reason to be pleased.

Night Watch from Philip Gibson was on an altogether different scale. The original request had come from Sarah Brown, wife of Gordon Brown, the British Chancellor of the Exchequer. Both had suffered grievously from the premature death of their baby daughter, Jennifer. Instead of wallowing in their grief, however, they turned it into a force for good by forming a new charity. First established in 2002, Piggy Bank Kids set out to build long-term security for the Jennifer Brown Research Laboratory, established to seek solutions to pregnancy difficulties and save new-born lives. Only 100 pieces of Night Watch were made. As a design, it was magnificent. Powerful in its night owl imagery, collectors watched the number of available pieces in the edition melt away before their eyes. Phil and Elise were invited to Downing Street to celebrate the success of a remarkable vase. Because of Hugh's illness, Maureen rep-

(Top) Forget-Me-Not (2004). Numbered Edn. (bottom left) Simeon Blue (2004). Diameter of charger 35cm (14")
(bottom right) Simeon Blue (2004). Height of tallest vase 23cm (9")

(Above) Inset of Dundela Orchard
FACING: *Dundela Orchard (2004). Tallest vase 20cm (8")*

resented her husband and herself. She was among friends. The words which passed between the Chancellor of the Exchequer, Elise and Phil are not for printing. Their conversation centred on Moorcroft, and both affirm that the art pottery was greatly admired by the Chancellor and his wife for its contribution to the applied arts.

While it had been relatively simple for Hugh to suggest to Phil that he bring out a blue version of his Simeon design in March 2004 as a special range of twelve pieces for the factory shop, the arrival of Forget-me-Not from Sandra Dance to celebrate Mother's Day was further proof enough, if any were needed, that special pieces were out of control. Forget-me-Not was a numbered edition, which eventually sold a mod-

*Open Weekend Collection (2004) Clockwise from Top: Athena Ltd.Edn.75, Burslem Twilight
Ltd. Edn.100, Wedding Bells Ltd.Edn.100 and Hera Ltd.Edn.50. Tallest vase 20cm (8")*

est 63 pieces. Keeping up the international momentum for special commissions,
Rob McIntosh in Canada asked for an apple design to be produced as an exclusive
range of five pieces. McIntosh apples had first been cultivated two hundred years
earlier at Dundela Orchard. Emma had always been comfortable designing fruit,
and her Canadian apple design was no exception. The range was called Dundela
Orchard, and it provided evidence of a totally new problem arising from exclusive
designs. Put simply, the more special commissions Moorcroft launched in the marketplace, the harder it became for collectors to track them down.

FACING: *(top left) La Tulipe Noire (2004). Height of lamp base 25cm (10") (top right) Anemone Tribute (2005)
Height of lamp base 25cm (10") (bottom left) Prairie Summer (2004). Diameter of lamp base 20cm (8")
(bottom right) Provence (2005). Height of lamp base 20cm (8")*

(Left) Open Weekend Collection (2004). Left to Right: Giant Pandas Ltd.Edn.150, Meconopsis Ltd.Edn.150 and Cloths of Heaven Ltd.Edn.250. Tallest vase 30cm (12") (right) Open Weekend mugs (2000-2005) Height 8.5cm (3.5")

Perhaps the biggest surprise of all arrived in 2004, and then again in 2005. The John Lewis Partnership asked to be included in the party, but this time for lamps rather than giftware. On the first occasion they commissioned an exclusive Prairie Summer lamp designed by Rachel, and a La Tulipe Noire lamp designed by Emma. Rather like Oliver Twist, JLP asked for more, and the following year the Partnership received an Anemone Tribute lamp from the tireless Emma and from Phil a diminutive Provence lamp.

As the spring of 2004 started to move towards a busy summer, the May Open Weekend arrived as something distinctly stable and familiar. David Holland was still talking happily about the quality of Nicky's Cloths of Heaven. It was an encouraging sign in a finance director, Hugh had observed dryly. Elise was looking forward to a strong turnout from collectors. To give them all a little push, she secured Jacob's Ladder as a free gift for those who booked a place and turned out for the occasion.

FACING: (top left) Jacobs Ladder (2004). Height 8cm (3") (top right) Jacobs Ladder (2004). Height 18cm (7") (bottom) Open Weekend Collection (2005). Clockwise from Top: The Vista Ltd.Edn.30, Pelargonium Ltd.Edn.50, Millie Ltd.Edn.100, Summer Hedgerow Ltd.Edn.75, Fallow Deer Ltd.Edn.150 and Wine Delight Ltd.Edn.50 Tallest vase 25cm (10")

Jacob's Ladder was a small vase designed by Alicia Amison, but even before Open Weekend came to a close, examples were being offered for sale on the Internet by dealers who attended Open Weekend disguised as collectors. To provide the now-familiar treat for collectors who travelled from overseas to attend Open Weekend, Elise asked Alicia to adapt her original Jacobs Ladder design to fit a larger vase. Overseas Club members were delighted. As one so aptly put it, the presentation made a welcome contribution towards the cost of the airfare!

As an experiment, the gift of Jacobs Ladder vases worked, even though some of the pleasure was lost when a group of dealers tried to corner the market by making multiple applications to attend the event. Inevitably there were a few Club members who simply turned up, ate their food, collected their free vase and then disappeared without trace; but that had been anticipated. A club is a club, and members are free to do what they like at Open Weekends. Certainly Club members attending the 2004 May Open Weekend enjoyed themselves. Sian's Athena and Giant Pandas both sold out. Rachel helped the occasion with Meconopsis, while Emma's little Hera vases vanished before collectors' eyes. Andrew Hull is a modeller who would have been instantly recognised by the late Robert Wallace Martin, one of the four famous Martin brothers. Eager to put his own distinctive mark on Moorcroft design in addition to his 'grotesque' bird models, Andrew offered Burslem Twilight. Everything about it was favourable with hints of Florian inspiration. It was a design for traditionalists if there ever was one, and they all loved it.

Phil had not been particularly pleased to see his Wedding Bells used for Open Weekend. He was still less pleased with the name attached to the design made up of fuchsias. Phil likes to keep firm control over names whenever he can. Pelargonium was specifically designed for the 2005 May Open Weekend, and Pelargonium was the name Phil attached to the vase. Every Pelargonium pot sold out. Collectors were equally enthusiastic about Sian's River Otters, every one of which disappeared. A handful were spotted in South Africa several months later – a country with an increasing appetite for Moorcroft. Nobody knows how they got there.

Hugh had known almost nothing about preparations for the River Otters' Open Weekend. Elise had been in charge, and another free vase, Ode to May from Sian Leeper, guaranteed the arrival of well over a thousand collectors during the four-day event. One of these was the Moorcroft chairman himself. Still hobbling along with a walking stick, Hugh was free to enjoy the occasion as a collector. Kerry Goodwin's tiny Fallow Deer bowl caught his eye. It had the word 'promising' written all over it. Hugh had been put under pressure by both Elise and Maureen to pay more attention

FACING: (top left) *Ode to May* (2005). Height 10cm (4") (top right) *River Otters* (2005) Ltd.Edn.150. Height 20cm (8") (bottom left) *Evening Sunset* (2004) Ltd.Edn.50. Height 35cm (14") (bottom right) *Summer Fruits* (2005). Ltd.Edn.25. Diameter of charger 35cm (14")

to Kerry and Sian, and it was Fallow Deer which convinced him that the two of them were right. There were three designs from Sian: her River Otters ginger jars, a limited edition charger called Summer Fruits and The Vista. As far as Hugh could see, Sian was working hard. Somehow he had to try and persuade her to change the way she worked. The amount of effort Sian put in would stay the same, but she would spend much more of her time on those pieces which had the highest perceived value.

Elise had every reason to be pleased with the way things turned out. Both Rachel and Emma had been persuaded to contribute new designs. From the senior designer came Summer Hedgerow, while Emma made an unobtrusive appearance with Wine Delight. Summer Hedgerow was a delicate mix of intricately tube-lined flowers and succulent blackberries, while Wine Delight featured rich, bold flowers with gold stamens. The quality of design that Open Weekend was high, but in future the number of designs on offer at Open Weekends had to fall. That was Hugh's conclusion.

Prestige House events are popular. They provide an impetus to collectors to travel to look at Moorcroft, and at the same time set up an opportunity to enjoy the facilities offered by the finest houses in the country. To mark the early autumn event at Waddesdon Manor, Emma designed three pieces: Waddesdon Waters featuring the famous Waddesdon Manor black swans; Baron Ferdinand with its crocus, dragonfly and ladybird; and Evelina, a floral pattern lifted from a wood panel on an antique piece of furniture in the main house. The manicured gardens at Waddesdon Manor with their hanging grapes, lemon and pear trees are a delight, as is the Rothschild family's wine shop! After wining and dining well on all three days, Hugh felt back in harness, and by the time the event came to a close those unmistakable surges of enthusiasm had returned. As Hugh and Maureen said goodbye, both had a strong feeling that something was missing. The truth was that a fox had been busy among the famous black swans. All of them vanished before the Moorcroft collectors arrived, but not a single person commented on the fact.

By midsummer, it was proving difficult for the Design Studio to cope. Nicky was away on her third maternity leave, and how it was that Elise managed to secure the attractive Millie vase from her for May Open Weekend was a genuine puzzle. The first real crunch came in March when a leading Moorcroft retailer, C.J. Beavis, asked for an exclusive design for a 'larger than normal' vase with a 'smaller than normal' edition number. Moorcroft delivered what was required of them in the form of Evening Sunset from Andrew Hull. By July, The Posthorn, a leading Moorcroft retailer based in Castle Douglas, Scotland, commissioned The Wild Brae with images inspired by the poet Robert Burns. Sian's slender jug had been a sensible shape to use, but once

FACING: *Waddesdon Manor Collection (2005). Left to Right: Evelina Ltd.Edn.50, Waddesdon Waters Ltd. Edn.100 and Baron Ferdinand Ltd.Edn.150. Tallest vase 23cm (9")*

again the retailer had prescribed the subject matter for the design. There was nothing wrong with that, but research and the quest for historical and reasonable botanical accuracy all took time. Sian found the commission difficult to refuse, as had Rachel when she accepted a request from Treeby and Bolton for an exclusive vase for their shop in the Lake District. Daffodils, water and mountains were a pleasing mix for the senior designer. With Rachel's signature on the base, Aira Force proved popular with casual visitors to the Lake District as well as regular Moorcroft collectors. Although it had always been an inescapable fact that special commissions from retailers compensated for autumnal falls in general trade orders, the price now paid by Moorcroft was too high. There were two solutions to the problem that Hugh could see. The first was to encourage overseas markets to grow. The second was to design something new, something which would involve those retailers worldwide who had shown enough courage to take on exclusive pieces. In this way the idea of a Shadow Collection was conceived. Moorcroft would change its approach fundamentally. It would grow its markets on a global basis, without increasing in size.

(Left) Aira Force (2005) Ltd.Edn.250. Height 20cm (8")
(right) The Wild Brae (2005) Ltd.Edn.200. Height 24cm (9.5")

TWENTY-FOUR

Going for Gold

Although production issues were still giving rise to enormous frustration among designers, in March 2004 Elise found time to orchestrate the arrival of four large pots. Dolphins leaping and gliding over the sea in joyous harmony saw Sian on familiar territory. Sea was also the central theme with Rachel and The Wave. The senior designer had used the movement of the ocean to conjure up sensations of powerful passion. The two pieces could not have been more different. It was the same with Emma's Evening Sky and Shirley Hayes' Delonix. Emma was still in the throes of preparing for her own special contribution to the new dawn. Evening Sky, taken straight from the catalogue, provided a temporary respite. Shirley decided to use a large plump vase much loved by collectors. The design itself was a rework of her successful Delonix range. This meant both Evening Sky and Delonix had an air of welcome familiarity about them, while Sian and Rachel's work on Dolphins and The Wave derived their strength from totally new inspiration. Dolphins heralded a new approach from Sian, although another prestige vase represented the old order. 'Pretty flowers round pots again', Hugh had muttered to Elise. The black backcloth against which the designer had set her pale pink and cream roses for Secret Garden was sufficiently dramatic to encourage a number of retailers to take the piece into stock. Nothing more was heard of Secret Garden, but one leading retailer pronounced that it was 'right for us'.

The new prestige pieces caused total mayhem in production. Hugh was not impressed, and made it clear that a further five new designs would soon make their appearance. It was at this point however, that his illness had taken hold, and it was not until May 2005 that Elise made a further push introducing two new prestige limited editions. Emma's White Rose was an awesome sight, but Rachel's Windflower vase was even more so in terms of pure drama. Both had been inspired by existing designs – Emma's from her own limited edition of the same name, and Rachel's

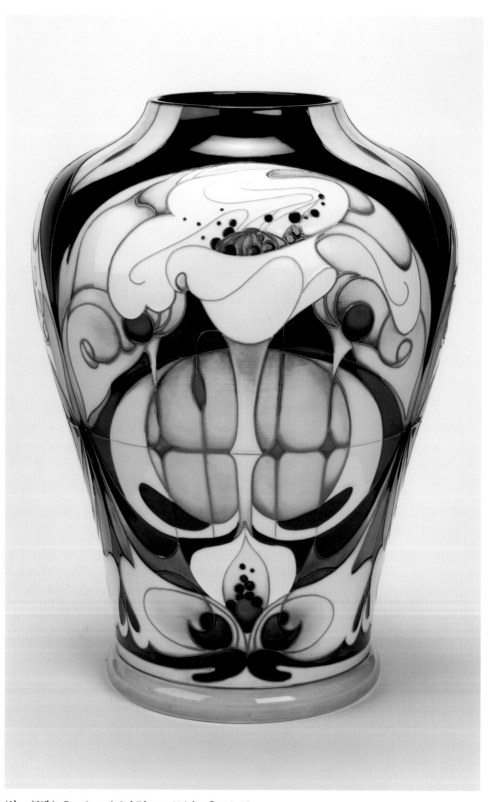

(Above) White Rose (2005). Ltd.Edn.25. Height 38cm (15")
FACING: (top left) Dolphins (2004) Ltd.Edn.10. Height 38cm (15") (top right) The Wave (2004) Ltd.Edn.15
Height 50cm (20") (bottom left) Evening Sky (2004) Ltd.Edn.10. Height 40cm (16")
(bottom right) Delonix (2004) Ltd.Edn.10. Height 38cm (15")

(Above) Secret Garden (2004) Ltd.Edn.15. Height 45cm (18")
FACING: Windflower (2005) Ltd.Edn.25. Height 40cm (16")

(Above) Caledonia (2004). Tallest vase 23cm (9") and inset

from her Windflower lamp range. Success was immediate, with a waiting list for
Windflower hopefuls arriving within three weeks.

A number of Scottish retailers made it clear to Donald Reid, Moorcroft's representative north of the border, that a 'wee range' exclusive to Scotland would be 'right
for us'. The message was passed on to the Design Studio. The simple truth was that
every designer was already busy on a multitude of projects. To deal with the request,
Hugh decided to speak with freelance designer Carole Lovatt. The result was Caledonia, a small range of five pieces. Inevitably thistles took centre stage in a design
coloured up with great finesse by that queen of colour, Wendy Mason herself. What
happened next was sad. After securing a design with a Scottish theme, most Scottish
retailers put their hands in their pockets and kept them there. As a result, Caledonia
still falls within the rare to very rare category of Moorcroft designs, with more pieces

(Left) Snowdon Lily (2004) Ltd.Edn.200. Height 15cm (6") (right) James Macintyre Collection (2005)
Clockwise from Top: Tribute to Trees Ltd.Edn.100, Floating Feathers Ltd.Edn.75, Florian Spirit Ltd.Edn.50 and
Hesperian Waters. Ltd.Edn.50. Tallest vase 23cm (9")

sold in the United States than in Scotland itself. It had all been one enormous waste
of time.

When Hugh returned to work, he found the whole design process in danger
of meltdown. Just Right of Denbigh, favoured retailers of distinction, asked for a
'Welsh something or other'. For Rachel, that turned out to be Snowdon Lily, which
sold very well indeed. On the day of its launch Rachel charmed every collector who
decided to pay a visit to Ceri and Terry Wild's famous shop. If either husband or
wife had said Snowdon Lily was 'Just Right for us', Hugh would almost certainly
have screamed. What Rachel actually received was a very genuine 'thank you' from
a grateful retailer for a design which had sold out. For Hugh it was even better. His
own letter from Just Right was the first letter of thanks he had ever received from a
retailer!

Crimson Cornflower (2005). Tallest vase 20cm (8")

If exclusive designs for retailers and the plethora of Moorcroft event pieces were to come gently to an end, one or two important customers had to be appraised of the fact. Robert Townsend, the new Head of Sales at Moorcroft, was given the unenviable task of travelling to Stratford-upon-Avon with Alan Wright to tell Barry Thornton the news, while Hugh himself set out to speak with his daughter Debbie, owner of James Macintyre & Co in Leeds. Hugh's task turned out to be the easier of the two. Debbie reacted positively and looked forward to the new Moorcroft approach planned to emerge during 2006. Macintyre's tenth birthday collection had gone down particularly well with collectors, with their tiny Crimson Cornflower range

FACING: *Marinka (2003) Ltd.Edn.300. Height 35cm (14")*

of just four pieces still a strong favourite. The whole collection had a distinctively 'Macintyre' feel about it, with shadowy images from early years of the last century well represented.

It had been Elise's idea, conceived and implemented before Hugh returned to work in June. Sian's Tribute to Trees sold out quickly, as did her Hesperian Waters. The former showed trees in the old Moorcroft style, while Hesperian Waters in shades of blue and purple picked up an old Moorcroft fish theme, with a style closer to the mid-1930s. That apart, the colours used in Hesperian Waters would have been familiar to Ostler & Co, retailers who originally commissioned early Macintyre Hes-

Trinity (2003) Numbered Edn.
Height 30cm (12")

perian design themes, including fish. For the same occasion Rachel offered Florian Spirit on the new 5/7 shape. It was vintage Rachel in Florian mode, with stylised poppies and tulips. Every Macintyre customer who walked through the door enthused about Florian Spirit. In the ordinary course of things, it should have been Rachel who introduced peacock feathers, but not this time. Emma's two-handled loving cup, Floating Feathers, provoked expressions of mild surprise, but the edition was purchased with enthusiasm.

The late summer release of the Design Studio's Innovation by Design Collection started well. It included Destiny, a design Rachel still considers her best work. Under any other circumstances, Rachel's Marinka would have fully justified lead piece status, but in 2003 Destiny reigned supreme. Phil also surpassed himself with one of his finest designs. Trinity had first appeared with a vibrant blue ground, but in its wisdom the design approval committee opted for a burgundy version instead. It was probably the correct choice, but the unique blue trial was snapped up at the December trial exhibition for a hefty sum. Sian was still in the process of cultivating a design style of her own, and her two-piece open edition Mountain Gold was a significant advance. Sales of Innovation by Design were strong

FACING: (top left) Moonlit Glade (2004) Ltd.Edn.30 (Sian Leeper)
Diameter of lidded box 15cm (6") (top right) Mountain Gold (2003). Tallest vase 20cm (8")
(bottom left) Meadow Charm (2003). Tallest vase 15cm (6")
(bottom right) Paradise Flower (2003). Numbered Edn. Height 13cm (5")

right up to the time the collection closed on the 31st July 2004, helped in no small way by Nicky's dainty Meadow Charm. All three pieces had the humble clover flower as their central design theme. The simplicity of Meadow Charm and its mouth-watering price levels showed just how popular small pieces could be.

Emma had been quiet for some time. She was feeling her way slowly towards her own great solo collection, learning as she did so. Her Birds of Paradise plaque actually offered some clues of what was to follow. Two pure white birds make up the central image, both framed by exotic fruit, leaves and delicate white and pink blossom. By 2005, this 'framing' technique had been honed to perfection. Emma's Para-

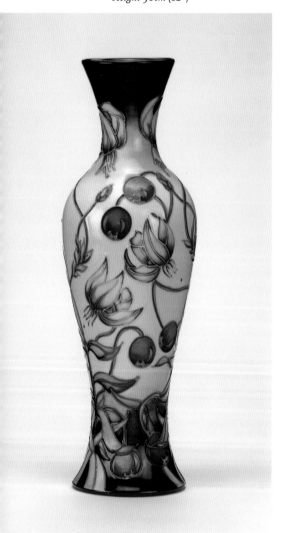

Party Piece (2003) Ltd.Edn.200
Height 30cm (12")

dise Flower was another powerful contribution to Innovation by Design. It was as if the designer were preparing to jump forward onto a much more dramatic platform of design achievement. The modest six-inch jar and cover startled Hugh with its bold white and cream magnolia flowers. To the trained eye, it might as well have been five metres high, so strong were the signals it gave out.

Against such quality it would be wrong to dismiss as lacking substance Sandra Dance's Party Piece, with its pale pink and white cranberry flowers and delicious fruit. Hugh says that those who have an example of Party Piece in their collection have understood the merit of simplicity in design. Over the past century, simplicity and not complexity has given Moorcroft its reputation. Anji Davenport's Nostalgia was complex, and the only piece in the entire Innovation by Design collection which was retrospective. All three images on the vase featured past work, and calling the vase 'Nostalgia' was Hugh's way of drawing attention to the fact.

Sian Leeper and Shirley Hayes rounded off the Innovation by Design collection, Shirley with her flamboyant and fiercely red Fleur Rouge and Sian, momentarily in monkey mode, with Cotton Top. Sian's design featured two cotton top tamarin monkeys peering curiously through lush jungle ferns, trees and flowers, with the prominent image of a rare white orchid and a brilliantly coloured lindley orchid with speckled, wine-coloured markings on the central petal. Despite mild retailer criticism about the size of the limited editions, the design approval committee seemed to have got its numbers right.

During a time of change, nothing can be more sacrosanct than the word 'Moorcroft' itself. Design had become the matrix, the essential ingredient of what is known in the business world as brand image. Hugh hated the word 'brand', but he was now almost twenty years into the Moorcroft phoenix years. The new Moorcroft imagery, as well as its hundred-year-old design style, were both here to stay. The

Peruvian Lily (2004). Length of name plaque 18cm (7")

Moorcroft name had to be protected. What had started to emerge from the design explosion of the phoenix years had been an acceptance that pretty patterns on their own were not enough. In a strange way, they were no longer seen as Moorcroft. Collectors' aspirations had grown beyond childish simplicity, or wallpaper work as Hugh once rather cruelly called complex flower designs in a fit of temper. After a number of conversations with her good friend Elise, Sian's Peruvian Lily appeared as an eight-piece range. As a follow-up, Sian drew Peruvian Lily on the triangular name plaque. The design survived the 2004 discontinuation exercise, and into 2005. 'More pretty flowers round pots', Hugh said the moment he saw Peruvian Lily. It was old-style Moorcroft. Sian had to change before the new dawn arrived. Tradition in design style was not sacrosanct. Design had to change like everything else.

In Hugh's new dawn there was colour and movement, designs with primary and secondary themes, a further extension of the Moorcroft colour palette, and design and colour inspiration lifted from mythology as well as distant parts of the world. Design would pay homage to a glorious living world slowly being desecrated in the name of 'progress'. Elise and Maureen had talked together about ways of bringing Hugh's design instincts to bear on Kerry Goodwin and Sian Leeper, just as he had done in the past with Rachel, who would probably deny it, and Emma, who would accept the statement. Once he had made up his mind on the pressures being brought to bear on him, Hugh acted. The moment he returned to work, he took Sian and Kerry under his wing. Between them they would work day in, day out at the Works, and define and then achieve a sizeable part of Hugh's new dawn. As in many other things, he had Maureen and Elise to thank.

Cotton Top (2003). Ltd.Edn.150. Height 23cm (9")

For Hugh, ceramic art had always been a visual expression of emotion. Good art will always challenge the emotions. Whenever something was felt to be good, it had to be encouraged to grow in stature and mature. This simple truth turned into the driving force behind prestige work at Moorcroft. It also served to explain Hugh's intolerance of one of the so-called 'Stoke diseases'. 'If it's difficult, you ignore it' was how the saying went, but not for Hugh. If it was difficult, he would pile on the pressure until everyone realised he would never give up.

Out there in the real world, Hugh once told Elise, there are collectors who think about Moorcroft morning, noon and night - and he was one of them. For those collectors, their hobby was a way of life, a means by which they all hoped to be judged by generations still to come. Elise was quick to reply. Out there in the big wide world, Boss, is a thing called the Internet with its electronic retailing and banking, and a capacity for passing around information like nothing else on earth. A computer illiterate himself, Hugh nodded. Elise was right. For those special Moorcroft collectors, a knight in shining armour arrived in the unlikely form of finance director, David Holland. 'They all need to be made to feel special', he suggested. 'How about Gold

FACING: *(above) Nostalgia (2003). Ltd.Edn.100. Height 23cm (9") (below) Fleur Rouge (2003) Ltd.Edn.50. Height 33cm (13")*

(Above) Golden Dream (2005). Height 24cm (9.5")
FACING: *Peruvian Lily (2004). Tallest vase 20cm (8")*

Christmas Collection (2004). Clockwise from Top: Christmas Tulip Ltd.Edn.100 (Sam Johnson), Gloriosa Lily Ltd.Edn.50 (Sian Leeper), Mulberry Wine Ltd.Edn.75 (Kerry Goodwin), Jack Frost Ltd.Edn.50 (Andrew Hull) and Festive Flame Ltd.Edn.100 (Kerry Goodwin). Tallest vase 30cm (12")

Membership within the Collectors' Club?' Elise thought about it. People who looked at balance sheets, banking, and profit and loss accounts were not supposed to be interested in customer care. At that moment the concept of Gold Membership within the Collectors' Club came into existence. The first vase to pass to those rare but special Moorcroft enthusiasts was Golden Dream designed by Nicola Slaney on a slender jug. In the new dawn, additional pieces of Moorcroft for Gold Members would follow. At a later date, other new Gold Members would be invited to join the select few who enhanced their Club membership status at the initial opportunity.

There were times when Hugh wondered how Elise had been able to cope with the design process during his absence, as well as continue to administer the Collectors' Club. Philip Gibson's complimentary 7/3 Holly vase had attracted a large number of club members to the 2004 Christmas Weekend. Only a few days later, Internet sales of Holly vases had already topped seventy pounds. Some collectors and a hardcore group of dealers had been selling their Christmas presents. Even so, the arrival of a free Holly vase ensured strong activity among the Christmas pieces on offer. As a direct result of the incessant pressure piling on Moorcroft designers, contributions from the Design Studio that year were thin on the ground. Support from freelance designers and staff helped Kerry and Sian. At the close of the event, both Kim and Elise concluded the mood had been one of light-hearted pleasure. A free pot made it feel even better, but not in 2005. Hugh was back in action and Moorcroft changed the rules. Chilean Crocus required a certain 'spend', as the sales team delicately put it, before a vase could be given away as a gift. The numbers attending the

(Above) Holly (2004). Height 8cm (3")
(below) Chilean Crocus (2005). Height 8cm (3")

Christmas Weekend remained as high as before, but the free pots had gone. Robert Townsend went further and asked for a significant number of Chilean Crocus vases for overseas retailers, with Moorcroft's compliments of the season. Things were really changing.

For Hugh and Elise, one design available that Christmas stood out all on its own. It was a favourite of both. Nicky Slaney's Candlelight appeared on nothing more than a small vase and a coaster. As the name Candlelight suggests, rays of golden light flow upwards from splashes of green, red and purple. Both pieces were released to retailers at large and sold merrily right through to Christmas. The following year, Candlelight became one of the first Moorcroft Christmas cards from Little Acorn Designs to be produced and sold on the open market.

Christmas Collection (2005): Clockwise from Top: Christmas Eve Ltd.Edn.50 (Kerry Goodwin),
Robin plaque Ltd.Edn.50 (Philip Gibson), Snowdrift Ltd.Edn.50 (Paul Hilditch), Robin Ltd.Edn.75 (Philip Gibson)
and Candlelight vase and coaster (Nicola Slaney). Tallest vase 35 cm (14")

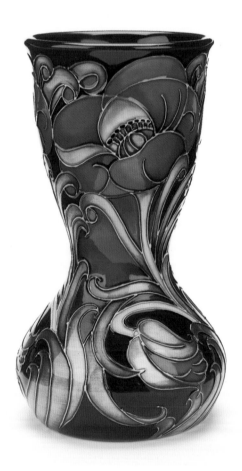

(Left) Fallowfield (2005). Height 20cm (8″) (right) Helen (2006). Height 18cm (7″)

TWENTY-FIVE

Bossons Blossoms

Back at work, Hugh reached a number of conclusions. No lingering doubts remained concerning Elise's ability to ensure that Moorcroft collectors enjoyed themselves pursuing their hobby or David Holland's skill at keeping tight financial controls. Head of Sales, Robert Townsend, was forging new relationships with retailers at home and overseas. Kim had adopted enterprising strategies to entice new visitors to the world of Moorcroft. Few are aware that The Potteries plays host to a significantly greater number of tourists than visit Stratford-upon-Avon, birthplace of William Shakespeare. These tourists come to explore the ceramic trail, the seventy-seven factory shops and three hundred and twelve companies in Stoke-on-Trent making pots of one kind or another. Now the jewel in the Potteries' crown, Moorcroft sits in the middle of it all, playing host and entertaining, as well as pleasing the eye with fine ceramic art.

By the end of 2003, the second series of Collectors' Days had come to an end, and for the Club secretary, 2005 looked as if it would be the right year to start a third. The theme for the next three years would be Moorcroft poppies, and who better to design poppy pots than the senior designer. Rachel was pleased to be asked. She saw it as a move back towards the old days when she designed vases for John Moorcroft to carry around from store to store throughout the United Kingdom. Hugh had called a halt to the John Moorcroft tours, because they gave rise to an erroneous public assumption that he was linked to the design process.

Rachel fell quickly into the scheme of things for the third series with Fallowfield, its vibrant red poppies dancing around a new vase in a style that would have been acceptable to old Florianware enthusiasts a century earlier. The following year Fallowfield disappeared, and Helen took its place. For Helen, Rachel decided on a mischievous choice of shape. Retailers almost invariably describe the 304 shape as being 'not for us' whenever it is used. Suddenly that same shape was held out as a magnet to attract collectors into their stores. The 304 is very much a collector's shape. The less in tune with collectors a retailer was, the less inclined that retailer would be to take it into stock. Rachel provided a one-off opportunity for this to change. Once again her poppies were a strong shade of red, but Helen had an unusual, albeit imaginary, flash of bright blue. In many ways the vase was even more striking than Fallowfield. It sold strongly and fulfilled its purpose, but so far Rachel maintains a discreet silence on the identity of the third and final poppy vase in the series scheduled to appear in 2007.

The simplicity of the concept of Collectors' Days makes them a feature of the new dawn, an era heralding not only a gentle return to some of the better ideas from the past, but also a time to provide clear pointers to the future. Electronic sales were part of that future. In some way Moorcroft had to reach out and embrace the Internet with more enthusiasm than it had done. For computer literate Elise, there were two major obstacles to this vision. The first arose from some of the more Internet-driven retailers who would howl with rage if the art pottery used the Internet to enhance its own retail sales. Moorcroft had given every retailer unrestricted access to its new website on www.moorcroft.com, with its auction facility, retailer web pages and hyperlink; plus, of course, the collectors' 'I Want' page. From the date the Moorcroft website first went 'live' in June 2002, there has been a Moorcroft Collectors' Locked Room, an on-line purchase facility for Club members only. The pots offered for sale in the Locked Room are not catalogue pieces, and while quality retailers had little to say about the limited, albeit exclusive, facilities of the Locked Room, rumbles of discontent surface from time to time.

There is a second and much more fundamental problem with electronic Internet sales. Moorcroft is very tactile. Some collectors say that when you hold a piece in your hand it is almost as if the pot is talking. To buy on-line is to deny the existence of that crucial tactility. As a result, fakes, forgeries and damaged pieces often slip into the hands of innocent and unsuspecting purchasers. For some years 'less than perfect' pieces produced at Moorcroft were marked with an incised silver sliver scored through either the designer's monogram or the Moorcroft mark on the base of each piece. Unfortunately, many less-than-honest people learned how to obliterate the metallic silver sliver, as a number of successful criminal prosecutions bear solemn witness. Those who still insist on buying at antique fairs or on the Internet do so at their own risk. To help bona fide retailers and collectors alike, the Moorcroft 'seconds' mark was changed in late January 2005, much to the chagrin of Internet pot peddlers. In place of the silver sliver, the red dot arrived. To mark pieces with a red dot, a small hole is drilled through the designer's monogram, filled with red paint and re-glazed before a light re-firing. Red dots are permanent and generally

FACING: *Website Locked Room Collection (2002-2005). Clockwise from Top: Cascade, Queen Nefertiti Ltd.Edn.50, Dawn Mist, Dream of a Dove, Cannonball Tree, Midnight Blue, Daisy Chain, Nigra, Moonlit Tulip coaster, Euphorbia Ltd.Edn.50, Rose of the Forest Ltd.Edn.50, Midnight Moonflower Ltd.Edn.50 and Moonlit Tulip jug. Tallest vase 30cm (12")*

disliked by 'the trade' as a result. Dealers seldom tell a potential customer that a red dot signals a blemish. Indeed, one regular dealer on the Internet recently described a piece put up for sale as 'having full Moorcroft marks including the red dot'!

During 2004 a number of criminal dealers were caught by Trading Standards Officers after rubbing out the silver sliver on some 'less that perfect' pieces before selling them on the Internet as perfect. The law in this area is tough, and a number were sentenced to several months in jail. At the end of the legal proceedings, the pots were confiscated by the Court and sent back to Moorcroft. With the approval of the Court, these pieces were handed over to the Douglas Macmillan Hospice and auctioned at a public event. The substantial proceeds of the sale all passed to the charity. For everyone at Moorcroft, the good news was made even better because each piece auctioned was sold with a brand new red dot!

There is less opportunity to redress wrongs perpetrated on the Internet than there should be, but if you are a Moorcroft collector living in Paraguay, the risk of slightly imperfect pots might still have attractions given the distance and the obvious cost advantages. Some form of compromise was essential. For Moorcroft retailers, it was the on-line catalogue, their auction page and an individual, personalised retailer page, plus the 'I want' facility. For Moorcroft it was the Locked Room. With these features in place, the Moorcroft website was launched into cyberspace by Webmaster Kardy. The following year Kerry Goodwin's Cannonball Tree and Phil's Dawn Mist made their debut. For Moorcroft designers the Locked Room was novel, and all of them were eager to bring forward Internet designs. Emma's futuristic Moonlit Tulip jug was followed by three September releases: Cascade from Sian Leeper, Daisy Chain, a Michelle Martin creation, and a small Moonlit Tulip coaster, also from Emma.

It was not until 2005 that four limited editions all appeared in the Locked Room at the same time. Queen Nefertiti found Sian in ancient Egyptian mode, while Kerry's Euphorbia was dramatic in the way colours had been applied. Indeed, both Queen Nefertiti and Euphorbia highlighted a novel problem arising from Internet sales. At best, Internet images tend to be less sharp than a photograph and at worst can appear shrouded in cyber fog. Moorcroft concluded that Internet pots had to be sharp and clear. Queen Nefertiti and Euphorbia both passed that test, as did Andrew Hull's Midnight Moonflower. A handful of purists asserted that Phil's Rose of the Forest with its rich red petals surrounded by a very subtle, pale pink edge was not sharp enough in its linework and colour for an Internet pot. Whatever the merits of that argument, Rose of the Forest sold out of the Locked Room, just as the other three

(Above) Left to Right: Royal Hakea and Kookaburra (2005) both Ltd.Edn.200. Tallest vase 25m (10")
(right) Sinensis (2005) Ltd.Edn.150. Height 30cm (12")

had done. Issues of Internet clarity continued to perplex Elise for well over a year, but on balance she veered towards the 'it must be clear cut' school of thought, rather than the 'anything goes' lobby. In saying this she had in mind the February release of Kerry Goodwin's Nigra which had added credibility to her 'clear cut' theory. Sales were vigorous from the outset – but then the design had a clean edge to it!

While Internet obligations neither helped nor hindered the design process at Moorcroft, their presence in the Locked Room provoked a fresh flurry of requests for exclusive retailer designs. Elise supervised the arrival of Phil's Sinensis with its pure white petals cascading down the sides of the classical Moorcroft ewer. Sinclairs snapped up the edition with alacrity, but some time later the delicious cream colour used by Phil for his free-falling flowers had its basic metallic oxide structure modified by the supplier. The Sinensis limited edition was never fully made and falls into the 'rare' category of Moorcroft designs as a result.

Quite independently, Goviers of Sidmouth's owner Alan Morganroth found himself drinking tea with Hugh in his room at the Works. It was mid-summer 2005, and what turned out to be almost the last special retailer commission ever accepted by Moorcroft came into existence as a result. Goviers' logo was a pineapple, a sign of hospitality and wealth in years gone by. It was also the Moorcroft year mark for 2005. Alan saw his opportunity and asked for a 'pineapple something or another'. What Kerry Goodwin designed for him was a small Pineapple collection made up of two vases and a lamp. Alan was delighted, and decided to take both vases as limited editions. For Moorcroft it was a good order to put on the books in September, while visitors to Hugh's house can hardly fail to notice a Govier pineapple lamp sitting on his writing desk.

Moorcroft occasionally finds itself assuming the role of entertainer. A prime example arose in the case of Phil's designer tour of Australia in November 2005. For his trip, Phil had designed Kookaburra and Royal Hakea. The Royal Hakea vase was particularly attractive. In some ways it looks like a colourful lettuce in shades of green, gold and burnt amber. It was pure design in the Moorcroft idiom, whereas Kookaburra veers towards picture image status. The birds were stylised, one on each side of the vase. In between were the branches and leaves of Eucalyptus trees. Kookaburra was probably not a picture in the accepted sense of the word. On this occasion Phil had seen the danger and had done his best to avoid it. As if to reassure Moorcroft, Australian collectors also saw it that way. Kookaburra totally sold out before Phil's tour closed. Royal Hakea was not far behind.

Those first few months back at Moorcroft were among the most exhilarating Hugh had ever experienced. On the one hand his absence had provided a unique opportunity for a young team to assume responsibility for the art pottery. On the other, his illness prompted a realisation that he had to make decisions about something he had loved with a passion for the greater part of his working life. The Design Studio had settled down to embrace a new order. Anji had left to start her own driving school. Shirley Hayes and Michelle Martin had also said goodbye. Deep in his heart Hugh wished all three of them well.

Emma was still there, of course, as modest and prolific as ever. The young artist on the shop floor had become a leading figure in the Moorcroft Design Studio, with so many successes to her name that even Elise and her computer lost count. On his return, Hugh was told how Emma was already designing a collection to be launched

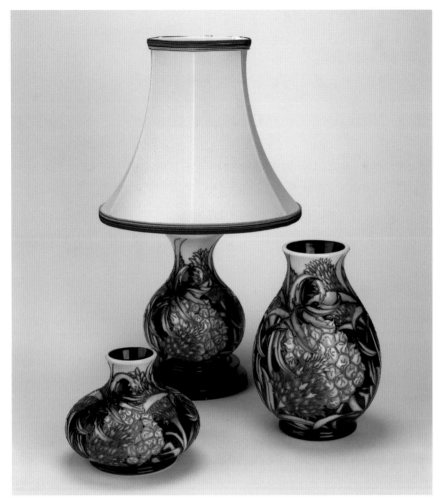

The Pineapple Collection (2005). Small Vase on Left: Ltd.Edn.250
Large Vase on Right: Ltd.Edn.150. Tallest vase 18cm (7")

in September 2005. That was good news. He had used Elise as messenger to tell Emma the time had come to make her greatest career move at Moorcroft so far. In some ways the past few years had turned into a rehearsal, a time to gather together her thoughts and emotions for a project more significant than anything she had ever undertaken. With brilliant solo collections from Rachel and Phil already in place, Emma's designs of a lifetime had to be totally extraordinary if they were to be successful.

Elise had facilitated the creation of a new shape not seen at Moorcroft since the mid-1920s. The square-lidded box had been a favoured shape of William Moorcroft, and was generally referred to by those operating in the secondary market as a 'bis-

Wild Meadow (2005)
Height of jug 18cm (7")

La Garenne (2005). Tallest vase 20cm (8")

cuit barrel'. That may or may not have been true, but for Trevor Critchlow the new box had been hard to model, block and case. Nobody thought to ask Emma why she wanted it. The designer was now working alone. There would be a prestige vase, a small collection of designs and other bits and pieces, Emma had announced airily. For Hugh it was just the tonic he needed. Emma had started to position herself in a way that would set the world of the applied arts on fire.

A chunky vase with three panels, one showing frogs, another a wicked-looking heron and the third a shoal of quaint fish made regular appearances. The main problem with the vase was its wealth of bulrushes and waterweeds. There were so many that each panel looked in serious danger of choking. During the course of his first working week, Hugh provided artistic secateurs. Out came many of the bulrushes and in came moonlight. Pondweed disappeared. Rippled water took its place. After nine trials, Shearwater Moon was ready for production. It was a masterpiece. The final trial left Hugh and Elise staring at each other in total silence. Before Hugh's return, Elise had initiated the arrival of Ariella. Rich purple clematis flowers swayed around the tall, elegant vase, while a black ground gave the design a fine edge, much loved by North American retailers who placed orders in large quantities. The name Ariella arrived via the daughter of the Edwards' adopted child, Lena; translated from ancient Hebrew it means 'lioness of the gods'.

One of the more curious aspects of making and selling art pottery is the way in which strict business theory often fails in practice. This proposition manifested itself with Ariella. There was no logical reason North American collectors should have shown such enthusiasm for the design. In contrast, the same collectors approached Emma's Sonoran Sunrise plaque with a surprising degree of reticence. The design on the plaque was wholly American in structure and subject matter. A blue butterfly, some exotic flowers and foliage created a design window together. In the distance

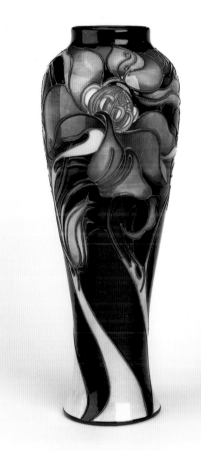

Sonoran Sunrise (2005). Ltd Edn.200
Height of plaque 30cm (12")

Ariella (2005) Ltd.Edn.250
Height 25cm (10")

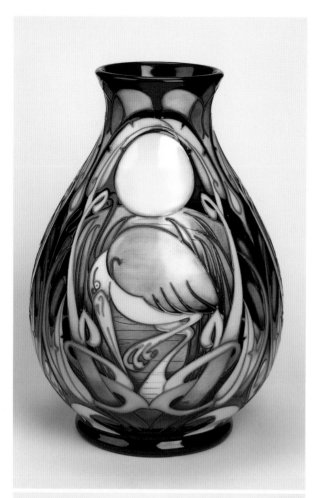

(Left) Shearwater Moon (2005)
First Panel with Heron. Ltd.Edn.150
Height 25cm (10")
(below) Shearwater Moon (2005)
Second Panel with Fish. Ltd.Edn.150
Height 25cm (10")

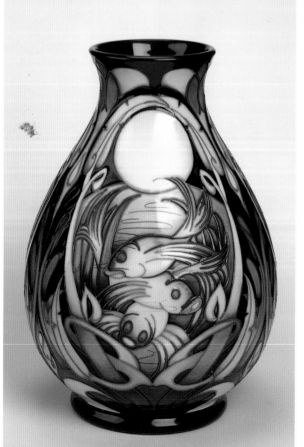

FACING: Shearwater Moon (2005)
Third Panel with Frog.
Ltd.Edn.150. Height 25cm (10")

was an arid desert and a sun-baked mesa stretching to the horizon. The plaque had been limited to a modest 200 pieces, all of which were enthusiastically snapped up by collectors in the United Kingdom: but not in the United States!

Wild Meadow was a pretty, gentle piece of ceramic art. Emma worked hard on it for those with a passion for wildflowers. Its eventual appearance on a smaller version of the perennial JU7 shape was a masterstroke. Emma knew her public. Very much in tune with Emma's more familiar style came an innovative design of stylised trees framing a rising sun. The colours were close to those William Moorcroft had used in his timeless Eventide design introduced in the early 1920s, but there all similarity ended. For Hugh and Elise the technique Emma brought into play created an artistic effect not unlike that of engraved glass. The shadow of Emile Gallé shone through as if the great French glass designer had supervised the process. Three modest vases and a slim plaque made up a small open collection. Hugh called it La Garenne after the Gallé family home in Nancy, France.

Greetings card manufacturer Anne Crowther of Little Acorn Designs had been impressed when she first set eyes on Tree Doves. For her it was a small miracle of perfection. Emma had drawn her images on the slender Moorcroft ewer, and after Anne Crowther's intervention, its arrival as a greetings

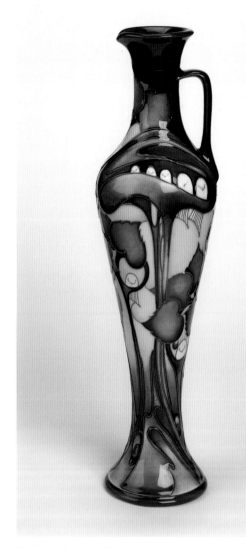

Tree Doves (2005) Ltd.Edn.200
Height 30cm (12")

card was inevitable. Several white doves lined themselves along a branch high in a stylised tree. Emma's colours paid homage to the past. The use of green and subtle splashes of yellow gave Tree Doves a faintly 'Hazledene' appearance. The late William Moorcroft would have approved. Tree Doves kept three painters busy right up to Christmas. By that time, every piece had been sold and dispatched to collectors' homes, pausing only momentarily on retailers' shelves during their journey.

One thing Emma was determined to do was show how much she had moved

FACING: *Edwardiana (2005) Numbered Edn. Height 20cm (8")*

forward as a designer during her ten years at Moorcroft. She had proved herself versatile with a number of design styles, and could look back to the past and into the future with equal confidence. Most of all she had an intuitive instinct for colour and a capacity for design images without any apparent limit. Several years earlier Victoriana had been a popular Collectors' Club piece, but at the time of its introduction Emma had been stung by one of Hugh's 'ring a ring of roses' jibes. She consoled herself in the knowledge that he had taken a piece home. It must have had some merit, even for Hugh. After thinking hard about it, Emma decided that the true merit of Victoriana lay in its colour palette rather than the design itself. To make her point, she designed Edwardiana using the same shape and colours as its predecessor. Only the linework changed. This time her chrysanthemums, Scotch roses and winter aconites came alive, weaving in and out over the surface of the vase in waves of joyous movement. Whether Emma's decision to call the piece Edwardiana was a dig at Hugh or the natural name for the successor to Victoriana, history will judge. For collectors, it was another remarkable vase in an even more remarkable collection.

The square biscuit barrel with its strap handles turned out to be the penultimate pot to appear at the Works. Colourful rhododendrons looked as if they had been thrown around the box's four panels with a skill that would have done credit to a magician. Pencarrow, Hugh called it. The name came to him after he recalled a visit Maureen and he had made to the famous West Country house with its mile-long carriage drive lined with masses of colourful rhododendrons. Orders for Pencarrow continued to arrive until well into 2006. All over the world collectors swooped on the biscuit barrels the moment one found itself sitting on a retailer's shelf. As an unnumbered piece of Moorcroft, Pencarrow was a phenomenon without precedent. In Hugh's new dawn, numbers would be relegated to their proper status of trivia. Pencarrow was leading the way.

Only when everyone else concluded that Emma's collection was complete did Hugh venture to ask about the prestige vase Emma had referred to at the outset. The designer smiled, but Hugh was puzzled. In the past, collections had often derived their content from images on a lead piece. Rachel's Centenary Collection vases carried images, all of which appeared on her centennial charger. Phil had produced the prestige Hidcote before moving on to smaller pieces which picked up the Hidcote design themes. Never in the history of Moorcroft had a designer completed a collection before turning to a large lead piece as a grand finale. When the massive RM3 vase arrived ten days later, it shook Hugh emotionally. Every design image was there – Pencarrow, La Garenne, Tree Doves and all the rest. Every part of Emma's

FACING: *Pencarrow (2005) Numbered Edn. Height 15cm (6")*

great vase carried a wealth of imagery hidden away in secluded places, all of them framed by secondary design work. For the man who thought he had seen everything that was excellent at Moorcroft, the vase was a dream come true. Hidden Dreams, Hugh called it. All fifty pieces of the massive 27-inch vase sold out within two weeks. The remainder of Emma's Hidden Dreams collection witnessed greater sales in both numbers and value than any other collection in Moorcroft history.

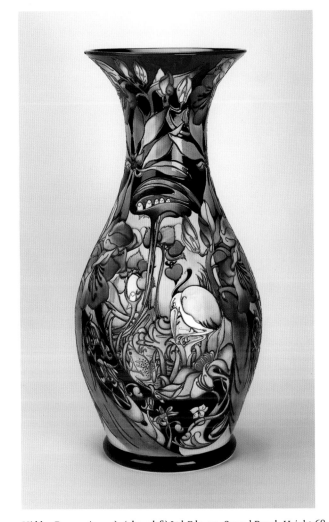 

Hidden Dreams (2005): (above left) Ltd.Edn.50. Second Panel. Height 68cm (27")
(right) Ltd.Edn.50. Third Panel. Height 68cm (27")

FACING: Hidden Dreams (2005) Ltd.Edn.50. First Panel. Height 68cm (27")

TWENTY-SIX

Dancing Toadstools

One of the more rewarding features of the 2006 catalogue was the greater contribution of Kerry Goodwin and Sian Leeper. Emma and Rachel were always going to be right there in the middle of it all. From Emma there was a range called Miss Alice, and no fewer than four limited editions. Rachel's Fly Away Home range was a celebration of simple elegance, to which she had added Fire Flower with four lamps and three vases. Two limited editions from the senior designer arrived like cream on a cake. What Rachel and Emma brought forward was par for the course, but the enhanced presence of Sian and Kerry was especially rewarding. By taking both designers under his wing, Hugh had honoured his promise to

Miss Alice (2006)
Tallest vase 25cm (10")

Maureen and Elise. As if to celebrate, the catalogue itself was re-designed from cover to cover, arriving with a totally new look. It was a modern showcase for a significant quantity of innovative work.

Kerry's dramatic Snapdragon Spell had its origins in ancient Tuareg legend, the mythical battle between the dragon, representing the forces of good, and the serpent, which symbolised evil. The dragon won, of course, but Moorcroft retailers were not happy. The diminutive size of the Snapdragon Spell edition brought howls of complaint from a number of them who made it clear they would like to have seen another hundred pieces. What they really meant was that another two or three pieces for themselves would go down well, provided other retailers stayed as they were.

The Gardeners broke new ground for Moorcroft in style and subject matter. Black scarab beetles occupied the base and shoulder of Kerry's elegant vase. Traditionalists who had seen early trials suggested that collectors would turn their backs on scarab beetles. Happily for Moorcroft they were wrong. The beetles pot, as The

FACING: *Miss Alice (2006). Tall Jug 24cm (9.5")*

Royal Gold (2006) Height of ginger jar 15 cm (6")

Gardeners became known at the Works, followed Snapdragon Spell and sold out almost before those in charge of sales had a chance to blink. Innovation in design had started to feature with increasing prominence in the new dawn at Moorcroft.

Emma's haunting Light on Waters was designed in a style echoing her Hidden Dreams collection the year before. It was a beautiful piece of work. Perceptive collectors seized the opportunity to place early orders with favourite retailers, and this time Moorcroft found itself rueing the day the edition had been fixed at a timid 100

FACING: *Snapdragon Spell (2006) Ltd.Edn.50. Height 33 cm (13")*

(Left) *Cow Parsley* (2006) Ltd.Edn.150. Height 30cm (12″)
(right) *Clematis Queen* (2006) Ltd.Edn.200. Height 30cm (12″)

pieces. The other two limited editions from Emma were said to appeal to the young and trendy (Cow Parsley) and connoisseurs of tradition (Clematis Queen). Over a cup of tea, Robert Townsend was heard to tell Hugh that the young and trendy were turning out to be a less powerful lobby than traditional connoisseurs. As a result, Clematis Queen moved powerfully off the block leaving its young and trendy stablemate, Cow Parsley, to follow at a more sedate pace.

By the time the new catalogue went to press, only one piece of Royal Gold out of a potential ten-piece range was passed for production. Rachel had done everything she could to ensure that Royal Gold was ready for the new year. After all the work she had put in on the other nine pieces, Rachel was bitterly disappointed. What the senior designer had not been told was that a new Shadow Collection was to be in-

FACING: *Fly Away Home* (2006). Tallest vase 35cm (14″)

troduced in June 2006. A Royal Gold range would be included in that collection. The news mollified Rachel, but Emma's new Florian Lilac design suffered an even worse fate. From a potential ten pieces, not one received approval, even as a limited edition. When the Shadow Collection finally arrived, Florian Lilac and Royal Gold were both unveiled as small ranges of equal size. They were joined by Can Can Birds from Kerry and Cloud Forest designed by Nicola Slaney. Can Can Birds was a hu-

FACING: *Light on Water (2006) Ltd.Edn.100. Height 20cm (8") (above) Reverse Side of Vase*

Royal Gold (2006) Ltd.Edn.100. Height 15cm (6")

morous successor to Kerry's Snapdragon Spell, with a pair of colourful birds leaping in tandem around the base of the vase, their colourful feathers flapping like Can Can skirts. Above them on the neck of the vase a third bird peers down in amazement, wondering whether to join in or not. Nicky's Cloud Forest was totally different in both mood and subject matter. The design took its inspiration from South American rainforest imagery, with rare orchids cascading from tree branches like giant white snowflakes. Cloud Forest is a haunting image, which can provoke remarkably profound emotional reactions.

To do what he could to ensure that designers achieve their best, Hugh would play to their strengths rather than their weaknesses; but there was an inherent danger in this strategy. For example, if a designer has an instinctive ability to draw poppies or grapes with their eyes shut, there is the risk of an endless stream of poppies or grapes until someone shouts stop! One of Sian's strengths lies in her deep understanding of the more exotic aspects of the living world. With this an accepted fact, she was actively encouraged to concentrate on coral reefs, African savannah, landscape and jungle. That encouragement secured the arrival of Coral Reef on an imposing ten-

FACING: *Florian Lilac (2006). Tallest vase 25cm (10")*

inch ginger jar and Shimba Hills on which giraffes make another welcome appearance. On a larger version of the strap-handled jug, Shimba Hills was an unabashed picture in the Moorcroft idiom. Retailers loved it, singing to Robert Townsend in perfect unison that Shimba Hills was 'right for us'. Coral Reef fell into the same category. In no time at all the dainty computer which accompanies the Head of Sales at Moorcroft on his travels almost died from an overload of emails, all gushing with praise for both designs.

Another owl vase from Phil stirred a certain amount of controversy. Twilight Hunter was a significant design, although after its introduction the picture purists started muttering under their breath once more. In a mood of exasperation Hugh asked one of the 'moaning minnies', as he called them, 'when have you ever seen an oak leaf the same size as a barn owl's head?'

To Kim, that custodian of all knowledge about what sells in shops and what does not, year plates were fast going out of fashion. Walter Moorcroft

*Cloud Forest (2006) Ltd.Edn.100
Height 20cm (8")*

had first introduced them in 1982, and 25 had appeared since that time. Emma's Sunbirds was approved as the 2006 year plate, and as a result of advice from Kim, the edition number was trimmed from 400 to a modest 200. Somewhere there had to be a collector with a complete set of twenty-five year plates, Elise had suggested to Moorcroft Museum advisor Kathy Niblett. 'If you find that person', was Kathy's quick reply, 'you have a ready-made exhibition'.

Although she found it hard to believe, Hugh had genuine sympathy for Rachel at her temporary loss of Royal Gold. The way the senior designer saw it, a single limited edition was cold comfort. As always, she decided to bury her feelings and worked hard on both Fly Away Home and Fire Flower. For Moorcroft, Fire Flower was something new and exciting. It was the first time in several years that Rachel had opted to use a celadon clay body for her work. Celadon would have the effect of calming down the red flowers and enhancing the visual impact of both the greenish yellow leaves and a carefully-chosen bramble blue ground. What was altogether new about

FACING: *Can Can Birds (2006) Ltd.Edn.200. Height 28cm (11")*

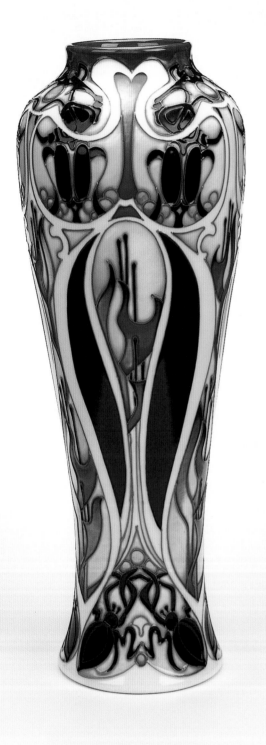

(Above left) *The Gardeners* (2006) Ltd.Edn.200. Height 35cm (14")
(right) *Shimba Hills* (2006) Ltd.Edn.300. Height 30cm (12")

Coral Reef (2006) Ltd.Edn.100. Height 20cm (8")

Fire Flower, however, was that the collection comprised four lamps and three seriously attractive giftware pieces. In the recent past, lamps and giftware had tended to appear separately. To emphasise the value of Rachel's new method of presentation, her Lamia design was concertinaed into a modest three lamps, a matching number of giftware pieces and a plaque. The plaque was subsequently photographed for use as one of Rachel's first greetings cards, and by June 2006 it had become the best-selling Moorcroft greetings card of them all.

Always someone who enjoys working his art on lamps, Phil designed Dancing Flame as a set of three lamps. The flowers were flame-red, and to ensure maximum contrast they were drawn on a pure ivory ground. Phil's approach was in complete

Fireflower (2006). Tallest vase 15cm (6″)

contrast to the one adopted by Rachel. By the end of the year, finance director David Holland would no doubt produce a raft of figures suggesting which of the two presentation techniques had been the most financially rewarding. More importantly, those same figures would show which approach collectors preferred.

When it came, Kerry had been taken aback at Hugh's stark warning that time was desperately short, and if she were to make any significant improvement on her catalogue contribution, she would have to commit herself to Moorcroft design twenty-four hours a day, seven days a week, until her work for 2006 was finished. It was a pressurised approach, but Hugh calculated it was necessary to turn Kerry into a consummate and successful designer. Speed and pressure of work applied to her profession as much as they did to everyone else. The knack was not to destroy a designer's creativity in the process. 'Go and design some dancing toadstools', Hugh barked at the hapless Kerry, 'and do them in a way that makes folk ask what sort of high you were on when you did the work: Put feet on them if you have to!' The result was Parasol Dance featuring surreal toadstools in a surreal landscape. At first, Kerry's toadstools were drawn with real feet and real toes. The design approval committee was not happy. Collectors were not ready for toadstools with feet, they said. That was that. Poor Kerry had to redraw her red toadstools without feet, which was perhaps just as well. At the December 2005 Trial Exhibition, all of the Parasol Dance toadstools without feet sold out. All those which had been drawn with feet remained unsold when the exhibition closed. In a fit of pique, Hugh seized a 'foot vase' as they were referred to in the factory shop, paid for it with considerable bad grace and took it home. It was the old collector in him who had made the mistake, not Kerry Goodwin. 'You put your foot in it, Boss!' Elise said. Hugh scowled.

Rachel had additional reasons to be less than happy at the treatment meted out to work into which she had invested a great deal of time and effort, and those feelings were made painfully clear to Hugh. He had asked her to redraw her Study in Blue onto the impressive 82/16 shape, largely on the ground that the original 3/8 vase

Twilight Hunter (2006)
(right) Ltd.Edn.75. Height 35cm (14")
(below) Reverse Side of Vase

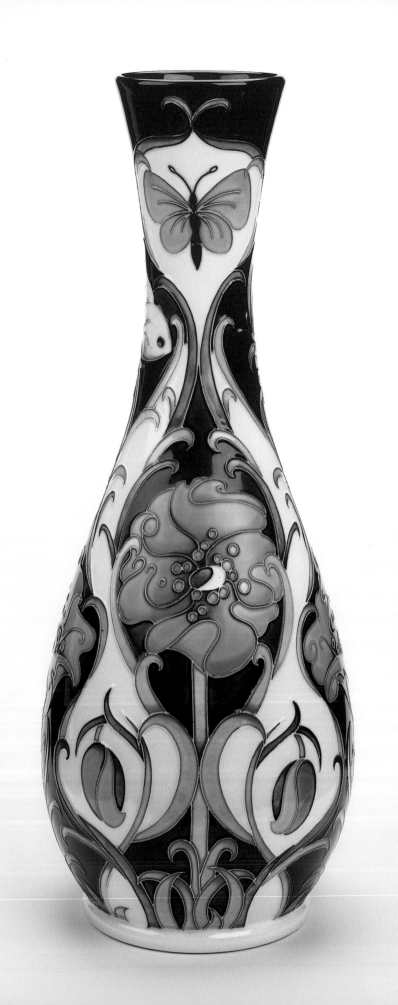

Parasol Dance (2006). Tallest vase 25cm (10″)

FACING: Study in Blue (2006) Ltd.Edn.250. Height 40cm (16″)

Dancing Flame (2006)
Height of Lamp Base 20cm (8")

selected was too small for the design. That was certainly one reason, but there was another. A number of new 3/8 pieces had been lining themselves up for the new year, including Emma's Light on Waters and a significant piece in Phil's Lagoon collection. Kerry put a 3/8 into Parasol Dance, and by the time Study in Blue arrived enough was enough. Elise decided to act. Rachel had already chosen to use a L3/8 in Fire Flower, and it fell to Hugh to ask the senior designer to reconsider her options. Rachel relented, and her magnificent sixteen-inch Study in Blue made a catalogue bow in place of the 3/8 vase originally proposed.

Fly Away Home was a joyous, almost fragile design made up of blue agapanthus flowers and the occasional ladybird. Originally Hugh had asked Rachel to design Fly Away Home as a single limited edition despite the fact that a range had always been her preferred option. This time it was Hugh's turn to relent. Any idea of using Fly Away Home as a limited edition would seem rather silly and the waste of a fine design. It made its appearance as a range of seven pieces. Almost overnight Fly Away Home was embraced by Moorcroft collectors with such enthusiasm that by the end of May seven painters were working on it.

Before the new year was more than a few weeks old, Moorcroft was humming with happiness. The reception of the new year's designs had been a tonic. Spring was fast approaching, and daffodils would soon be nodding their yellow heads in response to a wind that had gently blown away the agony that had erupted into Hugh's life more than a year earlier. For him, life seemed almost surreal. Fifteen months earlier he had been fighting for his life. Only a wife he adored, an unshakeable love of Moorcroft and the anticipation of spring had kept him going. As clearly as if it had been yesterday he recalled how a thin scattering of snow had melted away to reveal dark green daffodil shoots emerging from the cold earth at the bottom of his garden. All Hugh had been able to do at the time was to watch nature roll back winter. To walk a hundred yards was unthinkable, but with spring around the corner, Hugh

FACING: *Lagoon (2006) (Above) Clockwise from top: Ltd.Edn. 100, Ltd.Edn. 50, Ltd Edn. 75 and Ltd.Edn 75. Tallest vase 30cm (12")*
(Below) Clockwise from top: Ltd.Edn. 50, Ltd.Edn. 300, Ltd Edn. 50 and Ltd.Edn 50. Tallest vase 20cm (8")

Professor Hope (2006) Ltd.Edn.250. Height 28cm (11")

resolved to walk a hundred yards to the bottom of his garden and pick the first daffodil to unfold into flower. With support from Maureen, he succeeded.

A year later, over the inevitable cup of tea, Hugh and Rachel talked together. For the two of them the regal daffodil was the flower which soared above all other spring flowers in beauty, in elegance and in colour. They came to an understanding which left them happy. Rachel would design the daffodil vase of a lifetime. It would be the only piece to appear at the Spring Festival in 2006. No other designers would be present. On Easter Saturday, Rachel would hold court on her own. Hugh also gave the senior designer his solemn promise to be present himself, but for a very special reason. Those who work at Moorcroft acknowledge that he owes his life to the skill and dedication of a Cambridge doctor, Professor Stephen O'Rahilly. Rachel decided to dedicate her new daffodil vase to Professor O'Rahilly, and called it 'Professor Hope'. It stands for all time as her tribute to a remarkable physician.

Sunbirds (2006) Ltd.Edn.200
Diameter 15cm (6")

Christmas Time (2004) (Carole Lovatt)
Height 20cm (8")

TWENTY-SEVEN

Dawn Breaks

The months that followed the Waddesdon Manor event in October 2005 witnessed a considerable change of attitude at Moorcroft. Hugh had been uncompromising in his response to retailer requests for special pieces, and not one of them had persuaded him to change his mind. Even Barry Thornton failed in his attempt to start a third series of Shakespearian ginger jars. Robert Townsend and his sales team had done a thorough and courteous job. Apart from Liberty of London, there were no exceptions, and those retailers with lingering hopes gradually subsided into silence. Individual events hosted by retailers locally would be encouraged. It was a future in which the annual Moorcroft catalogue would reign supreme, where whole collections would be released from time to time, some to specially selected retailers and some to the world at large. Even at the Works, limited editions would be restricted. Collectors would start collecting again, enjoying the excitement of search and discovery. Liberty was an inevitable exception. It would continue to receive exclusive designs for as long as they were wanted. You cannot sustain a legendary trading relationship by failing to deliver your part of a mutual understanding which has helped sustain that relationship for more than a century. A significant part of Hugh's new dawn had arrived.

In other ways the Moorcroft vision of a new dawn was symbolised by Emma's Miss Alice, a design considered to have been too good for an 'in-house' release at Waddesdon Manor. Miss Alice had special international qualities which took it away from such a closed occasion as a Collectors' Club away weekend at a stately home. It was more suitable as a range to be sold by Moorcroft retailers worldwide. The design was a riot of coordinated colour with white, cream and orange flowers set against a dark blue ground. At the same time, its arrival sent out a clear signal that Emma's work on her famous Pencarrow box the previous year had come of age.

The unseen hand of an experienced collector had been the catalyst to Parasol Dance, and that same hand was there when Kerry completed Snapdragon Spell. Kerry told those with whom she worked closely that she had felt herself moving

FACING: *Landscape Medley (2006). Clockwise from Top: Woodland, Seashore, Riverbank, Moorland, Grassland and Mountain. Tallest vase 25cm (10")*

(Above) Duet (2006). Height 15cm (6")

(Left above) Apollo (2006)
Tallest vase 28cm (11")

(Below) Apollo (2006)
Tallest vase 23cm (9")

slowly but inevitably towards the Islamic colour palette and the ancient world of Arabic legend and myth. For Moorcroft, her Moroccan Myths was also different in style, colour and content. First, it was definitely a collection of individual pieces as opposed to a range. Each vase carried a separate image. There was the talking hare, which Elise still persists in calling a rabbit, the weasel fish, the devil's vulture, the ubiquitous sand thief and the mighty Atlas dragon bird. By the time she finished her work, every image had been framed with purple desert grass. As he talked Kerry through her Moroccan Myths project, it was Hugh the collector who offered a helping hand. Everything he had done in his first twenty years with the art pottery had been done with the mindset of a collector. The shapes chosen for Moroccan Myths were all down to Kerry, but the stories and dreams which lay behind each image were the product of imagination rather than knowledge.

As Hugh saw it, to own an example of every piece in Kerry's Moroccan Myths collection was to own pots each of which told a story. Two Californian collectors from Los Angeles had evidently seen it that way as well, and each placed orders for all five vases with their retailer. Robert Townsend was eager to tell everyone about the surge of enthusiasm for Moroccan Myths on the other side of the Atlantic. North American retailers loved it. It remained to be seen whether United Kingdom retailers would react in the same positive way. If they failed to do so, Hugh was ready to deal with the problem. Lessons had been learned as a result of the tribulations suffered by Rachel's Gypsy range. Moorcroft had to continue to move forward. It would no longer be acceptable to be wholly traditional, commercially timid or forever seeking a bargain.

In terms of design, none of this was new. When the first five trials appeared, Sian's embryonic Amazon Collection had a familiar ring about it. Exotic birds, flowers, animals and reptiles were all there, but first time around the images had all been lost in a suffocating jungle of leaves, ferns and creepers. Out came the design secateurs once more, as they had done with Emma's Shearwater Moon the year before. Most of the undergrowth was pruned, exposing a cheeky gecko in the process. The gecko became the common feature in all five pieces, with their gloriously bright rainforest colours. It was a collection for collectors, as was Sian's more tranquil Landscape Medley, designed for lovers of the countryside. In Landscape Medley the main design theme (landscape) is framed by a secondary design theme (waving corn). Both landscape and waving corn are design concepts drawn from Moorcroft history. Each landscape is different: grassland, moorland, mountains, river bank, seashore and woodland. Even more interesting is the fact that each scene comes with its own bird: kingfisher (riverbank), woodpecker (woodland), seagull (seashore), swallow (grassland), osprey (mountain), buzzard (moorland). Sian's objective was to ensure that collectors saw Landscape Medley as a collection, and not as a set of different shapes carrying the same design.

As he stood looking at the Moorcroft exhibition stand at the Birmingham 2006 International Spring Fair, Hugh found himself smiling. He had survived an appalling illness against all the odds, a new pay structure had replaced the pernicious system of 'average pay' which had almost brought Moorcroft to its knees, special designs for retailers had become a thing of the past and designers themselves had become ambassadors of the new dawn, the standard bearers of the Moorcroft name. Now the correct number of tube-liners fed the correct number of painters in the decorating shop, and prestige vases were being made, not ignored. What Hugh saw were retailers on the Moorcroft exhibition stand happily telling Robert's sales team how the new 2006 designs were 'right for us'. He was glad some of their little idiosyncrasies would never change.

The 21st April 2006 was Queen Elizabeth II's eightieth birthday. All his life Hugh had been proud of the Queen of his country, a diminutive but highly intelligent person who added grace and dignity to the United Kingdom throughout her reign. He had once sat opposite Her Majesty at lunch and found himself on the receiving end of a series of conversational questions ranging from roses to monuments built to commemorate great people of the past. In answer to a question, Hugh intimated that he preferred the idea of laser lights reaching up to the stars rather than monuments rising from the cold earth. The Queen made it clear that laser lights were 'not what We had in mind'.

It had been a pleasant occasion, and at the time of the loyal toast the Moorcroft chairman rose to his feet. Not knowing quite what to do next, he smiled at the small figure sitting opposite and raised his glass as much for everyone at Moorcroft as for himself. Hugh would remember that moment for the rest of his life. When the time arrived, everyone agreed that something special had to be done to commemorate Her Majesty's official eightieth birthday. After full discussion, a decision was made to design a special vase and plaque to commemorate the occasion, and it fell to Emma Bossons to do the honours. On her chosen vase there appeared a white rose enriched with a central flush of pale lilac. From his conversation with the Queen, Hugh had learned that white and lilac were among Her Majesty's preferred colours. Inevitably Emma's celebratory vase and co-ordinated plaque were called Elizabeth. The vase was released to the world, while the plaque was made available solely to

FACING: *Moroccan Myths (2006). Clockwise from Top: Desert Hare, Sand Thief, Weasel Fish, Devil's Snake and Atlas Dragon Bird. Tallest vase 25cm (10")*

(Top left) Inset of The Amazon Collection – Red Eyed Tree Frog (2006) (top right) Shearwater Moon Fish Model (2006) Height 18cm (7″) (bottom left) Shearwater Moon Frog Model (2006). Height 16cm (6.5″) (bottom right) Shearwater Moon Heron Model (2006). Height 19cm (7.5″)

FACING: The Amazon Collection (2006). Clockwise from Top: Ringed-Tailed Lemur, Cameleon, Gecko, Red-Eyed Tree Frog and Blue-Necked Tanager. Tallest vase 18cm (7″)

Gold Members in the Moorcroft Collectors' Club.

In Sandbach Road, plans were moving forward to convert William Moorcroft's old factory into a Heritage Visitor Centre, complete with restaurant, an enlarged museum and retail area. It was home to the designers, to Hugh and Elise, Robert and Kim, and it was home to the finest tube-liners and ceramic painters to be found anywhere in the world. Early in the New Year, Trevor Critchlow had collaborated with master sculptor Rob Tabbenor. Between them they had completed three new models, the form of which had been taken from images on Emma's Shearwater Moon vase – a shoal of fish, a frog and a heron. In March 2006, Emma had been with Moorcroft for ten years, and March was the month in which the models made their first appearance. Even though they had been the first models to emerge from Moorcroft for a long time, out of caution Robert Townsend and his sales team decided not to push retailers too hard. Elise had been enthusiastic about the models project from the outset. She knew from her records that within the last five years a red owl model made c1925 had sold in the secondary market at a figure in excess of twenty thousand pounds.

With the anniversary of his first twenty years at Moorcroft approaching relentlessly, Hugh was surprised at how strongly he still felt about the pots he had loved all his life. The old instincts of search and find were still alive inside him, just as they had been almost four decades earlier. He knew collectors would always find happiness and fulfilment finding something new or unexpected. Good fortune was looking favourably on Moorcroft yet again. A new breed of retailer had emerged, people who were happy to swap stories with collectors and saw it as their job to find out what was new and fill their shelves with interesting pots. Many of these retailers were collectors themselves with significant quantities of Moorcroft in their own homes to prove it. To collect is to seek out new pots wherever they might be hiding.

Almost twenty years earlier, on 16th September 1986, a much younger and extremely enthusiastic Hugh Edwards had entered the time warp that was Moorcroft. On 16th September 2006, his twentieth anniversary would arrive. It would be an occasion to be celebrated. Young faces were already moving around the art pottery. It was in good hands and in good health. Deep inside, Hugh felt a wave of sadness. Would he become a forgotten man? Would his first twenty-year contribution to Moorcroft stand the test of time as had the eras of William and Walter Moorcroft, father and son, with almost ninety years service between them? Twenty years seemed relatively insignificant in comparison, but they had been twenty dramatic years. The

FACING: *Elizabeth (2006) Both Numbered Edns. Height of vase 25cm (10")*

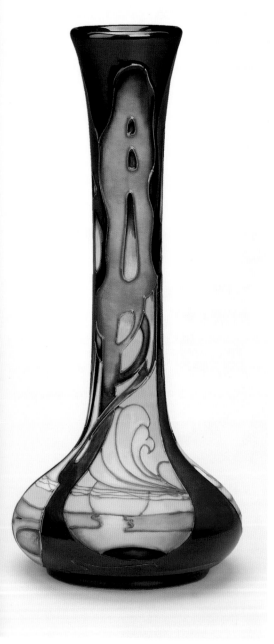

New Dawn (2006). Height 20cm (8")

winds of change had blown through the art pottery, and a new dawn was already shining like a bright light on the horizon. That new dawn would be his legacy, and the thought pleased him.

For the past nine years Hugh had worked alongside Elise Adams. Her 'it's only me' on the internal telephone was always welcome. The thought of Elise becoming custodian of the Moorcroft design matrix gave him great happiness. The matrix is a magical place where new pots are born deep in the heart of the art pottery. Just as it does with Hugh, the spirit of Moorcroft touches her soul. It is much more than a mere part of her life. Love and commitment are essential if Moorcroft is to survive. As long as Elise remains at the heart of Moorcroft, stories and dreams will continue to unfold. Hugh looked forward to sharing his remaining time at Moorcroft with her.

A Moorcroft collector was standing alone in the car park outside the Works in Sandbach Road enjoying the pale late winter sunshine which covered the bottle oven with an orange veil of soft light. Despite the deceptive warmth of the colours, it was chilly. Hugh shivered and shuffled his feet. A hand touched his arm. 'Can I see you? I've got something to show you'. It was Emma. Some things in a working life are remarkably consistent. With that, the two of them walked inside the Works together. Emma was carrying a slim vase decorated with silvery water, trees and a rising sun. 'For your book', she said. 'It's the New Dawn'.

Moorcroft Design Studio 2006. Clockwise from Top: Philip Gibson, Nicola Slaney,
Emma Bossons FRSA, Rachel Bishop (senior designer), Sian Leeper and Kerry Goodwin

Moorcroft Marks

TUBE-LINERS' MARKS

Alicia Amison
1998–present

Amanda Baker
2004–present

Janine Barrett
1999–2004

Alison Benson
1989–present

Tracey Bentley
2004–present

Tonia Billings
1999–present

Amanda Bourne
1994–present

Julie-Anne Bowen
1998–present

Jeanette Brammer
2002 – Present
(née Sneyd 1996–2002)

Tracey Weston
1999–2004

Debbie Clarke
2005–present
(née Harrison 2004–2005)

Helen Dale
1999–present

Pamela Deakes
2002–2005

Kelvin Dean
1996–2004

Katrina Dundas
2002–2004

Alison Edwards
2004–present

Sylvia Evans
2004–present

Ruth Fairweather
2004–2005
(née Luby 1998–2004)

Sue Griffin
1996–2003

Hayley Grocott-Smith
1995–2005

Linda Hammond
2004–2005

Julie Harrison-Statham
2001–2002
(née Harrison 1993–2001)

Sandra Hartshorne
1998–present

Caroline Hulme
1996–present

Gillian Johnson
1985–present

Julie Johnson
1998–2005

Paula Jones
1998–2004

Kath Keeling
1998–present

Louise Llewellyn
2003–2005

Clare Lowe
1999–2001

KDM Kerry Marshall
1999–2001
2002–present
KDE (Kerry Edgerton)
2001–2002

lm Lesley Myatt
1998–2004

mp Marie Penkethman
1990–present

Kp Karen Porter
2003–present
(née Potts 1989–2003)

GjP Gillian Powell
1998–present

Ks Kerry Shaw
2004–present

LS Lorraine Sherwin
2002–present

HS Heidi Simon
2002–present

CS Catherine Smith
1992–2004

DS Debbie Smith
1999–present

CES Clare Sneyd
1996–present

Ss Stephanie Snow
1998–present

JS Jackie Strode
2004–2005

VT Vicky Thorley
1998–present

SW Sarah Wild
Sp 2002–present
(née Pendlebury 1997–2002)

Aw Ailie Woodhead-Coates
1987–2004

LB Linda Worthington
1999–present

PAINTERS' MARKS

SA Sharon Austin
1989–present

AB Amanda Baggley
1995–present

AB Amanda Baker
1996–present

SB Sue Barnsley
1995–present

CB Chris Bell
1998–2004

EPB Emma Bossons
1996–present

Ste Steven Bourne
1997–2005

EB Emma Burton
ER 2002–2005
(née Rafferty 1994–2002)

N.C Naomi Caroll
1999–present

JC Jim Carroll
1999–2004

HC Hayley Cook
2003–present
HS (née Smith 1988–2003)

HD Helen Dale
2000–present

ADS Anji Davenport-Salmon
2003–2004
Anji (née Davenport 1995–2003)

℗	Julie Dolan 1984–present	ℎ	Peter Harrison 1998–present
LBE LB	Laura Earlam 2003–present (née Blight 1998–2003)	ℋ	Shirley Hayes 1992–2005
AE	Alison Edwards 1997–present	4H	Laura Hewitt 1998–present
JE	Julie Edwards 1999–2000	ℋ	Gwyneth Hibbett 1973–2001 2003–2003
LE	Louise Edwards 1999–2004	Ph	Paul Hilditch 1999–present
ʌE	Mary Etheridge 1987–2004	MH	Marjorie Hill 1987–2001 2003–2003
ℰ	Sylvia Evans 1991–present	ℋ	Heather Honeyfield 1998–present
SF	Sue Fairhead 1998–2005	kerri	Kerry Hopkinson 1998–present
Vf	Victoria Ford 1999–present	ℰH	Elizabeth Hughes 1997–2004
PG	Paula Gaitley 1990–2005	LK	Lorraine Knowles 1997–2005
DG	Donna Gerrard 1999–2002	Sian	Sian Leeper 1999–present
ℊ	Sue Gibbs 1984–2004	VL	Vicky Lovatt 1999–present
NG NW	Nicola Gilchrist 2003–2004 (née Woodward 1999–2003)	MM	Michelle Martin 2002–2004
KG	Kerry Goodwin 2000–present	W	Wendy Mason Thorne 1979–present
DW	Dawn Hall 1998–present	PM	Patricia May 1998–2004
DH	Debbie Hancock 1992–2004	JM	Joanne Megyesi 2001–present (née Morton 1994–2001)
JH	Jayne Hancock 1987–2005	KM	Karen Mellor 1995–present

Paula Mellor 1999–present		Glynn Simpson 1999–present	
Hayley Moore 1987–present		Deborah Smith 2001–present	
Jackie Moores 1998–present		Maggie Thompson 1991–2001	
Barbara Mountford 1987–2004		Karen Walker 1998–present	
Joanne Mountford 1993–present		Joanne Walton 1999–2004	
Alisa Phillips 1991–present		Chris Walton 1998–present	
Sue Pointon 1988–present		Joanne White 1997–present	
Carolyn Pugh 1997–present		Beverley Berry 2005–present (née Wilkes 1989–2005)	
Simon Quinn 2002–2004		Mandy Wood 1994–present	
Mandy Rashford-Jones 1999–present		Joanne Wootton 1999–2004	
Jackie Rowe 1992–2005		Linda Worthington 2001–present	
Claire Shelley 1999–present			

COLLECTORS' CLUB MARKS

Moorcroft Collectors' Club
M.C.C., Open Weekend and
Open Weekend auction
designs

1 Star Members' Design

2 Star Members' Design

3 Star Members' Design

4 Star Members' Design

5 Star Members' Design

DESIGNERS' MONOGRAMS

Alicia Amison

Rachel Bishop

Emma Bossons FRSA

Anji Davenport

Philip Gibson

Kerry Goodwin

Debbie Hancock

Shirley Hayes

Sian Leeper

Carol Lovatt

Nicola Slaney

RETAILERS' EXCLUSIVE DESIGN MARKS

Ashwood Nurseries
in Kingswinford

Ashwood Nurseries in
Kingswinford to celebrate 200
years of the RHS in 2004

BBC CHILDREN IN NEED
2003

BBC Children In Need
charity auction

LOVE'S LABOUR'S LOST
B & W THORNTON
STRATFORD-ON-AVON

B & W Thornton in
Stratford-Upon-Avon

OTHELLO
B & W THORNTON
STRATFORD-ON-AVON

B & W Thornton in
Stratford-Upon-Avon

ROMEO & JULIET
B & W THORNTON
STRATFORD-ON-AVON

B & W Thornton in
Stratford-Upon-Avon

THE TEMPEST
B & W THORNTON
STRATFORD-ON-AVON

B & W Thornton in
Stratford-Upon-Avon

TWELFTH NIGHT
B & W THORNTON
STRATFORD-ON-AVON

B & W Thornton in
Stratford-Upon-Avon

MADE
FOR
CERAMICA

Ceramica in Stoke-on-Trent

MADE FOR
COLLECTABLES

Collectables in
Newcastle-Upon-Tyne

Connaught House in
Nottingham

Dalbry Antiques in Australia

Dalbry Antiques in Australia

Dalbry Antiques in Australia

Douglas Macmillan in
Stoke-on-Trent

Goviers in Sidmouth

James Macintyre & Co
in Leeds

James Macintyre & Co
in Leeds

James Macintyre & Co
in Leeds

Liberty in London

Piggybankkids charity

Rob McIntosh in Canada

Sinclairs in Hale

William Sissons Gallery in
Helmsley and Weavers in
Saffron Walden

The China Shop in
New Zealand

The Posthorn in
Castle Douglas

SPECIAL MARKS

Made for Australia

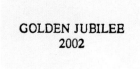

To celebrate Queen Elizabeth II's Golden Jubilee

Royal cipher granted on the occasion of Queen Elizabeth II's Golden Jubilee

A Trial Mark

Special 2004 designs made exclusively for the Moorcroft Heritage Visitor Centre

Pieces are impressed 'Moorcroft Made In Stoke-On-Trent England' (on pieces with small bases 'Moorcroft Made In England' is impressed). Pieces feature an impressed tube-liner's mark and year mark, and a painted decorator's mark

Limited edition designs feature designers' signatures, the number of the edition and the total edition run. Also illustrated are the impressed registered mark and design copyright mark

Numbered edition designs feature designers' signatures and an individual number

YEAR STAMPS

2001 Leaf

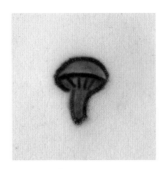

2002 Mushroom

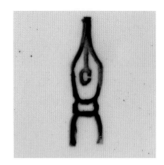

2003 Nib

2004 Octagon

2005 Pineapple

2006 (January–February)
Question Mark

2006 (March onwards) Q

Index